HELEN

HAD

A SISTER

Books by Penelope Haines

The Lost One
Helen Had a Sister
(previously published as Princess of Sparta)
Blood Never Lies

The Claire Hardcastle Series:
Death on D'Urville
Straight and Level
Stall Turns

HELEN

HAD

A SISTER

A Tale of Ancient Greece

PENELOPE HAINES

For information contact;

www.penelopehaines.com

Published by: Ithaca Publishing

ISBN 978-0-473-55135-3

To Quentin and Rupert.

My wonderful sons,

with all my love.

.

Map of Homeric Greece

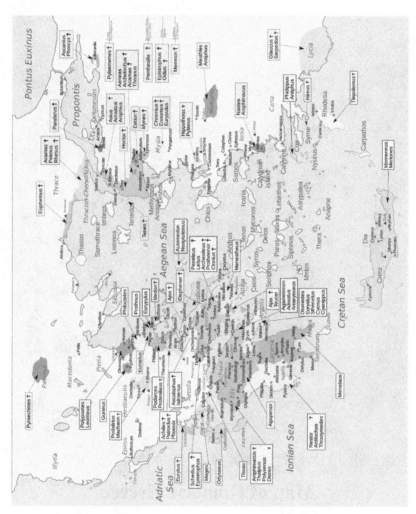

The Heroes of Ancient Greece

PROLOGUE

IT IS PLEASANTLY COOL ON THE terrace. The balustrade and pillars hold the warmth of the day's sun and press comfortably against my back as I sit on the railing here in the twilight. Beyond, in the shrubbery, I can hear the susurrations of little night creatures starting to go about their business. The scent of jasmine hangs in the still air and it is magically beautiful. Moonrise will be early tonight. Last night it was full and lit my room with its silver light.

The palace is hushed. The usual domestic sounds of food preparation, children wailing and slaves readying the house for the night are missing. Many of the servants have fled. Charis came in a while ago bringing a shawl, spiced wine and sweetened cakes, setting them out on the table as if laying places for guests. Perhaps she is. I would have refused the food, but I knew it kindly meant.

When she had finished, she came and knelt at my feet. "Lady, let me stay with you," she pleaded.

I looked at her kneeling form, reached out and touched her soft, dark hair. I love this girl, she is all I have left of my eldest daughter. "You cannot stay. This is for me alone, Charis. If you stay, you will be killed. You must go."

She looked up at me, her eyes red and swollen. "Lady, please, I beg you."

"Go, Charis." I was firm. "I need no innocents on this journey. Don't weep for me. All here is as it should be."

She sighed, but eventually left.

Aegisthus died some hours ago. The screams first alerted me. I sent Charis to investigate the uproar, and she came running back, white with shock, to report his bloody body lay in the forecourt. The slaves, after their initial outcry, faded from the scene. They will have found some safe place to hide and tomorrow will emerge to serve whoever survives the night.

My murderer is in the palace already. I wonder what he's been doing in these hours. Has he gone to the bathhouse to pay his respects to the shade of his father? Does he pray? Is he afraid of what he has come to do? He must know I will not resist him. Of all who ever lived, he is the one man forever safe from me.

I have loved him most truly, treasured his embraces, valued his opinions and rejoiced and shared in his goals. He left me seven years ago, and the pain of missing him has been the greatest grief to me.

I feel Aegisthus's presence, and it comforts me. He will wait until I join him so we can walk the dark road together. It won't be long now. I try in these moments to steady myself. I seek some pattern or meaning in the skein of my days, but my mind is restless, its processes near inchoate. I remember myself as queen, lover, mother and avenger. How did I become murderer and monster; hated by my children and reviled? At the end I will die as a victim. If there was some plan or working to make me what I am, I cannot see it. Truly, we may simply be the gods' playthings.

The sun set an hour ago, and I watched as its edge dipped below the horizon, knowing I saw it for the last time. I will not be alive when it rises tomorrow.

CHAPTER ONE

I WAS FOUR YEARS OLD WHEN MY mother, Leda, called my twin brother and me to meet our new siblings. We sat beside her on the bed as the nurse brought the babies across. Leda looked tired and a little rumpled, but she was smiling as she placed Helen in my arms, showing me how to support her head.

"Gently," she laughed, as I nearly dropped the baby. "You've got to be very careful with her."

I wondered, as I tried to balance the weight, that such a small creature was alive and was my sister. Castor held Pollux gingerly, looked him over with interest, but became bored quickly and handed him back to the nurse.

"Typical male," the nurse snorted in amusement as she took the baby back to its cradle.

Leda gave her gentle laugh, her face soft as she watched me with Helen.

I stayed, watching as Helen's swaddling bands were changed and Leda took her to her breast.

Castor and I had been the babies of the household, but now we were supplanted. He and I were children now, not infants, and our world was larger than the nursery.

With elegant efficiency Leda had borne four royal children for the House of Sparta from two pregnancies. Our father Tyndareus, who loved his wife and children, was delighted. Later, of course, there were rumours that Helen and Pollux had been sired by Zeus, who manifested as a swan. This was fuelled by the surprising symmetry of Leda's birthing patterns, and by the undeniable fact that Castor and I were dark like our father, while Helen and Pollux were fair, taking after our mother.

I doubt if my mother betrayed her husband, even if importuned by a god. Leda was the model of a good Grecian wife – loving, modest, elegant and dignified. She was astoundingly beautiful, though her reputation was to be eclipsed by her younger daughter. In various measure she passed her beauty on to all four of us children.

There was only one affliction in my childhood: the names in our family are straightforward – Helen, Pollux and Castor. Even Leda, our mother's name, runs straight and clean on the tongue. What inspired my parents to name their eldest daughter Clytemnestra? I blame Leda, of course. She probably wanted a fancy name for her eldest daughter and thought one with length would be imposing. As a small child, I couldn't get my tongue around my own name. I called myself Nestra, and the name stuck. Eventually, the only people to use my full name were my mother, when she was angry, and my husband, for much the same reason.

We grew up as happy Spartan children, and when seven-year-old Castor went off, proud as a young hawk, to the discipline of the agoge, I was just as happy and excited to enter the girls' school. I went skipping through the palace to tell Leda I was to start my education the next day.

I found her sitting with her women, twirling the spindle as she spun.

"Mother," I shouted happily, throwing myself against her legs. "I start school tomorrow."

Leda gave a slight grunt as she absorbed the shock of my

body against her knees, but kept up her steady rhythm with the spool. Calliope, one of Mother's youngest slaves, winked at me.

"You're a big girl now, all right," she said. "Going to learn to be a brave warrior princess?"

Calliope's support encouraged me. I levered myself off Leda's knees and picking up an empty spindle, I held it like a dagger and danced round the chamber, stabbing at invisible enemies. Hydra, the Minotaur, Cerberus were all one to me and fell beneath my onslaught.

"I've got one!" I shouted in triumph, stabbing it to death with determined enthusiasm.

Leda's reaction was unmistakable. She gave a gasp of horror. "No!" she exclaimed as she dropped her spindle, stood up and rushed off to confront her husband. I tagged along in her wake, unnerved by her response and worried I might not be allowed to go to school the next day.

All boys and girls of Sparta have a public education, and for girls, this includes studies in arts, dancing, poetry, music and physical education. During the latter, girls, like the boys, train outdoors unclothed, learn the basic drills and disciplines of fighting, and are encouraged to be brave and forthright.

We found my father in the great hall, where he had been all morning dispensing justice to the citizens of Sparta. He smiled at his wife as she entered, but his smile turned to a frown as she spoke.

"Husband," she said. "Nestra says she is to start her education. She must not. I refuse. No daughter of mine is going to a Spartan school. There is nothing such a place can teach them. The only things a young girl should be taught are spinning, weaving and household management, and they can learn that at home. You can't let a daughter of ours do physical training. No daughter of mine is going to be allowed to behave so immodestly."

My father, a true Spartan, was startled. He rose from the bench and came towards her. "Leda, this is what our girls do. It is how we bring them up. What is wrong that you find this so offensive?"

"It's immodest. No girl should go unclothed in public. And

why should a young woman train with sword and spear? Is she to be a warrior? Do you expect her to fight? And what happens when she's older? Do you want her, once she has her menses, to lie on the cold ground and steal and forage what she needs to stay alive along with a platoon of men? Is this a suitable upbringing for a princess?"

Tyndareus gave a little laugh. "All Sparta's daughters are reared this way. No, she won't be a soldier but she will be the mother of soldiers. Our young men learn the skills and discipline of warriors. Our young women learn to be strong in mind and body so they can breed warriors. Why do you think Sparta's armies rule supreme?"

Leda would not be moved. "She doesn't need those skills. She needs to know how to run and rule a household."

My father roared with laughter. "Why should any Spartan, let alone a princess, know such mundane matters? There is an endless supply of slaves who devote themselves to household tasks. Nestra doesn't have to waste her time on foolish things. She needs to learn to be brave and be the mother of kings. If she grows strong and healthy herself, then she will breed better children."

Leda's voice dropped. "But she will not be a princess in Sparta, my husband. It is the fate of princesses to be married to kings and princes from other lands, as was I." She took a deep breath. "I know you consider it appropriate for young women to walk freely, and talk with men, and have opinions and an education. It is not so in the rest of the Greek world. I had much to learn when I married you. You do your daughters a disservice if you do not teach them that other kingdoms will demand they stay in the women's quarters and deal with women's matters. Men will consider them coarse and unwomanly if they train with sword and spear. Worse, they will think them immodest whores. Do you wish your daughters to be the joke of Attica?"

I had never truly realised before this that my mother was a foreigner. I knew her father was Thestion of Aetolia. Such knowledge was part of our family tree. Where Aetolia was, or that their customs might be different, wasn't something I had considered. Leda's elegance and poise seemed innate, not the result of a very different upbringing.

Her speech must have hurt her husband. "Are you not happy here, wife?"

Leda's voice softened. "With you, my lord, I am always happy. You know that. But our daughters are not ours to keep forever. They will grow and marry. Not all husbands are as kind as you. You had to teach me to be bolder. Other men will want to teach our daughters to be quiet and submissive. I don't want them to have to learn through pain and misery."

I peered round the corner of the tapestry where I was sheltering. Leda had moved close to my father and put her arms around him. "A woman should be strong, but sometimes she needs to hide this. I don't have to dissemble with you, my lord, but other men may not be so understanding."

Her words had pulled Tyndareus up short. He spoke thoughtfully. "Nestra must be educated with others of her age, Leda. She is a princess of Sparta and will be educated as one. But I understand your fear." He pulled his wife closer into the embrace. "Nestra will train, but you will ensure she understands the duties of a household so she is not shamed if she marries into another kingdom." He kissed Leda lightly on the forehead. "It seems I will need to choose carefully which man I allow to marry my daughter. I will think on this matter. They must be as happy as the two of us."

Leda wasn't mollified. Her daughters' public nudity would remain a shame to her for the rest of our childhood, but she loved her husband and understood he had offered her a compromise. She was too wise to persist in a battle she couldn't win.

Consequently, in any time spare from my formal schooling, I was put to learning the slave duties of carding, spinning and weaving. I learned about brewing and butchering, and the proper ways of pleasing the gods. In short, everything a conventional Greek bride would be expected to know. Naturally I was furious. Not only did this extracurricular education take up my spare time, but it exposed me to mockery by my peers.

"Here comes the helot, Nestra is a helot," they would chant.

I had a miserable time until I taught them to respect my temper and my newly learned fighting skills. I felt deep shame at having to work with slaves - the real helots - and I grew sulky and rebellious with my mother, judging her responsible for my plight.

*   *   *

I enjoyed my public education. We were taught to run, to wrestle, to throw a discus and a javelin. If we were not training physically, we were learning to sing, dance and play instruments. Our teacher for the latter was an elderly woman from the polis. She had perfect pitch, elegant movement – and the foulest temper I have ever encountered in a woman. She watched our practice from the sidelines, leaning on her sturdy stick. The gods help any girl who moved out of sequence, or without grace – that stick would come cracking down on us wherever the old crone could lay it. I was talented at dance, but I felt the weight of that stick on several occasions.

The argument between Leda and Tyndareus had opened my eyes to the purpose of our education. Girls were supposed to be brave and strong so they could breed strong Spartan soldiers. I was too young to understand fully, but I understood that when we danced and played music, particularly with the boys, the purpose was to make us nimble and supple in warfare. The boys were being trained for the phalanx, that Spartan technique where the whole unit moves in unison. It is almost indestructible in battle, and the boys train for it endlessly.

Girls wouldn't normally be called on to go to war, but we knew very clearly that we were part of Sparta's defence. If called upon, every woman in Sparta had the knowledge to defend her land, her home and herself.

CHAPTER TWO

Five years later

IT WAS THE HOTTEST PART OF summer; Helen and I had been swimming. At the point the fast-flowing river turned a right angle, it had scoured a deep hole surrounded by steep banks that gave way on the southern side to a pebbly beach, providing easy access to the pool and a convenient spot for the building of small campfires. To access the swimming hole you had to scramble down a rough track, holding on to the shrubs that clung to the face of the bank. In the shade of the banks the river ran cool and deep and was a popular spot in the summer heat. All local children knew of this place, and Helen and I had been playing in the swift-flowing waters.

Now we sweated our way back up the path. The sun was blazingly hot, the track dry and dusty and we were out of breath as we reached the rise, close by the place where three roads met. Helen's eight-year-old limbs were shorter than mine, but she made no complaint as we struggled up the pebbled track through the straggles of thorny scrub.

A few lengths ahead of us a chariot had stopped by the side of the road. The occupants were talking. The horses hung their heads, grateful for a rest in the late afternoon heat. I watched one nibble experimentally at a shrub of dusty sage.

As we approached, the nearest man saw us and called out, "Oi, slave!"

Involuntarily I spun to see which helot had crept up behind us. There was none, and I realised the redheaded stranger was addressing me. The shock of the insult struck me to silence. I stared at the man as I felt my anger build. I had no weapon, but Spartans are taught unarmed combat.

Beside me Helen giggled. "She's not a slave," she called back to the chariot. "She's Clytemnestra, and I'm Helen. We're the daughters of King Tyndareus."

The man's dark-haired companion turned sharply and gazed at us. He said something under his breath to the other. The first speaker turned deep scarlet, his skin tone clashing violently with his red hair. If I hadn't been so angry, the reaction would have been funny.

"Princesses!" he exclaimed in horror. "Pray forgive me, I had no idea." He glanced round in desperation. "I didn't see your maids. I meant no insult." He ran out of words and stared at us in silent mortification.

After a moment the dark companion spoke. "What my brother is trying to say is that he is deeply shamed by his foolish words and begs your forgiveness." His lips quirked slightly. "We were seeking directions to King Tyndareus's palace. It was no part of our plan to insult his daughters. On behalf of my brother and myself, I apologise and beg your pardon."

My wits had slowly returned. "Who are you, and why do you want my father?" I allowed my tone to be arrogant. One apology doesn't necessarily make a truce.

The dark man hesitated, glanced at his silent brother and shrugged. "Agamemnon and Menelaus. We are brothers of the house of Atreus from Mycenae."

I nodded as if this meant something to me, although I had never heard of either. I realised they were both young, Agamemnon perhaps eighteen, and Menelaus, a year or two younger. They were travel-stained and dusty from the road, but their clothes were of fine quality and their chariot well made, cast with reliefs and decoration, the harness formed from supple leather that spoke of high-quality workmanship. Suddenly I felt shy in their presence, aware of my dusty feet and tangled, damp hair.

Helen said helpfully, "If you want the palace, you should take the left branch of the road just ahead of you."

I admired her eight-year-old poise and forced myself to say, "It's only a couple of miles further."

Agamemnon thanked us gravely.

We watched them drive ahead up the road.

"I want to get home quickly," said Helen. "I want to hear what they've got to say when they speak to Father."

We started running.

*   *   *

I had been looking forward to the feast that night. Alcman, our most famous poet, had returned on one of his cyclical visits. It was a celebration for all, as we assembled to hear his news, stories and scandals. Tomorrow he would be amongst the girls at school, teaching us the latest poems.

The addition of the visiting princes was a bonus. We take guests seriously in Sparta, and xenia, or providing for such visitors, is a sacred obligation. As I dressed for the feast, I wondered how their story would affect the poet's programme. I was attending as one of Leda's companions, which meant I would be near her at the high table and in a good position to hear what the princes had to say.

Agamemnon and Menelaus were escorted into the room and bowed before my father. They had cleaned themselves from their travels and changed. I could see again the quality of their clothes, and they bore themselves with the balance and grace of trained warriors. The redheaded one, Menelaus, had brushed his hair, and it gleamed deep gold in the torch lights. He saw me standing behind Leda's chair and nodded to me with a slightly embarrassed smile.

Tyndareus, seated beside Leda, rose to greet them. "Welcome strangers," he said formally. "You will join us and be entertained as our guests here tonight. After you have feasted, we ask that you will tell us your story, and let us know if we can help you in any way." Their formal recognition as guests having been dealt with, Tyndareus offered them seats at the table.

Leda leant forward and smiled at them. "I hope our maids looked after your comfort?"

"Very well, thank you," replied Agamemnon. "We travelled a long way in the heat, and it feels good to be clean and refreshed."

Leda nodded and sat back in her chair, satisfied.

Conversation ceased as the maids busied themselves bringing food to the table. Large platters of venison, flatbreads, olives, cheeses and flasks of wine were circulated by the servants. I noticed our guests behaved courteously enough but ate with a ferocity that suggested it had been a while since their last meal. As we ate our fill, conversation slowly started up again.

Warriors' conversations are always the same: raids or hunting, discussed for hours; about who had performed well or indifferently and what the catch or loot was. I could see our men taking the measure of the newcomers. A couple of questions were asked, and answered by Menelaus. Agamemnon was the more reserved, while his younger brother seemed to make friends easily. Whatever Menelaus replied seemed to please our men, as I saw a couple of approving nods. Perhaps he had cracked a joke, as there was a sudden gust of laughter from those sitting close to him.

The maids worked through the hall keeping wine cups replenished, cheerily slapping the hands of importunate warriors and clearing empty platters and trays. There was a deal of good-natured teasing going on. Everyone was excited by the presence of strangers at our feast and looking forward to the entertainment the poet would offer.

Eventually Tyndareus called for silence. "I now invite our guests to introduce themselves, and tell us what brings them to Sparta."

The two men stood, and Agamemnon bowed to my father. "Thank you, Tyndareus, and your gracious wife, for your welcome to us, travellers to your land. I am Agamemnon of the house of Atreus, and this, my brother Menelaus. Our father, King Atreus, has been killed by Aegisthus, his nephew, and we are fugitives from Mycenae."

There was a murmur of conversation that ran through the hall. This was news indeed.

"Aegisthus and his father Thyestes led an insurrection against our father. They now hold sway in Mycenae and rule our dead father's kingdom." Agamemnon paused for breath. "I ask, King Tyndareus, for sanctuary, until my brother and I can win our kingdom back. We place our swords at your disposal to serve in whatever way pleases you."

Tyndareus looked at Agamemnon thoughtfully. "Please sit, Prince Agamemnon. These are sad tidings indeed. We grieve with you for the death of your father. All here will give you welcome and comfort while you are our guests."

Agamemnon sat, and an elderly warrior at the back of the room stood.

Tyndareus waved to him to speak. "Adrastos."

Adrastos nodded to my father. "Prince Agamemnon, I heard a tale many years ago, which claimed Atreus's wife had an affair with her brother-in-law, your uncle, Thyestes. Atreus discovered this and in anger cooked Thyestes' children and served them to their father as a meal. Is it this act, perhaps, that Thyestes and his youngest surviving son have avenged by killing your father?"

I watched Agamemnon turn pale, but he stood and answered Adrastos firmly enough. "I have heard this story, though my brother and I are too young to know if it is accurate or even true. I have also heard that Aegisthus was bred by his father solely to destroy Atreus. That may also be true. Sometimes the gods drive men mad. My father never spoke of this to me. I knew him only as a noble, brave man who honoured the gods."

Adrastos sat down with the pleased look of a man who has done his duty. There was a shocked silence in the room. I saw Tyndareus examining Agamemnon thoughtfully. I knew he would respect the young man's poise, even if he loathed Atreus's actions.

I heard Leda mutter beside me. "What a monstrous, impious family. Cursed by the gods, indeed."

I felt sick. What sort of person cooks children? I looked across at Agamemnon. Frankly, I thought his uncle had good reason to murder the man who'd massacred his family so foully. I supposed the faithless wife must have been Agamemnon's mother, and wondered, with a shudder, what had happened to her.

Finally Agamemnon sat down.

A younger man, Fotis, stood, and my father nodded to him to speak.

"Prince Agamemnon and Prince Menelaus are our guests," Fotis began. "Our king has welcomed them, and it is not good to cause them distress. Stories and minstrels' tales may not always be true. Our best poets take facts and make them elaborate to please an audience. We hope for one of the best of them to perform here tonight. "

When he sat down there was a good deal of head-nodding in agreement. I wondered how many believed the story false, and how many simply wanted to forget its horror as soon as they decently could. We were lucky, I suppose, that we had eaten before hearing the tale. I couldn't have faced a platter of meats straight after tales of butchered children. My tummy felt queasy enough even now.

It was a relief when Alcman stood up to perform. Perhaps he, too, had been affected by the earlier tensions in the hall, as he chose to stay away from the more stirring tales in his repertoire. Instead he told the ancient story of Philemon and Baucis. This married couple loved each other so much they wished to die at the same moment, so neither had to grieve for the other. They prayed to the gods to grant them this boon. The gods, pleased with their piety, granted their wish and on their death transformed them into trees. Philemon became an oak and Baucis, a lime. Their boughs intertwined forever as a symbol of their everlasting love.

It was one of my favourite stories, and I saw my father

reach out for Leda's hand and squeeze it gently. I smiled at his unwarrior-like affection for his wife.

*   *   *

Both foreign princes were seasoned warriors and were accepted as such in the messes. They became an accepted feature of Tyndareus's court. Agamemnon was true to his word. His sword was there to aid Tyndareus in any mission or battle.

Sparta as a kingdom was never wholly at peace. What would be the point of that? There were always skirmishes with those peoples to the south and west who didn't move out of the way quickly, or pay their levies fast enough.

We were not a trading kingdom. Our wealth was our slaves, our strength was our army and our fortress the ring of mountains that surrounded our lands. Unlike other kingdoms there was no central, fortified palace to protect the royal family. We lived spread out through the land, protected by our geography and our warriors.

In contrast, as I came to learn, Mycenae's wealth was based on where it lay at the apex of the trade routes. Ships and traders came there from all quarters of the world with their goods to sell. By charging a small tax on each transaction, Mycenae grew rich. I had noticed the richness of Agamemnon's clothes when he and Menelaus were received by my father, but it was years before I fathomed just how wealthy that kingdom was. I came to understand that Sparta was unusual amongst the Greek kingdoms. Self-sufficient, but poor in luxury goods and great art, our culture was purely militaristic.

Slaves were a great asset but didn't necessarily translate into fine jewels, clothes and buildings, and the number of slaves Sparta owned was a problem in itself. I had heard my father comment that there were eight helots for every Spartan citizen. Slaves, for all their obvious usefulness, caused problems. Our warriors spent much of their time pursuing and disciplining the wayward and rebellious. Castor was immensely proud that he had killed two helots himself as part of his education.

Leda always treated her house slaves with unusual courtesy and kindness and ensured that Helen and I did the same. I didn't see why we should; a slave is a slave, after all, and not worth considering.

When I was seven, a slave stood in my way when I tried to climb over the balustrade high above the entrance to the palace gates.

"Little lady, you must not do this," he remonstrated as I put my foot over the railing.

I was filled with stories of Daedalus and Icarus and was determined to try flying for myself. When his words failed, and I persisted in my folly, the slave reached out and dragged me to safety. I was outraged, picked up a loose stone and threw it at his head, cutting him deeply on the temple.

Two things made this memorable. The first was, that night I went down with a fever and spent the next six weeks fighting for my life. Consequently I was forgiven my petulant action as it must have been a precursor to the illness. The second, the slave was flogged for grabbing at me.

I didn't hear of this until weeks later when I lay recovering on a pallet in my mother's room. Calliope let it slip while she was feeding me sweet gruel to tempt my appetite.

"He was old," she said. "It was nothing special as a flogging, but he died all the same. The physician said his heart gave out." She reached forward to wipe my chin, but I grabbed her hand.

"Are you saying the slave died because he warned me?" I asked, outraged.

Calliope looked startled.

"No, of course not, little mistress. He was flogged because he laid his hands on a member of Sparta's Royal Family. He died because his heart was weak, nothing more."

She was right, of course, but the guilty feeling remained. Perhaps it was worth noting that Leda's slaves were loyal, reliable and never caused trouble. I never admitted my childish guilt, but I made a point of not actively abusing slaves from then on.

CHAPTER
THREE

B Y THE TIME I WAS SIXTEEN, the princes had been with us for four years and had become an integral part of the palace and army. I think my father enjoyed their company. They were older than Castor and I, so he could deal with them as adults while treating them as surrogate sons. They represented a different set of values and culture, and Tyndareus, a wise man in many ways, valued widening his own knowledge and understanding.

I was old enough by then to know I was going to need a suitable husband in a few years, and was aware of a bond forming with Agamemnon. I saw him as he exercised in the training grounds, and I watched his technique, his power and the naked planes of his body. He was of stocky build, a function of muscle structure rather than weight. It made him a powerful wrestler, and he won several classes at the games.

Menelaus, lighter and taller, was better at running.

Agamemnon confessed that the warrior training he'd received as a boy in Mycenae was much less vigorous and harsh than a Spartan's. If so, it made him no less a warrior as far as I could see.

Helen had noticed my preoccupation with the prince.

"So, do you fancy Agamemnon?" she asked me with a grin. "You can't take your eyes off him."

I flushed a little. "Not really," I shrugged, as if unconcerned. "I just wondered how they train their men in Mycenae."

Helen giggled. "You mean they do things differently there?"

It wasn't the words, but her tone which made the statement sexually charged.

"You wouldn't understand," I said sharply. "You're too young."

She laughed at me and stuck her tongue out. "I'm not that young anymore," she chuckled.

*   *   *

Unfortunately, Leda had also noticed my interest in Agamemnon.

"Stop making cow's eyes at the man," she said to me sharply. "That's no way for a respectable girl to behave. Grow up, and stop acting like a trollop. Men will misunderstand if you go on like that. It's an open invitation for trouble."

I bowed my head obediently. Leda was not a woman to cross. Inside I seethed with embarrassed fury. This was a private matter, and I didn't appreciate anyone else speculating about my feelings.

Agamemnon's princely status automatically ensured he had his own troop of men, which was augmented by the refugees from Mycenae who had followed him to Sparta.

I was too shy to approach him directly, but Agamemnon fell into a friendly way of stopping to talk to me if we passed. Eventually I relaxed and learned to enjoy those casual encounters. He teased me about when I first met them and Menelaus had tried to summon me as a slave.

"You looked like an angry cat," he said. "I expected your tail to start twitching, just before you pounced on him for the kill."

I was shy, but smiled at him. "I'm not used to strange princes riding into my land."

"Well, you looked very able to defend all of Sparta by yourself," he said, grinning.

I grinned back.

He was a handsome man and there was enough humour in his manner to make him appealing.

Perhaps he, too, was thinking about his future marriage prospects. He was a refugee prince, but if ever he regained his kingdom, he would need a wife, and Sparta, with its formidable army, was a good ally to have.

The potential for an alliance and for romance was a heady brew. I indulged myself, imagining being Agamemnon's queen. Of course, he had yet to win the kingdom back, but I thought I would rather like to be queen of Mycenae. My mind was occupied by Mother's words from years ago about princesses being forced to marry away from their homes and all they were familiar with. At least Agamemnon wouldn't be unknown, and I could imagine loving him. My parents' marriage was my guide. Leda may have come from a culture that required submissiveness in a woman, but she had no difficulty imposing her will and personality on the palace when Tyndareus was away, and she served as his de facto regent in his absence. Loving and supportive of each other all through the years, their relationship survived Tyndareus's frequent absences in wars or raids.

* * *

It was the time of the annual Gymnopaedia, those sacred games dedicated to Apollo, and almost all the students were involved in the events.

I had entered and won a running race and was to participate in some dance performances. I watched Helen dance, compete in javelin throwing, and then run. She was deceptive. Blonde, pretty and blessed with an apparently sweet, undemanding nature, many wrote her off as too gentle to handle competition or conflict.

Those who thought so were wrong.

I watched as she ran, long hair and long legs flying. Helen was the most competitive person I knew. I smiled as I saw her tear down the track of the stadium to a well-deserved win. She was pure ambition, never to be swayed once she had set her heart on a prize.

A campsite had been set up outside the precincts of the temple. Immediately a market established itself in close proximity, with traders selling everything from wine and stuffed pastries to spare bedding and clothes. A makeshift hospital had been established to cope with those injured in the games, or, more prosaically, those victims of drunken stoushes in the camp itself. For a few days our quiet valley teemed with people.

Strangers from every level of society and from every kingdom came to join in the competitions and celebrations. At the start of the festival our head tutor gave all the students a speech. I could have summed it up in two words – keep away. Keep away, keep away.

Spartan scholars were not to risk their health, reputations and fortunes in the shanty town that followed the games. Of course, we ignored him and made our way into the fascinating market. There were sweetmeats to buy, wandering players to entertain us and exotic goods for sale. How could we stay away? For the majority of us it was the most exciting event of our young lives.

More important visitors stayed at the palace as guests. That year we hosted Theseus, King of Athens. He was supposed to be a great hero after his exploits defeating the Minotaur in Crete, but he didn't impress me. He was a short, wiry little man with an opportunist's face and a lecher's awareness of women. I was conscious of him among the spectators watching Helen as she competed and gave a shudder of revulsion. He ogled her so freely it was indecent.

I watched his behaviour that night when he dined in the hall with my parents. He expected a little too much adulation, which sat ill with us Spartans who were accustomed to understating our achievements in case we incited the gods' jealousy. He was particularly obnoxious in his attentions to Leda who deflected him with grace and charm, although I could tell she was offended.

When he was introduced to me I felt, as a physical force, his quick assessment of the body beneath my tunic. His oily words only completed my disgust.

We were all relieved when he elected to leave early.

No one noticed at first that Helen was missing. Usually her absence would have been noted immediately but the games had meant a relaxation in the strict disciplines and routines of our lives. It was next morning that a slave arrived at the palace from the school with the news that Helen had been missing for the night. Frantic questioning established that she hadn't been seen since the early afternoon of the previous day. Sparta's military were put on high alert. A systematic search of the visitors' campsite was undertaken, the occupants of every tent questioned.

I was with my distraught parents when a witness was brought in.

"He claims to be Gyras, from Athens," stated Fotis, who led the terrified man into the audience room. "He says he was camping besides a tent full of fellow Athenians and heard them talking."

Tyndareus stood up and approached the prisoner. "Tell us what you heard."

Gyras fell to his knees. "I didn't know anything was wrong. I haven't done anything," he said. "I just came for the games."

"Oh, stand up, man, and stop snivelling," said my father. "We just want to ask you a few questions. What did you hear from the Athenians?"

Gyras clambered to his feet. "They were talking about their King Theseus." He stopped abruptly.

"Go on," said Tyndareus patiently.

"They said he had seen this girl, the princess. They said he wants to marry the daughter of a god, because he is himself the son of Poseidon. He and his friend Pirithous have a bet that they can both get gods' daughters as their wives." His face was sly when he looked at Leda. "Everyone knows Zeus is the father of the princess Helen."

Leda had turned very pale, the knuckles of her hands white where they gripped the arm of her chair.

Tyndareus erupted. "What a complete load of horse shit.

Whichever minstrel thought up that tale needs a dagger across their throat. Helen is my child, and no more divine than any other princess. Are you saying Theseus stole my daughter?"

Gyras flinched. "I don't know, but that's what the men in the camp were talking about. I don't know anything else, I swear by the gods. I don't know whether King Theseus would actually steal her. Maybe he wanted to marry her?"

"Over my dead body, and the dead carcass of every man in the Spartan Army. That pompous, arrogant little bastard from Athens isn't good enough to wed a poxed whore from Piraeus. How dare he lift his eyes to a daughter of mine?"

Gyras collapsed back on his knees again. "I'm sorry, I'm sorry."

Tyndareus looked down at him with contempt. "Get this milksop out of here, Fotis, before I kick him to death."

"What do you want me to do with him?" asked Fotis cheerfully. "Flog him, spear him, or chuck him into a ravine?"

At this point an unfortunate wet patch appeared on Gyras's tunic as he lost control of his bladder.

"Just throw him out of the palace," said Tyndareus in disgust. "Get out of Sparta," he said to the grovelling man. "And don't ever come back. Do you understand?"

Gyras nodded his head as Fotis hauled him to his feet.

"Get a maid to clean the floor," Tyndareus shouted as Fotis dragged the man away.

Tyndareus's tone was gentle as he turned to his wife. "Are you all right?" he asked.

Leda bowed her head. "I had heard that tale, but I didn't actually think anyone believed it. I am sorry, my lord, for bringing such shame on you." Her eyes were wet, but she kept herself from crying.

Tyndareus knelt beside her and took hold of her hands. "Dear heart, you and I know who fathered our children, and we both enjoyed doing it very much." This drew a wan smile from my mother and an embarrassed squirm from me. If I hadn't been so worried about Helen I would have willed myself anywhere but here with my parents. Their tender affection mortified me.

"Don't waste your time on that nonsense, as I certainly won't." He kissed her hands and stood up. "Now we need to arrange for the return of our daughter. The sooner our troops are after that bastard Theseus, the sooner we will get Helen home."

He strode towards the door. "Fotis!"

"Father," I said.

He stopped and turned.

"Please let me go on this mission. Helen's my sister."

He looked at me for a minute.

"Please. You know I am good in a fight, and I'll have my bow and my javelins with me."

He nodded curtly, "Get your things," and strode out of the room.

I turned to Leda, who was now in open tears. I felt a moment of contempt. No proper Spartan woman should give way to crying.

"It will be all right, Mother. We'll get Helen back," I said awkwardly.

"But now I have to worry about you as well," she said softly. "Take care, Nestra, and come home safely."

I allowed her to hold me briefly in a damp embrace before I escaped to pack my kit.

*　*　*

The men assembled were chosen for their ability to move at speed. Theseus had a full day's lead on us, so every soldier and his charioteer would be involved in the race to catch up with them.

I stood uncertainly as the men paired up. I was trained as a Spartan warrior, and well able to carry my share of the fighting, but these men had lived together in barracks since they were seven. They were partners, some even lovers, of long standing and weren't about to yield that place to a girl, princess or no. I saw Castor glance my way and avert his gaze. Pollux was with another boy from his year. I felt a slow flush of shame start to burn as I wondered what to do.

A chariot pulled up beside me. "Do you want a ride?" Agamemnon enquired.

I nodded my thanks and scrambled up beside him, my relief and embarrassment making me uncharacteristically clumsy.

"Hold on," he said cheerfully. "This is going to be a wild ride."

We galloped the miles, following the easy line of the road as it ran out of our valley and turned up along the coastline. The mile markers flashed by. Looking eastward, I could see the far-distant sea. I realised I had never been this far from home before.

I gripped the edge of the chariot and spread my legs to hold my balance. I was very aware of Agamemnon standing close beside me. He was concentrating on driving, so there was no conversation, but I watched the muscles move beneath the tanned skin of his arms. The dark hair on his forearm fascinated me. I wanted to put my hand out and touch it. Occasionally the sway of the chariot would bring our bodies into contact. Once he turned to me, the excitement of the chase clear in his grin.

I focused on him to distract me from thoughts of what might be happening to Helen. True, she was warrior trained, tough and courageous. She was also twelve years old and alone in the hands of a man who already had a dubious reputation with women. I shuddered, and returned to studying Agamemnon.

We reached Troizen two days later.

CHAPTER FOUR

TROIZEN AND ATHENS LIE, OF COURSE, in opposite directions. We had assumed Theseus would take Helen directly to his capital, but at Argos we lost the trail. We waited at the crossroads for the scouts to return. They had gone north to Corinth but came back with no news of Theseus. The horses were tethered so we got down and stretched our legs.

I was aware of Agamemnon striking a ragwort that had dared grow at the base of the mile marker. He was staring up the road towards Mycenae. A palpable air of rage and frustration emanated from him. He threw his whip down and took a few steps up the road. I had lived around men in barracks long enough to know when not to talk, so I sat down on the abused milestone and picked the seeds off a stem of grass while we waited. Even among the various sounds of the war party, I could hear the harshness of his breathing.

"Moody bugger, isn't he." The charioteer on my right jerked his chin at Agamemnon's back. "Happy as a cricket one moment, then something sets him off. Don't let it worry you."

I sighed. "I won't. I suppose he misses Mycenae."

The charioteer grunted. "What he misses is common sense. We're not going to Mycenae today. Why waste your time pining over it?" He went off to rub his horses down. I smiled a little at his practical attitude. He was perfect warrior material.

Across the road was a wayside shrine to Artemis. I went and stood in front of it and offered prayers for the safe return of my sister. I promised the goddess a magnificent offering if Helen and I returned to Sparta safely. I believed Artemis to be my special protector, so I prayed with all the intensity a young woman could muster. There was no answer, but I took comfort in the words and ritual.

Eventually, after losing half a day casting round in other directions, one of the scouts picked up the trail, this time heading south-east.

We started in pursuit again but were warier. Eventually we came down the coastline and here had some luck. We stopped at a wayside inn, and one of the scouts learnt Theseus's mother lived in Troizen on a small property, set back in a valley away from the coast. The innkeeper, for a fee, described the layout of the farm and gave us clear directions to her estate.

We gathered some miles further on to plan the raid. There were older, more seasoned warriors, but this mission belonged to Castor. His sister had been abducted, and it was his responsibility to get her back. I felt the same weight, but no Spartan would allow a woman to lead a war band.

There was only an hour of daylight left as we gathered in the olive grove to the north of the farm. Lights were already burning in the house. Scouts checked the stables and farm buildings, but there was no evidence Theseus was in residence, although there were fresh horse droppings in the muck heap, as if several animals had been stabled overnight.

I gripped my javelins firmly. Agamemnon was somewhere on my right, beside Menelaus and my brothers. When the scouts gave the all-clear, Castor raised his arm and indicated we were to move forward. We crossed the open area between the trees and the house without being challenged. Castor and Pollux ran to the door, put their shoulders against it and burst into the house.

Too late the occupants realised they were under attack. Castor cut down a couple of men who tried to oppose him, but there was little resistance. These were farmhands, not warriors. A terrified housekeeper was hauled out from where she had taken shelter behind a door.

"Where is Theseus?" demanded Castor.

"He's not here," the old woman whimpered. "He left this morning with his men."

"What about my sister?"

"The girl? She's upstairs with Aethra."

"When will Theseus return?"

"I don't know. He went with his friend Pirithous."

Castor gave a grunt of exasperation and ran her through before shoving her aside. Her body collapsed to the floor. I had to jump over it as I followed him up the stairs. Others were there before him and had pushed open the door.

Helen was chained to a bed frame on the far side of the room. Beside her, two other women, obviously noble, frozen in the act of eating.

"Which one of you is Aethra?" Castor asked.

The older woman rose to her feet. "I am." She stood proud and tall, a princess in her own palace. "Who are you, and why do you invade my home?" She addressed me, I presume as the only woman present.

I ignored her and turned to the other woman. "Who are you?"

The girl wasn't much older than me, pretty in a pale, indoorsy way. Now she was shaking like a leaf. "I am Phisaides," she replied.

I shrugged my shoulders. "So, why are you here?"

"My brother is Pirithous, friend of Theseus. He brought me to help guard the capt-." She broke off suddenly as she realised who she was talking to. "I mean, to keep Princess Helen company."

I stalked passed her to Helen. She gave me a small grin, and I hugged her.

"Remove those chains from my sister," shouted Castor.

I examined Helen. There were bruises on her wrists and on her cheek. Her knees were grazed and her fingernails torn. I gave her a grim smile. "I take it you didn't go quietly?"

She smiled back, a little wavering smile. "They grabbed me before I realised what was happening. I fought with all I had, but I was unarmed."

Pollux came forwards with a hammer and chisel and worked his way through the links to free her. I helped her stand and hugged her to me, almost giddy with relief.

We drove the captive women before us down the stairs and into the kitchen. Others of our troop had arrived after checking the outbuildings. I saw Agamemnon among them and was pleased he was unscathed, although there had been little enough danger in our raid. The bodies of the dead servants had already been dragged out to the midden, leaving streaks of blood across the tiled floor.

"What are you going to do with the women?" Agamemnon asked my brother.

"I am going to do to them exactly what they planned to do with my sister," was the curt reply. Castor gestured to Pollux. "Put the chains on both of them."

He turned and faced Aethra. "Your son took my sister for his own pleasure. Now you will serve her, as a slave, for the rest of your life."

For the first time I saw Aethra rattled. "But Theseus never hurt her," she exclaimed. "He wanted to wed her but was prepared to wait until she was old enough. She is a maiden still."

I had heard enough. "Do you see the bruises on my sister?" I asked. "Do you see the cuts, grazes and scratches? Did you put the chain round her to bind her to your will?"

Aethra made a sort of choking noise. "But you can't make me a slave," she wailed.

I ignored her. "You will serve her, and serve her well, as my brother has decreed. If you or Phisaides ever fail in your duty, then you will die as slaves in a foreign land."

I felt a warm pair of hands on my shoulder and, turning my head, saw it was Agamemnon.

"I told you you could defend Sparta all on your own, little cat," he whispered softly so only I could hear.

Aethra's actions had raised such anger in me I was hard put to contain it. I struggled to control my breathing before I could turn and smile back at Agamemnon. "Always beware of a cat," I teased.

"For some they are good luck." His fingers gripped tighter before he released me.

We feasted that evening on the food meant for Aethra and her household. Pollux had discovered the wine store, and it was a happy, raucous group of Spartans who sat round the brazier in the courtyard.

Castor called to Aethra. "Woman. More wine for my cup, then serve the men."

"I am not a slave," she said stubbornly. "I am the daughter of a king. You can't make me a slave."

Castor's eyes narrowed. "Pour the wine." He spoke slowly, as to one who has difficulty understanding. I recognised the menace in his tone.

Aethra stood her ground. "If you hadn't slaughtered my servants, they could have waited on you. Let their corpses serve you, not I." She was all queenly attitude and disdain.

Castor leapt to his feet, crossed the distance between them in one stride and hit her so hard across the face that she flew several feet before sprawling on the ground.

"Pour the wine," he growled.

I watched Aethra very slowly stagger to her feet and stand, swaying. Her lip was split, her nose at a strange angle and a trickle of blood ran from it, pooling in the crease at the side of her mouth. Very slowly she gathered herself together.

"Pour!" demanded Castor again.

Aethra would have been much of an age as our own mother Leda. I forced the thought away.

The fight had gone out of her. With a choked sob she lifted the amphora and poured Castor his cup full then turned to Agamemnon.

Beside me Pollux snorted, "Stupid cow. She'll find it much easier if she just gets on with it."

I turned my head and looked at Phisaides, already pouring

wine like a dutiful slave. The drink had got to the men, and she was fending off groping hands with every sign of distress. As a Greek princess she would have been as gently reared as Helen and I. More gently in fact, for no one would have taught her to fight or kill. There would be a difficult night ahead for her, I guessed.

I looked back at Aethra, now serving our warriors, but crying silently as she bent beside each one to refill their cup.

We had been taught that pity is a weakness we could not afford. I was strong, I reminded myself. I was a Spartan princess. I was not weak. I summoned the image of Helen in chains and hardened my heart.

Later I lay in bed beside Helen, in a room overlooking the courtyard. The men still caroused below. They were singing now – barrack-room songs with easy tunes and filthy lyrics.

Later still, I heard an anguished scream. "Nooooooo!" followed by hysterical sobbing before it went quiet.

I rolled over and turned my back to the window in an unconscious gesture of rejection. I saw Helen was awake, her eyes wide in the gloom. I wondered suddenly whether I should say something to her, perhaps explain matters. She was, after all, only twelve years old.

"We aren't going to Athens, to kill Theseus for revenge, are we?" she asked. "Not now you've got me back."

"No," I said, grateful she hadn't asked me to explain the scene outside our window. "No point." There was a pause.

"So Theseus and Pirithous will get off unpunished? Even though they stole me from my father's kingdom?"

I shrugged. "I suppose so."

"Aethra didn't know anything about my abduction, you know. Theseus just turned up here yesterday afternoon and told his mother she had to care for me until I was old enough for a wedding."

"You had chains on your wrists," I said. My anger at the sight flooded through me again.

"She couldn't say no," said Helen. She always had been stubborn, and she spoke now with conviction. "She's his mother.

She didn't have a choice."

I said nothing.

"Why is it that the men who abducted me and hurt me are getting away with it, and the women who did nothing are the ones getting punished?"

"It's the way of things," I said curtly, although I really had no answer.

We lay in silence for quite a while.

"Aethra and Phisaides are also the daughters of kings," whispered Helen eventually. "Could this happen to us as well?"

"Don't be silly," I said. Her questions were making me cross; they echoed those in my own mind, and I couldn't afford to be gentle.

The silence was fraught. I could sense Helen's distress.

"Look, they will be well looked after when they reach Sparta," I said at last. This was true. No slave of Leda's was treated with anything other than courtesy and kindness. I couldn't remember any time my mother had beaten a slave.

"Go to sleep, Helen. We travel tomorrow, remember?"

We burned the homestead the next morning, piling the bodies of those we had killed onto the fire to turn to ashes in the conflagration. We had neither the time nor interest to bury the dead. I noticed Aethra standing stony-faced while her erstwhile home burned to the ground.

Phisaides' face was swollen and marked with tears. She moved with the stiffness of a crone. Aethra put her arm around her shoulders in comfort. The men rounded up the few cattle, sheep and goats from the farm and sent them on the road to Sparta.

It took us several days to reach home. Messengers had been sent ahead to let Leda and Tyndareus know the news of Helen's rescue. For the rest of us, the journey turned into a holiday. We covered miles each day but at a much slower pace. The stock moved at their own speed, which kept us to their rhythm. The two wretched women, tied to a cart, trudged in the dust behind the cattle. I refused to feel compassion for either of them. Every time I thought of Helen in chains I felt a surge of murderous rage. It wasn't Castor's intent, but he had been kinder to them than I would have been.

There was time in the chariot for Agamemnon and me to talk.

He told me his dreams of reclaiming his kingdom. I began to understand the depths of frustration he hid from us all. Years had gone by, and usurpers still sat on his father's throne. Why had I never realised his anger was so intense? His brother Menelaus was a happy-go-lucky type, just grateful for a warm billet and a group of supportive friends.

Menelaus could be happy anywhere, but I began to understand that Agamemnon would never be happy or content while he felt humiliated. I also began to understand how easy it was to generate that emotion in him.

I felt a deep sympathy. If I had dreaded being shipped off to a husband in a distant and different land, how galling must it be for a warrior to have to patiently endure exile while another took his place on the throne? I hoped there would be some way for Agamemnon to achieve his destiny.

Not all our conversations were serious. We fell into an easy way of talking to each other, which was flirtatious and enjoyable. He called me 'little cat'.

"I think you're insulting me," I complained. "I'm a warrior woman, but you make me sound like a tame pet."

He laughed out loud. "Maybe you're a wild mountain cat, a little lioness."

"Well, if I'm a cat, what does that make you?"

He thought for a while. "A boar," he said at last.

I was surprised. I had imagined a wolf, or maybe a bear.

"What makes you say that?"

He gave a smirk. "Because the boar is the most dangerous animal in our forests. It's quick, clever and just as likely to kill the hunter as to be killed itself. If you wound a boar it will come after you for revenge, and it can have a very long memory."

"Surely it can't be safe for a cat to travel with a boar?" I asked.

He gave a thoughtful pause and then laughed. "I think conflict between a mountain cat and a boar might be about equal. They're both very dangerous."

"So you declare a truce?"

"Let there be truce then between us," he agreed and grinned at me.

I was flattered, amused, and his attentions spurred me to being quicker, cleverer and wittier than was usual for me. I believe I gentled his angers. He was never anything but kind, amused and affectionate towards me.

We only once referred to the mission we had been on.

"Your sister is likely to pose a few problems over the next years," he remarked.

"Oh? Why?"

He looked at me sidewise as if unsure how to proceed. "Your sister is going to be very beautiful, and her rescue from Theseus is only going to add to her reputation for desirability," he remarked. "If I was your father, I'd get her betrothed as soon as possible."

I stared at him in surprise and some indignation. "She's only twelve," I said. "Spartan girls don't wed until they're eighteen or more. That's years away for Helen." I didn't add my equally clear thought that, for me, it was only two years away.

Agamemnon pulled me towards him suddenly in a close hug. "You know, you're a very unusual girl. Any other would have been furious I said your sister was attractive. You're just concerned that she would be too young for a betrothal."

I said nothing, but his words gave me pause. Of course Helen was beautiful. So was I. Leda had given each of us a portion of her beauty. I glanced at my sister riding in a chariot with Pollux. The twins made a very attractive pair with their wheaten hair and warm-toned skins. Menelaus had pulled up beside them. He must have said something funny, for Helen's head was thrown back, laughing at some shared joke. It showed the long, pale line of her throat.

Was there something special about Helen's looks? I had seen her only as my little sister.

Now it seemed men saw something else.

CHAPTER
FIVE

OUR VALLEY RETURNED TO SOLITUDE. THE men were back in barracks and training, and Helen and I returned to our studies. My lessons had become more demanding. At the age of eighteen, every Spartan girl is examined in physical fitness, dance, music, rhetoric and philosophical thought. This is the single key to our future. Pass, and we become full citizens of the state of Sparta. Fail, and we are relegated to the *perioikos*, the middle classes, never to be a true member of the state.

I am a princess of Sparta, but I would get no special treatment. If anything, I had to meet higher expectations. The thought of failure was intolerable.

Dance was my favourite subject, but now we were drilled to uniform perfection. Every girl moved in unison to the movements and the music. Every arm and placement of the foot precise.

I trained, until even my calloused hands blistered. I was more than competent with javelin and bow, but the sword had always been my weakest weapon. Now I worked through the drills for hours.

Sometimes Agamemnon would spar with me. Our movements became a complicated dance. I had been trained to look into the eyes of my foe, to predict their next move. When I gazed into Agamemnon's, what I saw invariably distracted me. His dark brown eyes gave me no indication of intent. The emotion – I later identified it as lust – drew me into its dark portals. I desired this man, I hated this man. In particular, I loathed losing to him because I knew some part of me wanted to yield.

I woke in the mid-reaches of the night and lay thinking of the match we would have the next day. I imagined thrust and defence for hours, until I fell into an uneasy sleep just before the horns blew to separate us from our beds.

I worked hard to achieve it, but one day a lucky stroke managed to get through Agamemnon's guard. He was gracious in his defeat and bowed to me with no irony.

"I was lucky to walk away from that last attack," he said. "A real foe would have had me butchered for a barbecue in seconds. You've improved, little cat. Each day you become more effective. If we ever go to war, you could be my shield bearer."

I gave him a slight smile, accepting the compliment, but wondering what had made him so abnormally careless.

*　　*　　*

Two weeks later I was in the palace with Leda. I resented the time spent learning silly domestic duties, but I was fed up with my studies and it did provide an opportunity to hear gossip which never made it as far as the barracks.

"Agamemnon must be looking forward to the coming war," said Leda.

"What war?" I asked. I hadn't heard any talk of war around the barracks, and Agamemnon hadn't said anything to me directly.

"Why, the invasion of Achea, of course. He's been talking with Tyndareus, and they've been planning it for weeks. They haven't released it to the men yet, just in case word gets out prematurely, but I believe it's planned for the next full moon."

Leda paused to examine a tunic in a pile of laundry. "This needs darning," she said and clicked her tongue in irritation.

I had been mulling over her words. "I suppose Agamemnon is wise to be careful. Many Myceneans followed him when he came here. Some may not be so loyal if he invades land where they still have family." I stopped to think through the implications.

A maid entered the room bringing chilled wine for us.

Leda showed her the tunic. "Why hasn't this been mended?" she asked.

"Sorry, mistress." The girl flushed and picked up the tunic.

"Go through the lot, and make sure you check properly this time."

The girl retreated with her pile of mending.

"Really," said Leda in exasperation, "we've got a houseful of slaves, and I still can't trust them to be reliable unless I'm there to supervise."

She poured us both a glass of the wine.

"When Helen returned safely, Tyndareus decided it was time to give Agamemnon the help he needs to win back his kingdom. The boys have been here long enough, and fought bravely for us. Also, your father thinks it would be good to have a future ally in Achea. Agamemnon has made him realise that Sparta could benefit from being more open to trade."

"He didn't say anything to me," I said. Surely Agamemnon should have known I was on his side, that he could trust me with his secrets. I was hurt.

"Your father? Well, he probably hasn't had the chance. Anyway, he wouldn't necessarily consider it women's business."

"Not father," I almost shouted in my exasperation.

There was silence, quite long enough for me to consider what I had inadvertently revealed. I looked up to see my mother staring at me with a stricken look.

"Are you saying that you expected Agamemnon to have confided in you?"

"No," I blustered.

She stared me down with the steely glare only she could muster.

"Well, maybe I thought he would have," I muttered eventually.

"Darling, are you saying there is something between you and Agamemnon?" Her voice was soft enough, but I could tell she disapproved.

I started to deny it, but she overrode me.

"Nestra, we've never talked about these things, but maybe we should. You are a grown woman now, and soon you'll be thinking about betrothal and marriage. Don't set your heart on Agamemnon. You are worthy of a much better man."

"How can you say that?" I was stung by the comment. "What's wrong with him? He's a prince. You've just said he's going to fight to get his throne back. Maybe he will be a king. What's wrong with that?"

I watched as Leda gathered her thoughts. She was a cool woman, my mother, not given to blurting out whatever first came to her mind. I saw her pause to form her argument.

"I want you to be happy," she said at last. "I want you to have as good a marriage as your father and I have had."

I nodded. Well, any mother would want that for her daughter, wouldn't they? I shrugged my shoulders.

"Agamemnon has been sleeping with Clymene," she said. "You know, Clymene, my maid?"

I felt a surge of anger wash through me. How dare a maid enjoy what I was denied? I knew Clymene as a perfectly pleasant young woman in my mother's service, but hearing she slept with the man I wanted made me hate her with an explosive anger.

"So?" I said, as arrogantly as I could to hide my pain and shock.

"He hits her," said Leda urgently. "I've seen her with a black eye. It may have happened more than once."

"She's a slave," I said. "She probably deserved it. What do you expect? If she didn't enjoy it, she wouldn't sleep with him."

Frankly, if I could have got my fingers on Clymene at that moment I'd have given her something a good deal worse than a black eye. A flogging at the very least.

Leda's voice hardened. "She's also a woman, which is something you would do well to consider. She probably had no choice in the matter. As you say, she's a slave, and though I try to keep them safe, I can't protect my maids against every man who orders them to their bed. He's a prince. How could she refuse? The point is, a man who hits one woman will go on to hit another. Nestra, please don't be blind or stupid about this. I want you to have joy in your marriage. You won't find that with a man who uses his fists on you when he gets frustrated."

I was furious. Why was my own mother so stupid she couldn't understand that I loved Agamemnon? He would be different with me. How could she rate a slave's welfare above my happiness?

We continued folding linen in silence. I thought I heard Leda sigh, but was in no mood to listen to anything else she had to say. I was happy when I was able to leave her and be alone to mull over the relationship between Clymene and Agamemnon. It had never occurred to me to be jealous of a slave before.

When Agamemnon joined me the next day I asked about the plans. I was hurt he hadn't seen fit to tell me himself. My feelings must have showed in my face, because he beckoned me to sit beside him on the wall surrounding the training ground. I glanced at him. His head was bent, staring at the engraving on the hilt of his sword.

At last he lifted his head and looked at me directly.

"Whatever happens, this attempt will define mine and Menelaus's entire lives," he said. "If I can defeat or kill Thyestes and Aegisthus, then I will have a kingdom of my own. I will inherit my father's crown, have status and a place among the kings of Greece." He made an odd little grimace. "If I fail, I remain a refugee. I will be a homeless mercenary doomed to wander Greece as a warrior for hire. I will have nothing to offer a wife."

I was about to say he would always have a place in Sparta, but stopped myself. Agamemnon needed no platitudes from me. We were taught from birth that death is better than dishonour. I was warrior trained myself and born to be the mother of warriors. I understood how galling it must be for him to live as a guest, however welcome.

"This is my test, Nestra," he said soberly. "Just as you must pass your exam to take your place in Sparta so, too, must I pass mine. If I succeed, I rule Mycenae; if I fail, I have nothing."

I nodded. We sat together quietly in the warm sun. I wondered whether to ask Apollo to stop time at this moment, when all was still hopeful and possible, or let it run on towards a dangerous, unknown future. I gave a slight shiver and decided it was time to break the mood.

I stood up. "Just as well you can practise with me then," I teased. "You are going to need to be at your peak when the battle starts."

He laughed and joined me on the grounds. We sparred, matching drilled move for drilled move. I thrust, he blocked. He returned my thrust and I spun sideways. There was a deadly intensity to our match. I thought I'd fought hard and well in previous bouts, but this was fighting above any level I had encountered before. Neither of us was prepared to lose. The pace grew faster, the blows heavier. My arms ached, the muscles at the back of my calves cramped with the constant movement and I had no breath left in my lungs. A god must have been with me, for none of this affected me. All I saw was Agamemnon. Each feint, each attack, lifted my skills to a new plane.

It had to end, of course. I had just blocked a particularly vicious attack on my offside and was spinning out of range when I became aware we had an audience. The sound of clapping and cheering penetrated my concentration. In that single instant Agamemnon swept forward and twisted the sword from my grasp. I looked down at the weapon on the ground then looked up at Agamemnon. He stared back at me. Suddenly a big grin split his face.

I was furious he should gloat over my defeat. Without thought I bent, picked up my weapon and leapt forward with vicious intent to stab him. I saw the flash of alarm in his eyes as he jumped to the side.

"Whoa!" he called. "Enough. Nestra, enough, we've finished."

"Enough," he said again.

His words penetrated, and I stepped back. I stood, catching

my breath, while I slowly climbed back down from wherever the fighting rage had taken me. As the elation died, it left me empty, with a sick feeling in my gut.

A deep flush of shame flooded my cheeks. Bad enough to lose the contest, without compounding my failure with treachery.

I turned away. My trainer was one of those watching. I expected a beating at the least for my actions. I started walking.

I hadn't taken two steps before Agamemnon grabbed my arm and spun me round to face him. I had expected fury, but instead his eyes were full of understanding. "You are a warrior, little cat. I've known few men fight like that, and no woman. Then, at the end, you still wouldn't give up! Do you know how hard that is to teach a warrior? You are magnificent!"

He had hold of my right arm. I gawped at him, sweating, flushed and shamed while he grinned at me. Then, turning to the audience, he slowly forced my arm up into a winner's salute. I tried to pull away but had no strength left in the arm. It waivered and quivered, but Agamemnon held it up in its defiant salute.

To my surprise the audience exploded into applause. I had no idea why. Somehow I had passed through that rage-filled mist and emerged in another country where no logic or reason applied any more.

Eventually he let my arm fall. I was so tired, I would have tottered if he hadn't held me up. The audience dispersed. There was no likelihood of further excitement.

At some point we were alone, back on the wall of the training grounds again.

I kept my head bent in apparent fascination at the lacing on my boots. I couldn't have looked at him if my life depended on it.

He sat with me in silence for a long time. I felt my shame, my exhaustion and the dangerous blood rage ebb. The sun was starting its descent, and it was the slight chill that stirred me. I turned to look at Agamemnon. He caught my gaze and grinned wryly back at me.

"I'm sorry," I said at last.

"No," he said. "You weren't in error. We prepare for battle

every day. All Greeks do so, and Spartans more than most. Very few are really ready when the time comes."

"But I forgot myself," I said. "I got lost, then found I had attacked you. I didn't mean to."

"That's the way it is," he said. "Do you think all battles are like the jaunt we took to rescue your sister? No. The one thing you've proved is that you are warrior through and through. When pushed to your limits, you weren't able to quit. I've known staunch men who could never be that brave and steadfast."

Suddenly I had the most terrible urge to cry. We got beaten for that in the barracks, so I ducked my head even lower and turned away from him. I don't think he was deceived, because he slid an arm around my shoulders. Eventually I subdued the tears and was able to relax into his embrace.

The sun had dipped below the horizon. Twilight is just a moment of time between light and dark, so his face was almost a shadow.

"Do you know why I need to win my kingdom back, Nestra?"

I shook my head. It was either obvious, or he referred to some imperative I didn't know.

"If I win, I will need a queen. To have that queen, I need a wife. To have a wife, I need someone I respect. But more than anything else, she must hold the keys to my heart. Do you understand?"

It was common sense. He would need a queen. I nodded wearily. No doubt, if he had a kingdom there would be girls in plenty queuing up for the privilege.

"If I win. If I am successful in winning back my throne, I want you as my wife, Nestra."

I froze. I was like a girl on my first hunting lesson: stay still, freeze into position like a tree, don't let even a breath disturb the integrity of the shape you let the prey see.

"Nestra? Nestra? Are you still with me?" His breath was warm against my forehead. "Will you let me ask your father for your hand?" I imagined, rather than felt, his lips moving over my hair.

"I won't ask until I return as King of Mycenae. But if I do, then I will be seeking your hand. There is no other woman alive

I love or trust as I do you."

"Are you sure?" The idiocy blurted from my lips before I could contain it.

He pulled me closer. "Oh yes, Nestra, I am very, very sure. When the days of my life are told, the gods will make it clear that Menelaus and I came to Sparta for no reason other than to win my bride."

I gave a hiccup of amusement. No doubt minstrels would make a similar tale: probably gods would be involved, all to make sure an awkward girl, and a man seeking refuge got together. Leda's talk of the usefulness of a liaison between Sparta and Mycenae, of trade, of allies, flashed through my mind. Agamemnon was a clever man. I already knew that. Knew he must have considered all these factors before his proposal, however romantic it was.

Well, I had considered them as well. He was a man I desired with all my being, and I had learned today I was a more complex creature than I had imagined. Agamemnon was someone I knew and wanted, so I wouldn't be doomed to the exile my mother had foretold. If this liaison came with advantages for all parties, then so much the better.

"I suppose you'd better talk to my father," I said turning towards him.

As a first kiss it wasn't bad. There were some adjustments to be made because our noses bunted in the middle of the attempt, but once I understood the angles involved, I was able to tilt my head and allow my lips to open to his in a very satisfactory manner.

CHAPTER
SIX

THE WAR TO RECLAIM MYCENAE WAS not what I had expected. I had been taught that battle-line supremacy depends on the strength of the phalanx and the courage of the warrior. I had imagined a campaign of spears, swords, death, courage and at the end, noble grief and loss. So deep is our respect for the heroic ideal, Spartan women tell their sons to come back carrying their shields, or borne upon them.

It took me some while to understand the words the messengers brought back, so foreign was this new way of thinking. This was a different type of war.

Scouts were sent to Mycenae to understand and assess the level of support for Thyestes and Aegisthus. Inevitably, there were noble houses who had been disadvantaged when Atreus had been usurped, and loss of wealth, land and status had caused resentments that had lasted years.

These prospective allies identified, Agamemnon's agents went in to make contact and sell the advantages of alliance with the true heir to the throne of Atreus. I don't believe these agents were subtle. Once the heir had been agreed on, any attempt to back away from totally committed support for Agamemnon was met with derision. Sitting on the fence was not an option. A failure to support Agamemnon could result in an unfortunate breach in security resulting in files of families and individual names falling into Thyestes' hands. This imperative spread, by some subtle process, into the general population.

Then a smear campaign launched through every tavern and brothel in the kingdom spread scandals about Thyestes and his son, and lauded the 'true' ruler, Agamemnon. The marketplaces, the gymnasiums, the temples and festivals were all opportunities for Agamemnon's agents to spread the word, and the words were foul: impiety and sacrilege were the least of the accusations. No wonder, went the gossip, Mycenae had been having a bad time with its weather, trade and the harvests. Thyestes and his son had angered the gods.

When Thyestes became aware of the scandals being circulated, it was too late for him to respond. Any attempt to counter such rumours sounded like weakness.

By the time Agamemnon's forces, augmented by Sparta's might, invaded Achea, the population was grateful to return to a simpler form of politics. The invasion was nearly bloodless apart from the assault on the palace itself. I believe Agamemnon would have felt cheated if he hadn't had to battle some actual foes.

The palace guards tried their best, but there was little they could do against the combined strength of Sparta and the Mycenean troops who had defected. There were few casualties as Agamemnon took Atreus's throne as his own. Thyestes' body was found in the palace, surrounded by those troops who had remained loyal. Aegisthus had fled.

*   *   *

When news of the successful rout of Thyestes arrived, I was ecstatic. I celebrated with my sisters in the mess, and then again with my parents. Naturally, there were more women than men present at the celebrations as our warriors were still away with

Agamemnon.

I grappled with the form the invasion had taken. I had envisaged a bloody campaign, with all the glory of heroic deeds and honourable combat. As itinerant messengers revealed aspects of the campaign, I felt less clear about Agamemnon's methods. This was success, but it wasn't the Spartan way. We understand and even applaud trickery and deceit. It is part of our warriors' training to live off the land and steal what is needed, punishment for such theft only occurring if caught. The war in Mycenae was, I supposed, an extension of the concept, but the campaign seemed less clean, less honourable and less manly than the war stories told by minstrels.

Where was the challenge of single combat? The drama of two heroes valiantly defending their kingdoms armed with their fighting skills and the favour of the gods?

I said as much to Leda. "It's not what I imagined being a warrior was all about."

She smiled at me. "It's called politics, Nestra. Men like to carry on about their warrior code but the truth is usually much more complex. We need the minstrels to burnish the tale and turn it into the heroic sagas we like to listen to."

I realised I was being a simple girl. Agamemnon had known what was best for the campaign, so I kept my thoughts to myself and tried to grow into a sophisticated woman who would understand this way of doing things. I wanted to make Agamemnon proud of the girl he would make his wife.

CHAPTER
SEVEN

I WAITED FOR A YEAR. FROM THE north we heard news that Agamemnon, having subdued his own capital, was now marching on neighbouring kingdoms, aggressively extending his territory. My father's Spartan troops were with him throughout his campaign.

I had passed my final school exams with distinction and was now a free and independent citizen of Sparta and ready for marriage. I had little to do but enjoy myself. I trained in the mornings to keep up my fitness and visited or picnicked with friends, most of whom were now promised in marriage. The next few months would be busy with wedding celebrations.

One day I caught my father watching me in a speculative way and imagined he was planning my future. I went willingly when he summoned me, assuming Agamemnon had finally asked for my hand.

Tyndareus was pacing up and down the hall in front of where Leda sat quiet and composed in her chair. Sun filtered through the window and turned her hair to gold. My father's shadow prowled the sunlit areas on the floor. He turned as I entered.

"You asked for me, Father."

"Yes, come in, Nestra." He stopped both his pacing and his speaking, as if he didn't quite know how to continue. He glanced at my mother before continuing. "I have received an offer of marriage for you."

I could hardly restrain my smile and was wondering how to phrase my willing acceptance when he continued, "It comes from Tantalus, King of Pisa, in the western Peloponnese."

"Who?" I blurted, too startled to phrase my question more elegantly.

"King Tantalus," said my mother drily. "He rules Pisa, as your father has just said."

I glanced at her. Her voice was flat, but her eyes sympathetic.

I stared at my parents in horror. "I've never heard of him. Why would he want to marry me?"

"He has heard that you are beautiful, dutiful and a pearl among women," said Tyndareus, apparently quoting something he had been told. "His messenger arrived this morning. He offers you his heart, his hand and his kingdom."

"But I don't know him. I don't want to marry a stranger, someone I've never met." I felt all my certainties and plans for the future fall away in a slide of terror. I knew daughters could, indeed, be forced to marry men they didn't know or love. Secure in the promises Agamemnon had made, I hadn't considered that possibility for myself.

"I don't know much about the man either," admitted my father. He looked at Leda. "I want to find out more about this suitor. We need to know what he offers, what sort of man he is and whether he would be a good match for our daughter."

Leda smiled at him. "I know you will choose wisely," she said. Then she looked at me. "You can trust your father, Nestra. He will not let you go to a bad or unloving husband."

"No," agreed Tyndareus. "Such arrangements and negotiations are not achieved in a couple of days. There is a lot involved in choosing the husband for a Spartan princess. There are alliances that can be brokered and need to be considered. There are so many benefits your marriage can achieve for your country," he said. I could see him firing up with enthusiasm.

"I will meet with the messenger again tomorrow to learn more about this proposal and about the king who sends it. It's the first offer, Nestra, and needs to be looked at carefully. I wanted you to know the process has started."

He looked again at his wife, as if seeking agreement. "I have decided to send messengers out to the kingdoms to announce that Sparta has a princess available to be wooed and won. The Gymnopaedia starts in a full moon's time. Guests will be invited to attend and present their case for your hand, and the successful suitor will be announced at the end of the games. We could receive other offers, better maybe, or some worse. I will consider carefully for you."

I hesitated, not wanting to be impertinent, then decided I had nothing to lose by speaking the truth. "Agamemnon told me he would offer for me. He told me that before he went off to Mycenae."

"Agamemnon?" Tyndareus paused for thought. "Well, that could be a good match, I suppose. I like the boy, although I would have thought that for you it would be like marrying a brother." He must have seen something in my face. "No? We have many political interests in common, of course, and our troops have campaigned together in the war with Mycenae over the last few months. Yes, we could consider an offer from Agamemnon."

Leda shifted in her seat but said nothing.

"But he hasn't asked me for your hand, Nestra. It's possible he has changed his mind. He's been gone a year. Don't set your heart on someone you may not win, my girl."

He looked at my downcast face and added, "But the messengers will be going to Mycenae as well as to the other kingdoms. If Agamemnon is truly interested, now is the time for him to declare himself."

With that I had no choice but to smile politely and leave my parents to their planning. I wondered if Leda had engineered this approach from Tantalus. I couldn't fathom how she could have done so, but I knew she didn't favour Agamemnon.

I was so panicked I felt sick. I rushed back to the quiet of my room and struggled for calm. The future I had considered a certainty was at risk. I weighed up my options for some time.

They came down to only two choices. I could send a courier to Agamemnon asking him to redeem the pledge he had given me, or I could accept whichever king or princeling my parents chose from the pool of suitors.

Neither appealed. Was I to beg Agamemnon to honour his promise? I thought not. He'd had a year or more to send word to Tyndareus. If I counted so little in his plans, then maybe I was better off without him. There might, after all, be some adventure in securing a new lover.

At this point I found myself in tears. I was trying to use the logic imprinted by our schooling, but it was failing me badly. I had thought Agamemnon cherished me; I thought he loved me, wanted me.

Try as I might, I couldn't put Sparta's needs above my own. I thought marriage to Agamemnon would satisfy all the requirements. With the exception of Leda, and possibly of the slave Clymene, who didn't count, I thought we would all be happy.

Now there was the strong probability that, within a month, I would be a stranger's bride and end up in some wretched, distant kingdom, with no hope of ever seeing my home again. I felt, with some stringency, the way Leda's life had panned out. She had never been back to the place she had, in her childhood, called home. I wondered if she missed it, if there was some part of her that felt forever an alien in Sparta.

Eventually I collapsed face first onto my bed and remained there, refusing comfort or contact for some hours.

Later, my maids, silly as they were, decided the only way to break my self-imposed isolation was to ask my family to intervene. I was, I suppose, fortunate they approached Helen. If they had tackled my mother, then maybe our futures would have been different.

* * *

Helen arrived an hour later with her maid Aethra in tow, the latter carrying a flagon of chilled wine. I had never managed to feel comfortable around her or Phisiades, but I understood they served Helen well. As I had predicted, they were safe and comfortable in Leda's household and appeared to have adapted to their fate.

Helen listened to what Tyndareus had said. She gave a grin when I mentioned my agreement with Agamemnon. "What if two sisters married two brothers?" she murmured.

"What do you mean?" I asked, confused.

"Nothing," giggled Helen, "just an idle thought, of no importance. What are you going to do?"

"I don't know," I confessed. "I thought perhaps I should send a message to Agamemnon, reminding him of his words."

"By Aphrodite, no," said my sister. "If he doesn't want you as his wife then pestering him isn't going to change his mind, and you'll only look foolish. You mustn't put yourself in that position." She grinned at me. "Men have to desire us. We have to be chaste and chased."

I rolled my eyes. The wretched girl was only fourteen. Still, as Agamemnon had predicted, Helen was turning into a very beautiful woman and developing a range of skills to cope with the admiration she received. For all my four-year seniority, there were times when Helen appeared the more experienced.

"What do you suggest?" I asked.

"You shouldn't do anything," she advised. "Just concentrate on making yourself beautiful and desirable so you get plenty of attention. You need to keep an open mind about the suitors who offer for you. If Agamemnon does turn up and asks for you, then you can assess his offer against his competitors'. Even if you still choose him, and if Father allows that, you want to keep Agamemnon in some doubt. He'll value you the more for it. Men want what they can't get, so don't be a pushover."

I sighed but accepted the wisdom of her advice.

The Gymnopaedia seemed a long time to wait before I discovered my fate.

CHAPTER EIGHT

L EDA ENTERED INTO ARRANGEMENTS WITH
ENTHUSIASM. I was absolutely forbidden from
participating in the games as a competitor.

"We aren't presenting you to your suitors as a Spartan warrior
woman," she said firmly. "You will be a decorous, charming and
desirable princess, fit to adorn any court, and you are not going
to scare off potential offers by proving yourself stronger, fitter or
more skilled with weapons than your suitors."

I didn't protest. I had never felt self-conscious about my body,
but now I was the focus of strangers' eyes and felt suddenly
shy. I would have liked a close friend to talk to, but although
my barrack mates were my sisters, there was an unbridgeable
divide between the king's daughter and his subjects. I could have
friends, but only if that friendship didn't compromise the dignity
of the royal house. My pre-wedding hopes and fears could later
be used in a political context, so I remained discreet.

Our cousin Penelope came to visit. Two years younger than
me, she divided the age gap between Helen and myself, and
accordingly became friend to both of us. As a king's daughter

she also understood the need for discretion and enjoyed the intimacy of our company.

She was a quiet girl, not one to put herself forward, a quality my mother noted with approval. I passed on Leda's words of praise and was rewarded with a grin.

"Haven't you heard it's the quiet ones who need to be watched most closely?" she asked. "Just because I'm quiet doesn't mean I'm not thinking. My father would be horrified if he knew some of my thoughts."

We were sitting in the courtyard of the palace with good open space around us and no need to fear that we were being overheard. I leaned back on my couch and considered her. She was a pretty girl, with a soft, gentle face that became beautiful when she smiled.

I gathered her relationship with her father was a rocky one, and Penelope was frank about her intent to find a suitor as quickly as possible so she could escape her childhood home.

"Don't you wonder whether a husband might not treat you well?" I asked. This thought had occurred to me far too frequently in the last few weeks.

"I believe I can make a husband love me," she said. "It isn't very difficult to make a man happy. All it takes is attention to what pleases them, and I am happy to pay them that attention. Remember, I want to escape my home, so almost any man will do. Of course, I'd like it if they had a brain, and I'd prefer it even more if they loved me, but that may be more than I can ever expect." She gave me an apologetic smile. "I'm sorry, I'm not romantic, but I think I can be happy if I'm sensible about my marriage."

"So you've never been in love?" asked Helen.

I watched with fascination as a deep flush of red crept up from Penelope's neckline to her face. Her body was determined to betray her, regardless of her prosaic words.

"There is someone, isn't there?" urged Helen, who could see the same signs. "Who is he? Is he suitable? What does your family think?"

"Enough", laughed Penelope. "No, there isn't anyone, really.

There was a man I liked, but really, he lives on a rocky island, so he's not a great catch. Something about him made me listen, and I liked his mind. He was clever and subtle, but not conceited. You know what I mean? But that doesn't mean he would be interested in me. I don't have a large dowry."

Helen and I stared at her. She had raised so many different points for us to consider, and her approach was so far removed from our own it was hard to know what to say.

"Who do you pray to? Who's your favourite god or goddess?" I asked at last to lighten the mood. "What about you, Helen?"

"Aphrodite, of course," said Helen. "The goddess of love. Who else should a young woman pray to?" She stretched her arms out in a dramatic gesture, as if surrendering herself to the sun.

Helen's voice dropped a tone and went soft and dreamy as she spoke. "Wouldn't you just love to be swept away on a wave of passion that caught you up and changed your life? Imagine how wonderful that would be."

I rolled my eyes at Penelope. It was just as well Helen wasn't old enough to get married for four years.

Penelope snorted with derision. "I can't think of anything worse. The wave would recede and you'd be left, dumped like wrack along the seashore after a storm. You wouldn't even be able to control where you ended up. I didn't think Spartan warrior girls had thoughts like that anyway."

Well, I hadn't thought so either. I studied Helen with some surprise. Sometimes I was amazed by the things she said. She was young, but she had never before given any indication of being silly.

Helen gave a sigh. "I think there can be nothing more lovely than a man who is prepared to sacrifice everything for the love of you. Think of it, being valued for your own self, not for your dowry, your kingdom or your army. Just pure love. It's why I pray to Aphrodite."

"That sounds like some nonsense a poet might write," I said, laughing at her. "Penelope's right, I don't think that would work out very well in real life. Anyway, I pray to Artemis, and I don't think waves of passion come very high in her regard."

"What about you, Penelope?" asked Helen. "Who do you pray to?"

"Hera," said Penelope. "I pray to a goddess who will give me a safe marriage and a family. I suppose that's what I want for my life."

We all fell quiet, contemplating our futures.

The silence went on a little too long before Penelope turned to me. "What do you want from your marriage, Nestra?"

"I just want to love my husband and to have him love me," I said, wondering if I would be so lucky.

"What about wealth and power and status?" asked Penelope. "Those things are important to our parents. Tyndareus may be thinking of that more than who we love."

"He's promised me that happiness is something he wants for me, so I hope he thinks about more than wealth," I said. "Otherwise I'll be packed off to some old rich man."

"Ugh," said Helen.

"Ugh indeed," murmured Penelope.

There was another thoughtful silence, broken by Helen's sudden laughter. "Look at us all, so gloomy and depressed. I bet within ten years we'll all be happily married to men who adore us. How could they not, when we are as wonderful as we are?"

*   *   *

The first suitors began to arrive a week before the festival. I was walking in the olive grove with Leda when we saw the first chariots arrive and drew back into the shade of the tree to see who it was. I didn't recognise the man.

"Who is it?" I asked my mother.

"Tantalus of Pisa," she replied.

I looked at him carefully. This was the man who had initiated the process of finding me a husband. I wondered how he felt now his wooing had turned into a competition.

"Isn't that Odysseus as well?" I asked.

"Yes, King of Ithaca. They must have come together," she

said. I noticed she was careful to give each man his full title as if their role as potential suitors had increased their dignity.

They were followed a day later by the King of Lydia. I had been afraid no contenders for my hand would turn up and I would be humiliated, so I greeted all comers with more warmth than I intended.

When most of our guests had arrived, Tyndareus welcomed them all to his palace and set out the rules for the various contenders for my hand. They were to make their approach to Tyndareus, with details of their exploits, their kingdom's assets and political intentions. They could discuss with my father what they could bring to the marriage and how this union would benefit both families and kingdoms.

"But," said Tyndareus, "when I have selected a shortlist of suitable candidates, the final decision will be Clytemnestra's. If you cannot win my daughter's affections, then you will not wed her."

This caused something of a stir, and there was some muttering among the suitors. When had it become custom that women were consulted, let alone allowed to choose for themselves? A few glanced my way as if seeing me for the first time. Plainly they hadn't factored the need to charm me into their bid for my hand and were now assessing how to deal with my father's requirement.

I was sitting beside Leda, watching proceedings. Helen and Penelope were seated behind us. I looked at the men, trying to read them. My future depended on these suitors, and I knew so little about them all.

Tantalus was an attractive man, tall, well made with unruly, bushy hair and smiling eyes. I suppose any woman takes an interest in a man who shows an interest in her, and Tantalus followed up the compliments he had paid me on his initial approach to my father with real and evidently sincere admiration in person. He seemed an intelligent man, one determined to rule his kingdom fairly.

If I had to marry someone other than Agamemnon, I could do worse.

We had still had no news from Mycenae.

I was less impressed with the King of Lydia. He strutted into the palace like a short, round pigeon expecting Tyndareus and me to be grateful for his attention. The man was impossible on all counts. His only claim to my attention was the large double-bladed axe he brought as a gift. Called a labrys, it was a heavy, sharp, vicious-looking weapon. I admired it immensely and when I lifted it was impressed to find the weapon balanced so finely I could swing it with ease. I gave it a twirl or two before I looked up to see Leda glaring at me. I put the axe down in a hurry with a muttered word of thanks to its donor.

We attended the Gymnopaedia with our guests. It seemed strange to sit in the stands rather than compete in the stadium below. I watched the running with a pang of regret. I wasn't a little girl any more.

Odysseus, seated on my left, although courteous and charming, clearly wasn't interested in me, and I wondered why he had attended the games. Helen, seated behind me leant forward and whispered that he had acknowledged Penelope when he arrived, and that Penelope had looked flustered. I paid closer attention to the King of Ithaca. He seemed popular with the other guests, and I could hear my father, on the far side, laughing at some of his comments.

I turned to Tantalus, seated beside me, and asked, "Where does Odysseus come from?"

"Ithaca," he replied. "It's a rocky island stuck out in the western sea. Why?" His tone was lightly charged with concern. Did he think me interested in the man?

I hurried to reassure him. "He seems to know my cousin, so I wondered where he was from."

Abruptly Tantalus lost interest in Odysseus and began to narrate a story about a wild boar hunt. I listened with half an ear and turned to watch Penelope. If I remembered properly, she had mentioned a man from a rocky island. Helen had been right. Our cousin was more than interested in the King of Ithaca. She kept her eyes down and her head modestly covered, but I could read the tension in her slender shoulders and observed the way her body was inclined towards his. I hoped she would be lucky in her choice of suitor.

The next day the men went into the hills hunting, which left the palace empty for a few hours. I blessed the silence around me until Leda used the time to remind me of my obligations.

"You are not to make a spectacle of yourself," she chided. "I couldn't believe it when I saw you waving that axe around yesterday. You must control yourself, Nestra." I nodded sulkily. "What is acceptable in Sparta isn't universal, you know."

Well, what could I say? I was enjoying flirting with Tantalus. Frankly, of the available suitors he was clearly the best. He demonstrated a calm appreciation of all that Sparta's armies could offer him, and a genuine appreciation of me.

I didn't love him, but in lieu of a better offer I imagined I could make a go of marriage to him.

Penelope's calm, prosaic wisdom coloured my decisions. Lacking love and passion, I would make do with kindness, shared objectives and someone who valued me. Clearly Agamemnon couldn't be bothered following up on the words he had spoken. I hoped he rotted in Hades.

CHAPTER
NINE

AGAMEMNON AND MENELAUS ARRIVED THE EVENING of the penultimate day of the Gymnopaedia. The suitors, who had enjoyed a strenuous day hunting boar in our mountains, were relaxed and raucous. Few noticed as the newcomers entered the hall.

I saw Agamemnon immediately. Common sense dictated I should have seen his brother's flaming red hair before anything else, but I had been waiting for Agamemnon for a year now. For the past two months I had looked hourly for his message and his return. I was a mass of frustrated energy, and watching him stroll, so casually, across the floor of the hall towards my father, I was filled with a murderous rage.

Menelaus waved happily to Helen, embraced Leda and grasped my father firmly by the hand. He was everyone's friend and boon companion. I smiled at Menlaus's uncomplicated enthusiasm – and ignored Agamemnon. Did he really expect me to greet him in a friendly fashion now?

I seethed with the humiliation I had suffered. I had embarrassed myself by declaring my affection for him to my family, only to hear nothing from the wretched man for over a year. Did he honestly think he could swan in now as if none of it mattered?

Leda greeted him with a cool courtesy that was nothing like the warm hug she had given Menelaus, and I followed her example. I thought Agamemnon looked a bit miffed by my coolness, and rather more annoyed when I turned immediately afterwards to Tantalus and gave him my full attention.

Later that evening I sat with Penelope and Helen. It was cool and peaceful in the women's quarters. My mother had led the women away from the feasting when the happy, drunk men began to be rowdy.

I was feeling wretched. "What do I do now?" I asked. "What am I supposed to say if he asks Father for me? He hasn't tried to woo me, or in any way advance his cause. Whatever I thought before the suitors arrived, the situation is different now. Even that stupid Lydian king has tried to be nice to me. Agamemnon can't just expect me to come to heel like a hunting hound when he hasn't put any effort into winning me."

Helen poured a goblet of wine and thrust it into my hand. "Have a drink. You'll feel better with that inside you."

I could have thrown the cup at her, but instead I took a deep breath then a deep swallow of the wine. "Thank you," I managed to say eventually.

I watched Penelope's clear face as she prepared to speak. "Who do you want? Tyndareus has left the decision up to you, after all. It's your choice."

"I don't know," I said. "Agamemnon told me once that he wanted me as his wife, and I treasured that, and wanted it more than anything else. In a way, I still do. But Tantalus also says he loves me and wants to wed me; and I like him a lot. My mother doesn't like Agamemnon – not that I would let that sway me if my own mind was clear, but now I don't know what to do or what I want. Agamemnon could hardly have treated me with less respect. What sort of suitor turns up at the last minute to woo a bride?"

*   *   *

"I thought you'd be here."

I turned, mid-movement, his words breaking my concentration on the drill.

Agamemnon leant against the door frame of the gymnasium. I wondered how long he'd been there, watching me.

It was very early, sunrise barely a promise in the lightening sky. I had slipped out of the palace and made my way to the training grounds. I knew none of my suitors were likely to be up, having caroused the night away in the hall.

I had spent a sleepless night, my thoughts tangled and troubled. Today was the day I would have to give Tyndareus my choice of husband, and I was still no clearer or closer to a decision. I had tried to follow Penelope's instructions, putting present emotions to one side while I chose for a long-term future, but I had failed to achieve either clarity or peace. At last, in frustration, I had come down to the gymnasium to work out as hard as I could, until physical exhaustion forced my brain back into quietude and discipline.

I straightened up. "Good morning, Agamemnon."

He gave a sort of a grunt and came closer. "Why are you avoiding me?"

"What makes you think I'm avoiding you? I came down to do some training, that's all."

"I mean last night. You barely said hello. You were all wrapped up with that man from Pisa."

I looked at Agamemnon squarely. "Tantalus, that man from Pisa is, as you well know, one of the men competing for my hand in marriage. He has been very attentive and pleasant over the last two weeks."

"You've already said you would marry me!"

"Oh, by the gods, Agamemnon, that was over a year ago." I felt my hold on my temper slipping. "Since that day, I haven't heard from you. Not one single message. You never asked my father for my hand, and he decided it was time for me to get a husband. What's so odd about him inviting suitable candidates to make their case known to him? What was I supposed to do? Refuse to obey my father because of something you said a year ago? I believe you were invited to attend as well, but you couldn't even be bothered to turn up, let alone press your claim. How did I know whether you still wanted me or not? For all I knew, you could have changed your mind."

"I was busy, Nestra. I've been fighting ever since I took back Mycenae. It's been a year of constant marching and campaigns. I couldn't come back here until things had settled down, you must know that."

To my surprise he sounded like a sulky boy. Where was the passion, or even the affection I thought we shared?

"Well, I've been busy too," I said, resisting the urge to stamp my foot. "I've been growing up, and today I have to choose a husband."

"But you can't be serious? You're supposed to marry me."

He still didn't get it.

I finally lost the last shreds of control I'd been clinging to. "I'm not *supposed* to do anything," I shouted. "I am *going* to choose the man I marry today, and there are some very worthy candidates. If you'd arrived one day later, I'd already be pledged to another man and we wouldn't be having this conversation. You had as much of a chance as anyone else, Agamemnon, but you couldn't even be bothered turning up to try and win me." I was shaking with anger. I couldn't believe his stupidity.

Apparently I'd hit a nerve, because suddenly he was very angry indeed.

"I didn't think I had to compete for you, Nestra. I thought you'd already made a commitment to me and that we'd agreed to share our lives. Are you so fickle and faithless that you couldn't wait a year? A year during which I was winning back the kingdom you agreed to share with me. I warn you, Nestra, I expect you to honour your word. If you dare try and pick another suitor, I'll bundle you up in my chariot and steal you away. Bride-capture; that's one of your fine Spartan traditions, isn't it?"

I glared at him. "Don't you dare try and threaten me."

He moved closer, put his hands on my shoulders and drew me towards him. I stiffened angrily, but his hands were gently insistent, and although I stood rigid, I let him pull me against his shoulder.

"Don't fight with me, Nestra. I'm sorry I couldn't be here earlier, but I thought you knew my intentions and would trust me. I am speaking with Tyndareus this morning. You and I are meant to be together. We share too much to abandon each other."

I'd been spoilt and flattered by the attention I had received from Tantalus and the other suitors. I wouldn't get that flirtation or flattery from Agamemnon. We had known each other too long.

I could feel his heart beating against me as I leant into him. Was this what I wanted? I supposed it was. I felt secure with Agamemnon, and he offered me the life I had planned. I thought about Tantalus briefly and sighed. He was such a *nice* man. It had been fun envisaging a different future for a few weeks. I wasn't looking forward to watching his disappointment when Tyndareus announced my choice.

When Agamemnon made me lift my face, I kissed him willingly enough – and then rather more than willingly. He tasted right, felt right. The tension between us diffused, and at last we smiled at each other.

"It might be an interesting marriage, little cat, if we're going to fight like this," he murmured, "but at least making up is going to be fun."

CHAPTER
TEN

IT WAS A BEAUTIFUL AFTERNOON WHEN we drove into Mycenae. The baggage train with my luggage and maids were an hour behind us on the road, but Agamemnon had wanted to press ahead. The road turned and twisted through rocky ravines beneath a mountain range.

"I want to show you my palace," he said. "I want you to see your new home."

I laughed at his enthusiasm but was silenced when we turned a corner of the road and saw the citadel ahead of us on the hill. Set in a nook in the pine-covered hills, it was a natural fortress. Huge blocks of stone formed protective walls around the town and guarded the palace on the summit. I had never seen a city so large. The walls couldn't even contain all the dwellings and shops, and they sprawled down the hill beyond the city in an unending stretch of buildings. We seemed to be driving through built-up areas for ages before we even reached the city gate.

We entered through the main gate and climbed the ramp that led upwards. I was aware of people watching our progress. Agamemnon waved and smiled, and many waved back.

"See, they want to welcome my queen," he said, waving once again.

I smiled at him. "I hope they like me," I said. I was apprehensive. Leda had explained in detail how critical it was to ensure the populace loved me.

"Remember," she'd said, "Agamemnon's only been their king for a year. They won't have the inbuilt loyalty to him they would have if he'd been a little prince growing up in the town. To them, he's just their current ruler." She'd been standing, watching the maids pack the last of my gowns. "A good and popular wife can help his situation enormously. Wave to them; stop and speak to them and, above all, let them think you care about them. That's what makes a queen popular with the people."

Now without my mother there to support me, I was nervous and turned to my new husband for reassurance.

He grinned at me. "Of course they'll love you. You represent a new future for us all, and the promise of peace and stability after the war we had last year."

We had pulled to a stop outside the palace. Slaves rushed to hold the horses and assist me to alight. Agamemnon took my arm and led me up the steps to the door. As we reached it a man stepped through. He was dressed in priestly robes so I inclined my head in respect. It never pays to offend those who serve the gods.

"Calchas," exclaimed Agamemnon cheerfully. "How auspicious. You are the first to greet my queen. Clytemnestra, meet Calchas, who is our priest and soothsayer."

The man was dirty, and I got a whiff of stale sweat, urine and foul breath when he began to speak. I smiled politely, although repelled by him. I was startled by the malevolence he brought to bear on me when he returned my gaze.

He gave a hiss of disgust, drew himself up as tall and impressive as he could and pointed at me. "I studied the omens this morning," he said loudly. "This woman is cursed."

I gasped. "Well, really …" I began, but the man cut me off.

"I have seen the signs," he declaimed. "The gods have spoken clearly. This woman will be your destruction, Agamemnon. You should never have brought her here. She will be your ruin."

I heard a low murmur from the servants who surrounded us. Other onlookers were joining the group, excited by the unexpected drama playing out.

I felt Agamemnon move uneasily beside me. "You must be mistaken, Calchas. Clytemnestra is my bride and our union blessed by the gods at our wedding in Sparta. The priests there read the omens and prophesied great happiness and success for our marriage."

The priest looked at me again. I'd seen my mother look at vermin with more warmth.

"I'm never wrong. The signs never lie," he said. "If other priests can't divine and read the portents, that doesn't make what I say wrong."

"Well, you are wrong this time," said Agamemnon. I could hear the quick anger in his voice. "I don't want to hear another word. She is your queen and my wife. How dare you try cause trouble and spoil her welcome to Mycenae?"

"You cannot hide from the gods," said Calchas in mournful tones.

I was beginning to get angry. I could feel him milking every shred of attention from the audience. This wasn't a prophecy, it was a deliberate attempt to eliminate any influence I might have before I had even entered the palace.

Agamemnon swore rudely just beneath his breath and gave Calchas such a foul look the priest took a step backwards.

"Whatever you think, don't ever try to tell me this nonsense again. Otherwise, Calchas, you will be out of a living in Mycenae. Do you understand me?"

I looked the priest square in the eye. If he wanted a fight for Agamemnon's attention, I would give him one.

I turned to my husband and smiled. "I have a prophecy as well," I said firmly and loudly. I wanted every person present to hear me. "I foresee our marriage will be celebrated in song and poetry for hundreds of years. We will be known throughout history for our marriage. Playwrights will write dramas of our love and our family, and no priest can change that." Then I deliberately reached up and kissed Agamemnon squarely on the lips. I heard Calchas hiss.

The crowd cheered. I pulled back from my husband and waved to them. No pesky priest was going to spoil my entry into the palace. It was a secondary consideration that I might be behaving immodestly in front of Mycenae's citizens.

Agamemnon gave a strangled gasp, turned to me and took my arm. "Come, Nestra," he said and yanked me through the enormous doors and into the palace.

I could feel the priest's eyes on my back as we walked away. I knew I had made an enemy already and wondered what it would mean.

I was out of breath by the time Agamemnon stopped. Propelled by his fury, he had dragged me through the better part of the palace, through great meeting halls, up flights of stairs and past chambers and halls. He had given a garbled description of each room and feature, but I hadn't taken it in. I knew I would never remember the route we took. Now we were on a balcony, looking over the city below. In the distance we could see across the Argolid to the Saronic Gulf.

I stood quietly, looking at the terraces of the palace set out below us. I was out of breath and shaking. The priest's words had disturbed me deeply. What had I done to deserve his hostility? I could think of no reason. I made a mental note to steer well clear of the man. Artemis had always been my favourite goddess, and I had no reason to doubt her protection and support. She must have a shrine somewhere in the city where I could worship.

I wasn't sure what to say to Agamemnon. I knew he was angered by the priest's words, but was he also angry with me? It was blighting to be told our marriage was doomed when it was only five days old.

At last Agamemnon turned to me. "Bugger Calchas," he said. "Stupid fool's probably been fasting or taken some potion best kept in the temple. He must have been staring at his divinations for too long." He grunted and pulled me towards him. "That was no proper greeting for my queen. I am ashamed of my city. I hope you aren't too upset?"

"I'm fine," I lied. "Do many such priests live in Mycenae?"

Agamemnon grinned. "No, thank the gods. Although Calchas has been very useful in the past. He swung a large number of people against the usurper Thyestes prior to me retaking the throne. He'll come round. He's probably afraid your presence means his influence over me might decline. Once he realises you pose no threat to him, he'll be fine."

I thought about that. I wasn't as certain. "But what about his divination?" I wondered. "Do you think the gods are really trying to say something?"

"Nonsense. I don't think the gods are going to doom our marriage when it's barely begun, do you? For the rest, it's up to us."

Servants entered then with refreshments. I wondered how they had tracked our progress around this enormous palace. Presumably they knew shortcuts I had yet to learn.

We sat on the terrace with a meal of olives, bread and wine. It was a beautiful palace, and the view over the plains below was magnificent. Soothed by the food and wine I began to relax and see the funny side of the incident. Poor Calchas. Was he really threatened by the presence of a young bride? I smiled to myself and stretched in the sun. Silly man, I thought.

CHAPTER ELEVEN

I HAD UNDERSTOOD AGAMEMNON WAS WEALTHY, BUT the luxury of his palace, the richness of materials, jewelry, food and comfort was a revelation. The walls of the palace were painted with fine frescoes, the floors were tiled mosaic. I had never seen art used so freely as a house decoration. I gradually came to understand that Spartans deserved their reputation for being rough, uncouth, provincial and ill-mannered. We had nothing to compare with the fineness of design and artefact that was commonplace here.

The freedoms natural to Spartan women, though, were absent in Mycenae, and I ruffled a few feathers with my independence. I heard several mutters from shocked nobles when I dined in the great hall beside Agamemnon. On the first evening, a horrified slave had tried to steer me towards the women's quarters.

"My lady, it's not proper for you to eat with the men." I looked at the bowed head of the wretched maid.

"I am Queen of Mycenae, and this queen dines with her husband," I said.

She saw I would not take her refusal. She looked miserable

but eventually led me to a place beside Agamemnon, who smiled at me. Some of the men made comments just loud enough for me to hear. I heard one particularly crude remark and turned towards the speaker, making it clear I had heard. He flushed and backed off. A few moments later the man beside him, emboldened by his companion's utterances, made an observation about Spartan harlots, which was clearly audible across the hall. I raised my chin and stared the man down, but this time Agamemnon had heard. I knew his meeting with Calchas had left him primed for a fight, and I wasn't wrong. Agamemnon stood, pointed at the offending courtier and demanded he be removed by the attending servants.

I watched the man go, through slitted eyes. I would remember him.

"The wife of Agamemnon, is Queen of Mycenae," Agamemnon declared to the suddenly silent hall. "If it is good enough for Agamemnon to have his queen beside him, then it had better be acceptable to the people who dine here on our generosity."

There was an uncomfortable silence for a moment, before the diners discovered the need to lower their gaze and talk to their neighbour who, unexpectedly, had such fascinating anecdotes.

The moment passed. Agamemnon's support had ensured my status. I was grateful but confused. Leda dined with her husband on a nightly basis. It had never posed a problem in Sparta. Clearly there were new rules here I would have to learn and understand.

I wondered briefly whether I should modify my ways in case I embarrassed my husband. Then common sense reasserted itself. I was the queen, and appropriate behaviour would be modelled on what *I* thought proper. Agamemnon was used to the way we did things in Sparta. I would start as I intended to continue.

I found myself profoundly grateful for Leda's lessons. No woman she had reared could fail to be gracious and elegant when it suited them so to be. I drew heavily on everything she had taught me. I would be more queenly than any consort Mycenae had ever had, and I would do it on my own terms.

* * *

Agamemnon was sprawled across our bed, his body striped with lines of sun and shade filtering through from the balcony beyond the window. He liked to join me in the early hours after noon for a time of intimacy and companionship.

"I'll place Myrto in charge while I'm away," he said drowsily.

He was planning to be away a lot, stamping his mark on the new territories he had taken. Mycenae thrived economically, his subjects were content and, at least in the capital itself, we had peace.

I hadn't expected this. Leda always managed Tyndareus's affairs when he was absent, and I saw no reason why I shouldn't do the same for Agamemnon. It was one of the most basic assumptions Spartan women lived by – the obligation to keep the place going when men were away at war. I was about to reply hotly when a newfound caution made me consider my words. I sat beside him on the bed and stroked his thigh. "You know, Agamemnon, I've been thinking. Mycenae has only recently started to heal after a civil war."

He half rolled over and looked at me. "So?"

"Well, if it were me going away with our fighting force, then I'd want to know the person left in charge at home was totally on my side."

"Are you accusing Myrto of something?" Agamemnon spoke sharply. "I thought you barely knew him."

I smiled at my husband. "No, I know nothing about Myrto. I'm sure he is a fine man. But there is only one person you can trust totally to have your best interests at heart, and that is your wife."

I saw Agamemnon think the argument through. "But you're a woman," he replied.

Honestly, I wondered sometimes why I didn't kick him. He'd known me for years. What did being a woman have to do with it when I rode with him to rescue Helen? He knew I could fight as well as a man. I was about to make a caustic comment to that effect when I paused. Leda never allowed herself to quarrel with Tyndareus. It seemed I had new marital skills to learn if I wanted to achieve my purpose.

I bit my tongue and said sweetly, "I'm glad you noticed, otherwise I've wasted my time this afternoon."

He grinned in a self-satisfied manner and lay back on the bed with his arms behind his head, his magnificent, if currently detumescent, manhood on full display.

I suppressed a secret smile. "Spartan women, as you know, are trained to hold the fort when their men go away to fight. Let me do what I've been trained for. You won't find a more loyal second-in-command."

He mulled it over for a while. "It might cause problems with the men," he said doubtfully.

"Have Myrto report to me. We can work together. He and I can talk together about problems as they come up. If necessary, he can deal with anything that needs a man to handle it. You've got the security of knowing I have your back at all times and a man there to enforce any discipline needed."

After a while Agamemnon nodded. "All right. We'll try it. I won't be away long anyway."

I held my tongue. I had achieved my purpose; now I had to prove my worth.

Leda had never appeared to have any problems controlling affairs in my father's absence. She had the loyal support of the citizens and any troops left at home to ensure affairs ran smoothly. She had relied on men like Adrastos to get practical work done. I realised that Myrto and I were going to have to become friends. His willing support would be crucial to my success.

I asked my maids about him and learned he was married and his wife had given birth a week earlier to his firstborn son. At dinner that evening I made it my business to congratulate him.

He was tall, in his mid-thirties. His muscles spoke of a man's strength, although his palpable energy meant there was something still youthful about him. He accepted my good wishes gracefully, and a moment passed when we studied each other. I realised Agamemnon had already spoken to him, and he was as curious as I to know who he would be working with.

"I think we will yoke together as a good team, Myrto." I smiled at him and he nodded, not yet ready to commit himself. I liked him for his caution; it indicated a man who would think before he acted.

I've never admired those who try too hard to please.

I watched Agamemnon and the troops depart. Calchas went with them to ensure no gods were offended during the campaign. He had read the omens and declared them good. I was glad he was going, for though I disliked his influence on my husband, I was sure he would cause trouble for me had he stayed.

I was confident I could redress the balance of influence over Agamemnon in my favour when he returned. It was too early to tell my husband, but I had missed my courses for three weeks. I hoped to have good news for him when he returned.

"Abantes was picked up drunk again last night."

I groaned. "That's the third time this week. What was he doing this time?"

"He was refused entry to the wine shop because he was too drunk. So he decided to climb onto the roof and urinate on the customers."

I stifled a giggle. "What have you done with him?"

"Given him the choice of working for the next few weeks with the team that's extending the drainage ditches, or being locked up until Agamemnon gets back and deals with him."

I thought about that. "What did he choose?"

Myrto grinned. "Digging ditches, of course. He didn't fancy being imprisoned for an unspecified length of time, nor the flogging Agamemnon would sentence him to. He may be a pisshead, but Abantes has never been stupid when it comes to self-interest."

I smiled. I enjoyed Myrto's company. He was intelligent, efficient, and I liked his pungent comments. We met most mornings to discuss events. There had been few significant issues, but we had proved we could work together and had established a template for managing Agamemnon's future absences.

I had formed the habit of going for a walk through the town in the early hours of the morning, when porters were still delivering fish, vegetables and flowers to the market, and artisans were busy warming up their fires or, depending on their craft, sharpening their tools. I liked the haphazard arrangement of a town still barely awake. Shopkeepers, still sleepy and relaxed, rolled their awnings up and arranged their wares. The casual informality of the scene suited me.

Bearing Leda's instructions in mind, I waved and smiled, and as my confidence grew, stopped to exchange words with people I passed. In a short while I knew that Milos's shop served the best pomegranate tea in town, and Arianna's honey-sweetened pastries were always worth stopping for. I was introduced to their young children and their aged parents. I began to develop a mind map of the city. The citizens worked hard, for long hours, and most were law-abiding. They were shy about discussing their politics, but I was building up enough of a picture from diverse gossip to realise with some surprise just how distressing the civil war of the last couple of years had been to ordinary people.

Arianna finally plucked up the courage to say, "No one benefited, my lady. Well, maybe some of the nobles. Down here in the town we lost business as the war took hold, and some lost their lives. All we want is peace. May the gods protect your husband and give him a long reign."

Praxis, her husband, butted in. "Warriors only want war and glory, and they see each other, nothing else. They don't know us working people exist until they wonder why they can't get food or goods any more because they've killed us and destroyed our livelihoods. All I've got to say is we can live without warriors, but no one lives very long without farmers producing food and merchants selling it."

"What about when our troops go off to conquer other kingdoms?" I asked, mindful of Agamemnon's intent to expand Mycaenae's territory.

Praxis shrugged. "Then it's not my worry. As long as it's not affecting my family or business, that's fine."

I smiled at his pragmatism and moved on. Like the warriors,

I had never previously noticed townspeople, either here or at home in Sparta. I had taken them for granted, like the helots, and never considered they might have their own opinions on the doings of the great and noble.

Clustered up on the hill near the palace were the villas of the nobles. This was a different world to the noisy town just a few blocks away. I saw few citizens on my perambulations here and almost no women. Upper-class wives lived very cloistered lives, rarely being seen beyond the confines of their homes. The only women on the street were maids, already busy sweeping out doorways or receiving grocery deliveries. I waved to them and to the doorkeepers, receiving some strange looks in return. I was, of course, always accompanied by my own maids, and frequently by Myrto, but the sight of their queen freely wandering through the streets was a novelty. I left them to make what they would of it. I wanted to change Mycenean ideas of what women could do. Even if they would never enjoy the liberty a Spartan woman took for granted, I thought any relaxation of their rigid rules separating women from society would only be good.

The current occupants of these affluent homes were those who had pitched their lot in with my husband. They had displaced Thyestes' and Aegisthus's supporters, and their continued loyalty for my husband depended on the wealth and power they could accumulate under Agamemnon's rule. While I felt safe walking through the market and the poorer streets of our town, I felt exposed and vulnerable when dealing with these nobles. They tacitly supported my husband, but it didn't take a lot of intelligence to see how tenuous this loyalty was. They currently allowed me to operate unmolested, but I wouldn't have trusted any of them within a spear's length of my person if they felt their privileges were being threatened. Agamemnon, no fool in these matters, had a premium regiment made up exclusively of young lordling warriors from these houses.

"Are they so good that you give them elite status?" I had asked him in some confusion.

Agamemnon snorted. "They'd run if they were faced with a real enemy who knew how to fight, but they've had basic warrior training and grown up hunting stag, wolf and boar. They understand no gentleman can act like a coward so they stand firmly enough together. The elements of warrior pride are there for me to build on, and it's a good way of my gaining their loyalty. They'll be all right once they're battle hardened. In the meantime, they are hostages for their families' good behaviour – although I would never say that to anyone other than you."

The troops returned, and the city once again filled with men. Agamemnon was in a foul mood. They had sustained a small but significant loss outside of Sicyon when a ragtag group of desperate fighters had ambushed Agamemnon's troops. They had tackled them in rough terrain and attacked, using the topography to great effect. Mycenean troops, used to the brute force of the phalanx, were completely unprepared for a foe that crept up in the dark, attacked viciously and from some distance with bows and arrows, then melted back into crevices and gullies where our troops couldn't follow.

Agamemnon was used to winning his battles, and the blow to his pride was considerable. Consequently, he sulked and blamed anyone and anything he could for the defeat – his hoplite captains for failing to adapt to this more mobile form of warfare; Calchas for not warning him of the disaster; the gods for failing to support him. I'm sure he'd have blamed me if he could. I noticed he didn't blame himself.

I trod round him warily. After his fifth retelling of the disaster I was increasingly bored with the story. I tried to pacify him. "Warfare is what it is: sometimes you win, sometimes you lose. Like hunting, much of the thrill is in the uncertainty of the outcome. This is the first defeat you've had in a year or more of conflict. By anyone's standards that is exceptional."

Agamemnon glared at me. "We lost good men to those scum. Who uses a bow for warfare? It's a coward's ploy to kill a warrior at range who can't fight back."

I thought it had been a very effective technique and would bear thinking about, but possibly this wasn't the time to discuss battlefield strategy with my husband, so I gave a mental shrug and began to undress for the night.

Agamemnon strode around the room ranting about the unfairness of troublesome natives, the treachery of defeated people and the importance of maintaining the Mycenean way. I listened with half an ear as I twisted a heavy bracelet off my wrist. The carving on it was quite exquisite.

Suddenly I heard a loud crash. In his vigorous pacing, Agamemnon had managed to knock over the pile of armour freshly returned from the smith. He stood for a moment in horror before stooping and gathering his gear together. He couldn't have displayed more concern if he had been examining his favourite child. His breastplate and shield were fortunately unscathed, but his helmet, having taken the brunt of the fall, was dented.

I moved to stand beside him, and we both surveyed the damage. I could see his distress. The damage to the helmet was significant and would require a return to the smith to beat it smooth and polish it again.

"It's ruined. Look at it. It's ruined," he kept repeating.

I felt his anguish was disproportionate, but I endured it for several minutes.

Finally, bored with the pointlessness of his reiteration, I said, as soothingly as I could, "It can be fixed. It will be as good as new once the smith has mended it."

"What would you know?"

Agamemnon swung round towards me, his eyes a blaze of hate, raised his right hand and smashed it into my face. I fell in a heap to the ground.

I sat up, staring at him in shock, feeling my cheek begin to swell. Then, to my eternal shame, I burst into tears, climbed to my feet and ran from the room.

As I fled I heard him cry, "Nestra ..."

* * *

I hid in the small room we used for storing linen and cried as if my heart was broken. Such an easy thing to say, but I suppose it was true. I cried for love lost and the trust he had betrayed.

I cried for my stupidity; I cried for Leda's advice, which I had ignored. Mostly, although I didn't know it, I cried for the girlish innocence gone in that blow. I was such a tangle of emotion I couldn't think or reason. The physical pain was slight; the pain of ripped love was incalculable.

Sometime later Agamemnon opened the door of the closet and found me. "Nestra." His voice was heavy with grief and tears. "Nestra, I am so sorry. I don't know what came over me. I'm sorry, so sorry. Please forgive me. I didn't hurt you, did I?"

His childlike grief and distress found a partner in my own. I let him pull me into his arms. "I'm so sorry, Nestra. My horrible temper. I promise I won't ever do that again. I don't know how I came to lose it, but I shouldn't have taken it out on you. Please say you'll forgive me."

"Please, please." His grovelling and begging went on and on, and I felt a sick swell of contempt at his self-abasement.

Eventually I let him propel me back to our room and bed. All I wanted was to be left alone, but I was in a city still strange to me, and I had nowhere else to go.

I lay beside him in the dark, wondering how the person I thought I was had allowed herself to be defeated so utterly. I had no idea what to do now.

*   *   *

In the morning Agamemnon left early. We were both subdued, not knowing what to say to each other. I checked my reflection in his bronze shield and saw the bruise had spread into the tissues of my eye socket, swelling the lid and blackening my eye. The maids came in, and I tried to turn my cheek from them to hide the mark. It was foolish, for there was no way to hide the damage, but I was ashamed. The younger girl, barely twelve years old, glanced at me as she reached to do my hair, and I watched her freeze as she took in the state of my face, although she made no comment.

The older maid, busy straightening the bed, didn't notice at first. Then she turned to say something, saw the marks and stopped dead. "Zeus! What happened, my lady?"

I gave a light laugh. "Oh, nothing. I was clumsy."

She shook her head. "No, lady, you were not. Someone hit you," she said flatly.

I tried to deny it, but she pressed on. "Who was it? Your husband?"

She took my silence for agreement.

"Bastard!"

I looked at her in some surprise. Her name was Chryseis. Mother had chosen her as one of the servants in my wedding train to accompany me from Sparta, and I had discovered she was a good worker. I knew no more of her than that. I hadn't expected sympathy from a slave.

I ducked my head. "Well, what's done is done." I tried to sound casual and composed. "It's nothing, really."

She looked at me shrewdly. "Madam, it is not a 'nothing'. It can happen, but it is not lawful for a man to beat his wife."

I shook my head. "There was no beating. Just a slap, nothing more."

I saw in her eyes she disagreed, but she said nothing, took a soft cloth soaked in cold water and held it against the bruise.

"Hold it in place, Io. I will be back with a tincture."

I was embarrassed by the attention, but Chryseis's competence was soothing. She returned in a few minutes with a bottle of oil from which she tipped a few drops onto another pad.

"What is it?" I asked.

"Hypericium, my lady. It will help the bruise disperse and heal. You should hold a pad of this against the bruise four times a day until it disappears."

"Are you a healer?" I asked in surprise.

"I learnt some healing when I was a child, a long time ago," she smiled. "I was thirteen when the slavers took me, but my grandmother had taught me well."

I nodded my thanks and held the pad against my face while Io put my hair up. I could feel my skin tightening. My eye felt a more natural size as the swelling from the bruise diminished.

I gave my thanks as I dismissed them. I had never before

thought to value a slave's comfort.

Agamemnon found me at noon and called me away from the women with whom I was winding thread for weaving. He led me onto the long terrace that surrounded the palace, far enough away to avoid being overheard.

"Nestra, about last night …"

I watched him fidgeting, his eyes not quite meeting mine.

"I want you to know I have never felt so ashamed of myself. I don't know why I lost my temper, but it won't happen again. I am so sorry, and I need you to forgive me. Please say you will."

I stared at him in silence. I wasn't being obstructive, I simply didn't know what to say, didn't know how I felt. There was a sense of boundaries needing to be redrawn between us, and I was uncertain how to do this.

I saw he was unnerved.

"Nestra, please forgive me. I've got you this as an apology. I want you to know I'm really sorry."

He held a leather pouch out. I reached towards him as he opened it and poured a necklace into my hands.

I gasped. The jewel glittered in the noonday sun.

"Let me put it round your neck."

I let him do the clasp, and the necklace hung heavy against my breast. I looked down and saw it lying on my skin.

"It is magnificent," he said. "You are magnificent. Nestra, I love you so much. Please try and forget last night and forgive me. I love you. It will never happen again, I promise."

Perhaps he was honest. We all make mistakes, and I had some petty guilt myself around my own failures to be a perfect wife. How could I judge him? Maybe this was a situation from which we had both learnt a lesson.

What were my options? I could go home to Sparta. My parents would probably receive me kindly; but then what? Sparta was my childhood and belonged in my past. Mycenae was my future and my life, for me to make of it what I could. I tried not to flinch as I imagined the look in Leda's eyes. She had been right to caution me. I had set my heart on this marriage and ignored her advice.

Agamemnon was the man I had chosen from all the suitors who had vied for my hand. I loved him, or at least I had loved him. I wasn't sure what I felt now. I had loved the companionship we shared, the warmth of late-night passion in our bed, the laughter shared memories brought. Was one blow to cancel all of that?

It was a silly thought, but had Agamemnon and I been quarrelling, or had I done something wrong, I could have accepted the chastisement. But I had not provoked him. I couldn't fathom the divide between the vicious hate that had propelled the blow and the love Agamemnon professed, although I believed both emotions were genuine. The ambiguity made me feel uneasy and adrift from my own certainties. I had lost confidence in my own judgment. It was simpler to try and put the incident behind us and hope it never happened again.

I sighed.

"I forgive you," I said finally. "Just don't ever let it happen again."

He gave a great laugh and gathered me into his arms, twirling me around like a dizzy girl in a dance.

That night I sat beside my husband at the feast held in the great hall for the returned troops. There were some who grumbled, or pretended to be shocked, that a woman sat openly at such a public event, but I ignored them. They should be used to my ways by now.

"I am your wife, and your nobles can like it or lump it," I had told Agamemnon when he raised his eyebrows in question. "I am your queen and the only woman who will host feasts in my own house." I kept to myself any embarrassment about being seen with a bruised face. The slaves had done what they could to disguise the marks.

He shrugged his shoulders. "Why not, after all? I like having my beautiful bride at my side."

Agamemnon was being particularly considerate since the events of the afternoon. We had gone to bed, of course, to seal our reconciliation, and I had told him we were to have a child. As I had predicted, he was delighted.

"I can't promise you a son," I said cautiously, although I

hoped for one.

"If it's a boy, he will be tough and strong like his father," he said. "If it's a girl, then she'll be beautiful and brave like her mother. Either way, it will be wonderful."

I smiled at him.

CHAPTER TWELVE

I WATCHED AGAMEMNON CRADLE OUR FIRSTBORN IN his arms.

"She is so beautiful," he said. His face was soft as he looked at his daughter.

"Iphigenia," he said, trying out the name, "I declare you the most beautiful creature born in Mycenae this year."

I laughed at him gently, moved by an unexpected tenderness. Some might have felt regret their firstborn wasn't a son, but Agamemnon's delight was transparent. I lay back in the bed enjoying the sight of my family. My husband sat beside me cooing at the baby.

Leda leant over and looked at the child. "She looks just like you did, Nestra. She's got your mouth."

"How can anyone see who a newborn baby looks like?" Agamemnon enquired. "She just looks like a baby to me."

"Oh, if you look carefully, you can tell," replied Leda, bending and kissing the little head.

Leda had arrived two weeks before for the lying in. I appreciated having her with me. She brought news of the family: Helen and Pollux were in their last year of schooling and preparing for exams; Castor was out on the border, sorting out boundary squabbles with neighbouring Tegea; Tyndareus had been very ill over the autumn but was recovering.

"Father is all right now, though, isn't he?" I asked, concerned. I couldn't remember my father ever being seriously ill.

"Fine," she reassured me. "He doesn't look after himself of course, so if he gets sick it tends to be serious."

I looked at my mother, realising my parents were getting older. She was standing by the window, and the clear morning light showed her fair hair had paled, the colour softened by grey. The hands holding the shawl for Iphigenia were still elegant but showed their age in the raised veins on their backs. Leda was a beautiful woman and always would be; her bone structure ensured she would be lovely whatever her age. But there were new lines on her face, and the quality of her skin had changed.

It was two years since I had left Sparta. I wondered what Helen looked like now.

"She's stunning," said Leda. "I don't like to talk about it in case I make some god jealous, but she's exceptionally beautiful. She causes disruption simply by walking into a roomful of men. Your father is worried, of course. He has to find her husband. He already has offers, but she isn't yet eighteen."

I frowned a little. "Do you mean she's provocative?" I found the thought disturbing. I knew she wasn't a child any more, but it was hard to imagine my little sister as a temptress.

"No, not at all," replied Leda. "As far as I can see, she doesn't flirt or encourage men in any way, but there's something about her that draws all eyes to her. Even women watch her avidly."

I smiled. "Father will cope. He'd better do what he did for me. Invite them all to come and visit, then make a choice."

Leda sniffed. "There are likely to be so many suitors, it'll bankrupt us trying to feed them, not to mention all the guest gifts we have to find. Actually, I think your father is more concerned that the competitors might come to blows."

"Let me know when the bidding starts," I asked. "We'll come and visit so I can see who my little sister will marry."

*　　*　　*

A little over a year later I sat in the hall beside Helen and looked out over the assembled guests. The sight was unnerving. The hall was packed with enthusiastic suitors, all vying for Helen's attention.

I shifted in the uncomfortable chair and looked at my sister. "Zeus," I muttered. "How is Father going to choose from this lot?"

Helen shrugged. "How does anyone choose?"

I watched fat little Diomedes eyeing up Helen's breasts and felt sick. "Isn't it a bit disconcerting?" I asked. "All these men slavering over you? It's positively indecent." I could almost feel the lust present in the room as the men eyed my sister.

She laughed out loud. "Now I know you're getting old, Nestra. It's exciting. Think of the power it gives me. I could ask them for anything, and they would do it for me."

I looked at her.

"I'll prove it," she said.

"I'm thirsty," she called over to Diomedes. "Please could you get me some wine?"

He rushed away to serve her.

I glowered beside Helen.

"This isn't worthy of you or of any Spartan woman," I scolded. "What happens when your power wanes? There's bound to be a price to pay. You're humiliating them. They're not even behaving like men anymore."

Diomedes returned with a glass of cold wine.

I felt nauseated as Helen thanked him with a warm smile.

She shrugged. "The future is the future. At the moment I'm learning things about myself, and about men, that I didn't know before. Let it be, Nestra."

"It may be fine now, but having to compete as one of this rabble must be terrifying for any man, and one of them is going to be your husband. You'd better hope he's not the jealous sort otherwise you're likely to be shut away in the women's quarter of some provincial palace and never be allowed to see the light of day again."

Helen smiled with youthful certainty. "No man is ever going to mistreat me, Nestra. I wouldn't let him."

I winced. Three months after the birth of Iphigenia, Agamemnon had struck me again. This time we had been supporting different contestants in the games. His player lost, I had laughed and he backhanded me. This time I came back fighting and snarled and spat at him in my rage. He was again apologetic and contrite, and his present was a golden bracelet. If his behaviour continued, I would end up with a significant collection of jewellery.

There had been another couple of episodes subsequently; all followed a similar pattern. I came to realise that Agamemnon never abused me when someone whose opinion he valued could see him. He didn't value slaves so had felt free to kick me in front of Io on one occasion.

It would have made more sense to me if he had been punishing me for something I had done. If I had dropped the helmet on that memorable first occasion, I could perhaps have understood and forgiven him. Instead, it was his frustration at whatever troubled him that was the spur. He deflected stress by making something hurt in his place. All too often, the something was me, although I'd also watched him saw at a horse's mouth. Not, I think, to hurt the horse, so much as his knowledge that I was watching, and the wanton cruelty upset me.

I looked at Helen's confident face and sighed. "So how do you explain what happened to Aethra and Phisiades?" I asked. "I imagine Aethra said the same things you are saying now."

Helen shrugged. "It's not the same situation."

I let it go. Maybe Helen's life would be easier than mine. I hoped she'd find a better man than I had.

I never got a final tally of how many suitors there were, but it must have been well over thirty, and of course each candidate had brought a retinue. I remembered Leda's sour words about the cost of feeding this crowd and smiled. The servants would be busy. Castor and Pollux were responsible for entertaining the visitors and took them hunting into our hills most days. On another occasion they set up games in the old training grounds and had the men compete at javelin and discus throwing. Those who didn't attend spent the day making appointments with Tyndareus or trying to waylay Helen.

I spent any time I could spare in the nursery with Iphigenia. It was strange seeing my own daughter in the home I had grown up in. She had taken to Tyndareus who had become a very proud grandfather. I realised how nice it was that we were close enough for these occasional visits and wondered again what Leda's family had been like.

To my surprise, Odysseus was one of the suitors. I remembered him from my own wooing and stopped to speak with him.

"Lady Clytemnestra," he replied to my greeting. "How is the Queen of Mycenae?"

"Well, thank you. Are you competing for Helen's hand?"

He smiled. "I came here upon another matter. I hope to win your father's support for a venture I have in mind."

I was surprised. "He's likely to be busy for a while with the matter of Helen's wedding. You may have misjudged your time."

"I don't think so," he answered. An amused grin spread across his face. "I believe I may have judged the time and circumstances perfectly. Do you think Tyndareus is finding this competition stressful?"

"Very," I said ruefully. "I think he's worried about what's going to happen when he announces the winner. All Hades could break loose among the losers."

"That's what I thought," he said cheerfully. "I might give him a hand."

It was an odd conversation. I watched him walk away and wondered if I'd missed something. I had the feeling Odysseus was more intelligent than me, and if he were planning something, the outcome would be interesting.

That evening, in the great hall, Tyndareus stood to welcome everyone to the meal. "I have an announcement to our guests," he began. "You are all here to compete for the hand of my daughter Helen, princess of Sparta. I have given much thought, not just to who wins her, but to the problem that will arise when I make that choice. In this hall we have some of the finest warriors of Greece. Fine Ajax, noble Diomedes, Odysseus, Menelaus, Idomeneus … You are so many I cannot name you all, and you are our most notable fighters. It worries me that I will offend so many when I choose who will wed my daughter and this will be the source of quarrels between us all. I do not want my daughter to be the cause of bloodshed or a war. I do not know how to resolve this."

There was a stir from the body of the hall as Odysseus stood. "I can solve this problem for you, Tyndareus," he said confidently.

I turned to look at him. He had said something like that earlier in the day.

"How are you going to achieve this?" asked my father.

I could read scepticism in his face.

Odysseus smiled. "I propose a trade, good Tyndareus. I need your help. If I give you the solution to your problem, will you give me your support when I court Penelope, the daughter of Icarius?"

There was a murmur round the hall.

Beside me I heard Helen chuckle. "Excellently done, Odysseus," she murmured.

Tyndareus smiled. "If you can give me a solution I agree with, Odysseus, I will most certainly help you when you apply to Icarius. What is more, I think every man in this hall will support you, if it means one less suitor for Helen."

There was a laugh from them all, and some cheers.

"Give us the benefit of your wisdom," said my father.

"The solution is simple," said Odysseus. "All suitors, indeed all men here, will swear a pact, a most solemn, binding oath, to defend the husband of Helen against anyone who tries to quarrel with him or take Helen from him. This oath stands not just for today, or for the time of the journey as we return to our lands. It stands for all time. There will be no retaliation against whoever is chosen as Helen's husband, and if any man should seek to steal Helen from him, then we are all bound to aid her husband to get her back. Tomorrow, we will go to the temple and sacrifice to the gods and get them to witness our oath as a sign of this pact's importance."

You could have heard a pin drop in the hall as each man considered the plan. I turned it over in my mind and could see no flaw in its elegant simplicity.

My father must have reached the same conclusion. He reached over, grabbed Odysseus by the shoulder and pumped his hand up and down. "I've always admired your subtle brain, Odysseus, but I think this time you've surpassed yourself. I believe this may be our solution. Do the rest of you agree?"

There was discussion of about the precise wording of the oath, but general agreement that Odysseus had found a way out of a tricky situation. I imagine Tyndareus hadn't been the only one worried about the possibility of endless quarrels and feuds. After a lot of arguing, a final draft was agreed on. The situation was unprecedented, and traditional rivals had just agreed to a truce. I saw a few suitors look sideways, assessing each other's reactions.

"One further thing, Tyndareus."

My father turned to Odysseus. "Yes?"

"To ensure no man claims you have wronged him in this, I have one more suggestion. Your daughter Helen must make the choice herself, here, now and before us in this hall. After all," Odysseus smiled, "that was the privilege you allowed Clytemnestra."

I turned to Helen to see how she was reacting. She had given me no indication of a preference. I even wondered whether she had spoken to all the contenders. She was smiling slightly.

Tyndareus looked across at her. "Is that your will, Helen?" he asked. "You don't have to agree to this if you don't want to, or if you are not certain." He had always loved his children, and his tone was gentle in his concern for her.

Helen stood. She was composed as she stepped beside Father. "I agree to this." Her poise gave the statement the formality of an oracle. "This choice will be mine, and mine alone."

Tyndareus studied her for a minute. I saw him glance across

at Leda, but if she responded I couldn't tell.

"So be it," he said as Helen returned to her seat.

The oath was agreed, and the suitors stood to take it. A couple had sent proxies, each of whom swore on his master's behalf. All agreed to the terms, bound by honour, for life.

Finally Tyndareus turned to Helen again. "Daughter. Speak your mind. Which man is your choice?"

She rose and stepped forward. I was proud of Helen. She looked every inch a princess of Sparta as she stood there in front of them all. There was a short pause as she gathered herself to speak and a rustling of clothing as every man in the hall leaned forward to hear her.

"I choose Menelaus to be my husband," she said clearly. "That is my freely given choice."

After a moment's silence the mass of suitors erupted. I saw the wisdom then of Odysseus's oath, for there would surely have been blood spilled otherwise. There were some who stepped forward to congratulate a stunned Menelaus, but many were scowling. It had cost them a good deal of money to enter the contest for Helen – money spent on their appearance, presents and retainers to present themselves appropriately as suitable candidates. No doubt some of the more impoverished kingdoms could ill afford the investment.

Helen returned quietly to her seat.

I turned to her. "Menelaus? You chose my husband's brother?" I couldn't keep the surprise from my voice.

She smiled. "I've always been fond of him, from the time we were children. I thought you knew that. I've had a crush on him since I was eight." She bent her head and pleated the fabric of her skirt of a few moments. She looked up again at me and gave a small grin. "Besides, it strengthens the position of Sparta, of Mycenae and all Laconia if we are united, and it means I don't have to travel to some far-off, alien land. Imagine if I'd married Idomeneus. I'd have had to go to Crete. I wouldn't even be on the same landmass as the rest of you." She rolled her eyes at me.

I cast around for something to say. "But you'll have red-haired children," I said for no obvious reason.

Helen gave an inelegant snort, and suddenly we were both giggling like a pair of schoolgirls.

I looked up to see Menelaus bearing down on us.

"Oh, Menelaus," I said, trying to collect myself. "Congratulations. I wish you and my sister every happiness."

He nodded at me then reached out to Helen who was drying her eyes.

"Thank you, Helen," he said softly. He was smiling down at her. I watched Helen blush beneath his gaze as he pulled her to her feet. For the first time she looked shy. "You've made me a very happy man," he said.

I heard Leda, who had come up beside me, give a sentimental sigh.

"Congratulations to you both," she said.

CHAPTER THIRTEEN

Fifteen Years Later

IPHIGENIA SAT ON THE BALUSTRADE PLAYING her flute. Helen's daughter Hermione sat in front of her, watching her every move. I saw Iphigenia stop, explain the sequence to the younger girl and hand her the flute. Hermione frowned in concentration as she tried the piece. I smiled at the two heads, one dark, one golden, bent over the instrument. I rather thought Hermione had a crush on her older cousin. She had been shadowing Iphigenia all week.

Electra and Orestes squabbled on the mosaic floor at their feet, oblivious to the trills of music going on above their heads.

"You're such a baby," said Electra disparagingly as Orestes burst into tears.

I picked him up and shushed him. "You were a baby once, Electra, and it wasn't that long ago," I scolded. "Don't be mean to him. Give me that ball." She pulled a mulish face but handed it over. "It's not fair to tease him."

Happily distracted, Orestes stopped his wailing and I put him back on the ground where he sucked enthusiastically on the rag ball.

"We all have to try and get on with each other." – which platitude all four children chose to ignore.

"That was effective," drawled Helen, watching me from where she sat in the shade.

"Well, you've got to try," I retorted.

Helen and her family were visiting. Menelaus and Agamemnon were running joint training exercises with their warriors in the hills, while Helen and I caught up on family news and her child played on the terrace with mine. We saw each other rarely enough, and we had a lot of gossip to catch up on.

I smiled at my little family. I was proud of them. Iphigenia was growing beautiful, and Agamemnon would soon need to find her a husband. Girls married earlier here in Mycenae than we did in Sparta, and at fifteen she was considered old enough. I hoped I could keep her a little longer. I had loved her from the moment they laid her in my arms. She was my firstborn, and we were very close, quite unlike the prickly nature of my dealings with Leda.

Electra, ten years younger than her sister, had a very different temperament. She and I scratched each other at every turn. I dreaded to think what she would be like at fourteen. I sighed, wondering if we were too similar. We clashed at every opportunity. It sometimes seemed she opposed everything I said. She was her daddy's girl, and Agamemnon could do no wrong in her eyes. She followed him round whenever she could, which was unfortunate as he had little time for her. Nor, now she was older, for Iphigenia.

Agamemnon had lost interest in his children when he found he had to share my attentions with them. From the moment I had held Iphigenia in my arms, they had become the most important thing in my life. On them I poured the unconditional love I had once reserved for my husband. His blows and tantrums had changed that, although we still had a workable marriage. I reasoned that Agamemnon, as my husband and my equal, could look after himself, as I did. My children, entirely dependent on me, were entitled to first place in my priorities.

Orestes, my baby, had been born two years earlier. Finally, after all those years of marriage, I had given Mycenae a male heir. Orestes was an easy-going, laughing little boy. As the youngest, he simply adapted to everyone around him. I was discovering that little boys are different to little girls, and he had me wound round his little finger.

Agamemnon adored him. "My little warrior," he would exclaim as he picked him up and cuddled him. Orestes would squeal with delight as his father lifted him above his head and tossed him in his arms.

I returned to Helen and sat beside her. "We've got an attractive brood between us," I remarked. Helen's daughter Hermione was a little replica of her mother, her blonde hair gleaming in the sunlight.

"How the years go by," said Helen. She sounded dejected.

I looked at her. "That sounded rather morbid," I commented.

"Mm," she hesitated. "Do you sometimes worry that our lives may be over?"

I had a sudden presentiment. "You're not sick or something, are you? You would tell me, wouldn't you?"

Helen shook her head. "No, nothing like that but … Don't you sometimes feel life is passing us by and we don't have a great deal to show for it?"

I laughed. "Well, you may have a point, but I'm usually too busy to let it worry me."

* * *

Ever since my first efforts at governing Mycenae in Agamemnon's absence, I had retained an interest in such civil duties. Spending a morning doing nothing was a rare luxury for me. Agamemnon's interests as a ruler revolved entirely around annual tax take figures, trade surpluses and protecting or extending Mycenae's borders. Or, as I came to term them, the three P's – Profit, Plunder and Power.

As a girl I had watched my father hold weekly courts where

cases could be debated in front of him. He had passed judgment in disputes, administered justice to the guilty and kept a firm finger on the pulse of Sparta's domestic life. It appalled me that Agamemnon would not do the same for Mycenae. When I asked him about it he shrugged. He had functionaries whose job it was to manage anything that didn't interest him.

I had been suspicious of these uncontrolled officers, reasoning that without proper supervision they were natural targets for corruption and cupidity. Once, in the early days of my watch, I had happened upon an ugly scene: A townsman complaining he had received short measure from a trader, a charge the trader was denying vehemently. A crowd gathered, and in short order, the military police arrived to drag the plaintiff away and administer summary justice.

I was about to turn away when, almost on instinct, I stepped forward, and said, "Let the trader show us his weights. Let the captain here hold them up so everyone can see. That way the trader proves his honesty to us all."

The crowd, who were enjoying the excitement, cheered the suggestion.

I called a seller from a different stall to bring his weights so that comparison could be made. The weights were put on the scales, one by one, and it was clear our trader's weights were lighter. I picked one up to examine it and saw the core of each disk had been drilled away. "I think the plaintiff is in the right," I declared. "Release him immediately, and take up this dishonest wretch in his place."

The captain had no choice but to arrest the protesting trader.

"I paid for protection," the wretched man was shrieking at the captain as they hustled him off. "You have no right to arrest me, I paid." The captain silenced him with a blow, but I'd heard the trader, and the captain knew it.

After that I made sure I oversaw justice in Mycenae. I took my place in the hall each week to hear arguments and administer fairness, and I made sure I was impartial. It didn't hurt to keep appointed officials on their toes, and I taught dishonest ones to fear me. I let Agamemnon's functionaries do their jobs, but they never knew when I would choose to turn up to check on them or run an audit of their work.

It was very much the work Leda had taught me in managing a household but on a larger scale.

I drifted back to the present and Helen's misery. "I suppose you could claim we have nothing to show for our lives – well, apart from our children, and that we are both queens in our lands. I can see how empty your life must be." I allowed the sarcasm to be overt, although I was concerned. It wasn't like Helen to be gloomy.

"I just feel a bit pointless, as if the most exciting part of my life is over and there's nothing left but to grow old and die," she said. "I'm barely in my thirties, and I feel like an old crone."

I resisted saying the obviously consoling things – that she was beautiful, had a lovely daughter and a loving husband. "You've probably got too much time on your hands," I said. "We weren't reared to be passive. You need to find a cause you can be passionate about."

A long silence filled the gap between us as I mulled over her words.

"Ignore me," she said at last. "I'm just being maudlin. It's probably the time of the month," she shrugged.

"Is everything all right between you and Menelaus?" I asked.

She hesitated, then shrugged again. "As well as any marriage after all these years. We rub along together, but it's not like you and Agamemnon."

I stared at her. "You aren't suggesting that my marriage is wonderful, surely?"

"Well, isn't it?"

I gave a little laugh. "Where do I begin? In our early years he used to hit me if something distressed him. Not, you understand, to punish me for something I had done wrong, but simply as a way of relieving his own frustration."

Helen's eyes opened in wide horror. "I never knew. Why didn't you say something?"

"Partly because I was ashamed, and partly because I always hoped it was a one-off and he would stop. Anyway, he hasn't hit me in years. Now he throws tantrums instead. Again, the purpose is to cause me distress, but at least it's not physical. Well, not to me any more. He smashed a rather nice marble statue of Athena last time he was in a rage. Then he was upset it was broken and had another tantrum because he couldn't get all the pieces to stick back together. It was funny in a rather sad way."

"What about the children? Do they know?"

"Iphigenia has seen him in action and, I suspect, now feels contempt for him. As of course do I; or at least for that part of his personality. He looks so strong, strutting around in his armour as our war leader, but inside he's really a weak man. He genuinely wants everyone to be happy, but if things don't go the way he plans, he doesn't take control of the situation and manage it through to the result he wants; he just goes to pieces and takes it out on me."

Helen put her hand on mine. "That's terrible. I always thought you two got on."

"The odd thing is, we do. He could be a great man if he didn't allow himself to behave like a spoilt child."

"Why don't you leave him?"

"Because there is a lot about him I still like," I said slowly. "He's the father of my children and has rights over them. If I left, I would lose the children, and I could never do that; it would cause them terrible distress. Anyway, I've always thought it best for everyone if I just carry on. Agamemnon and I are fond of each other in our own way, and as you said, after all these years, what do we expect?"

Helen sighed. "To think I thought I had problems."

"Not real problems," I hastened to reassure her. "I suppose every marriage is different."

We sat in companionable silence for a while, both following our own thoughts.

"The worst thing is I can't really complain that Menelaus does anything wrong. He is still the man I married. Everybody's friend and drinking companion, popular in the mess, always cheerful."

"So what's the problem?" I asked.

Helen turned to me. "I feel he's never grown up. People

describe him as youthful for his age, but the truth is he's still a boy in everything he does. Sometimes I feel I want an adult, not a child." She bit her bottom lip. "I don't think he's terribly intelligent."

I choked back a laugh. I had never thought Menelaus intelligent, but he had always been well meaning. I looked at my sister thoughtfully. "There isn't someone else, is there? You've never spoken like this before."

"I suppose we've both admitted things today that we've never told each other," she said. "No, there isn't anyone else." She gave a sad little laugh.

"I live in Sparta, remember? Wall-to-wall warriors with no ambition beyond the next boar hunt or raid. I've considered them to see if there was anyone there I fancied, but no. Not a one."

I was relieved. "Maybe this is just a phase that will pass. Perhaps Menelaus will grow up. He must be nearing forty."

Helen nodded but said nothing. We returned to watching the children.

"To tell you the truth," said Helen eventually, "Sparta has been having a rough time. You asked if I was sick. I'm not, but we've had plague over the last year, and it seems unstoppable. One of the reasons Menelaus wanted to visit and talk to Agamemnon was to see whether he had any suggestions. The healers are at their wits' end. There's an uneasy mood amongst the people that we've offended the gods, although how, I don't know."

"Well, if Agamemnon has no suggestions, I imagine he'll ask Calchas," I said. "If anyone can interpret the signs, it will be him. He's famous for it."

Calchas had managed to retain his influence on my husband. I disliked the man and still avoided him whenever possible, but I had come to realise his importance to Agamemnon and the people of Mycenae. In the early days of my marriage I had tried to win him over but failed. I smiled at him when we passed in the street but was rebuffed or ignored; I met him once at a feast and sought to engage him in conversation. He had ignored me until I persisted. Then I read scorn in his eyes and was forced to listen once again while he intoned the grim prophecy that

I would be Agamemnon's doom. The guests around me were entranced, and several enjoyed my public embarrassment. From then on I left the priest alone if I encountered him in the town, and he continued to ignore me. We were both wary of each other's influence over Agamemnon, and I was unwilling to push the issue to open warfare and force Agamemnon to take sides. There was universal faith in Mycenae that Calchas spoke with the words of the gods and that he would warn us of any danger. Frankly, it said little for the good taste of the gods if they used such a revolting man as their mouthpiece.

I thought he was a fake, that most of his famous prophecies were invented for his own purposes, and that he was a mean-spirited individual.

When the men returned from their manoeuvres it was obvious our husbands had spoken together. At dinner Agamemnon announced Calchas would interpret the omens on the following morning, and Menelaus would be guided by the words of the seer.

Accordingly, bright and early the next morning we all stood in the temple to watch Calchas scry. After Agamemnon had dispatched a sheep in sacrifice, Calchas withdrew into the inner sanctum to riffle through the dead sheep's intestines, interpret what he saw there and consult with the gods. He was away for some time, and I was becoming impatient. Iphigenia stood by my side, but I had left the younger children with Io and Chryseis. I knew they would be well cared for, but I hated leaving them too long, and I didn't trust Electra not to find some new mischief.

At last the seer returned.

"The gods have spoken," he cried.

Obediently the nobles and warriors quieted down to listen.

"There is disagreement among the gods, and their quarrels and fighting are causing pain among their worshippers. The oracle is clear; Menelaus must go to Troy. He must observe propitiatory rites at the graves of Lycus and Chimaereus, sons of Prometheus, who are buried there. Only by doing so can he lift the plague from the land of Sparta."

"Troy?" murmured Helen beside me. "Where's Troy?"

I didn't know, but I had heard of it.

"Somewhere out in the eastern sea, I believe. Agamemnon is always complaining that the Trojans ruin our trade. It's a fabulously wealthy place, and he maintains that they control the trade routes, so all we get are their leavings."

"Sounds exciting," said Helen. "I wonder whether Menelaus will let me go with him. I'd love to travel. I'll ask him."

Apparently the answer was no. The next day, Helen, Hermione and the Spartans hastily packed up to return home to prepare for Menelaus's mission.

"Bastard," commented Helen as she hugged me goodbye. "He could at least have said yes. Ah well, back to being a dutiful wife. Next time it's your turn to come and visit us."

I hugged her back. "Give my love to our parents."

We waved them away from the palace, then I climbed to the top level of the palace so I could watch them in the distance. I saw sunlight flash on one of the chariot's panels as they rounded the bend and went out of sight.

It was the last glimpse I would ever have of my sister.

CHAPTER
FOURTEEN

"THE JOINT EXERCISES WITH MENELAUS'S MEN were useful," Agamemnon said to me the next evening, "but the truth is, our warriors need a decent war to shake them up and motivate them again. They're bored. We need a good, hard skirmish to sharpen them up, otherwise they'll run off and cause trouble in the town."

Agamemnon had managed to subdue most of the surrounding kingdoms, either by directly annexing them, or by treaties and trade deals with their terrified rulers. No sensible neighbour was going to take on the might of Mycenae.

I told Agamemnon so. "They call you the 'Great King'; no one's going to challenge that."

Agamemnon sighed. "A generation ago we mounted a campaign against Crete and conquered them. That's what we need now. It's too quiet for warriors. They won't win glory sitting in barracks polishing their armour."

I sniggered. "Send your warriors home to plough their paddocks and grow crops. We can live in the Elysium fields."

Agamemnon snorted. "I'd be dishonouring the gods if I were

that feeble a king. We need challenges so the men can strive to be heroes. At the moment all they aim for is who can piss highest up the wall in the latrine."

I laughed at that. Sometimes it amazed me that, after the vicissitudes of our married life, the two of us could still enjoy each other's company and share our thoughts so easily.

He smiled at me and held my gaze. Married couples have ways of inviting intimacy without need of words. We ended up in the large bed. We still pleased each other well enough. Everything about this man was familiar, his scent, taste, touch and his moves. Afterwards we slept.

Chryseis had asked, many years ago, whether I understood Agamemnon. I remembered my surprise when I couldn't answer the question. Surely a woman should understand her husband? But I didn't. I had never plumbed the depths of his complexity. He was loving, affectionate, loyal, intelligent and honourable. He was also vicious, unkind, unpredictable, childish and stupid. He was a visionary, a charismatic man full of ideas that could change the world. He never listened to what people tried to tell him and lived in a world where what he imagined was more real to him than reality. I had married two different men and never knew which of them I would wake up with in the morning.

*   *   *

We received word from Sparta that Menelaus had departed on his pilgrimage to Troy.

"Do you think Calchas really received a message from the gods?" I asked Agamemnon.

"Maybe, maybe not. Who can say? But Calchas can seem uncanny. I've watched him as he divines, and it's as if something otherworldly takes hold of him. He's made some very effective prophecies."

"He's made a few mistakes as well," I said. "Remember what he said about me when I first arrived in Mycenae? He got that wrong."

Agamemnon shrugged. "No man can be right all the time. I

suppose even Calchas must be allowed a few errors."

"Hm. Well, let's hope he's right this time." I was thinking about Helen and her frustration at not going away with her husband.

"There's another reason I'm glad Menelaus is going to Troy," said Agamemnon. "I want him to have a look around at what is going on there. A trader came to me the other day with excuses for not being able to supply the tin and copper we need. Tells me he sold his entire shipment to Troy so had nothing for the rest of his customers. I'm hearing this story over and over again and across a wide range of commodities that we need."

"Can't you persuade the traders to go round their clients in a different order?" I asked. "At least that way others would get a chance to buy supplies."

"It doesn't work like that. Traders go where the market is easiest. And there's another problem. New weapons and materials are coming out of Anatolia, north of us, but near-neighbour to Troy. A trader showed me a knife with an odd-coloured blade. I thought it an ornament, but he let me use it, and it was more powerful than bronze and kept its edge. We need this technology if we are to hold our dominant position, but the Trojans have it in their capability to ensure we never get it. Can you imagine the imbalance of power in the region if Troy manages to equip an army with these new weapons?"

I thought Agamemnon was probably overstating the problem. Greeks had used bronze weapons for hundreds of years; no doubt we would use them for hundreds more. It would be like my husband to work himself up over nothing. I shrugged and went off to manage my family and maids.

The next word from Menelaus was that he had returned from Troy, having successfully completed his mission. Appropriate rites of propitiation had been performed, and the plague in Sparta should resolve itself. His message contained some of the information Agamemnon had asked for but was very light on detail.

"Why couldn't he understand the importance of what I asked

for?" stormed my husband. "I asked for trade and armaments figures. I want a detailed description of Troy's defences, and instead I'm told how generously Menelaus is treated by the Trojan royal family, how hospitable they were, and how he's brought some princeling back with him to help him with purification rites. The man's an idiot."

I grinned. "I'm glad he had a nice time. What does the prince want purification for?"

Agamemnon glared at me. I wondered if he was about to be unpleasant, but he relented.

"Apparently the man accidentally killed his best friend in an athletic contest so he needs purification, and Menelaus has offered to have it performed for him. What a waste of time."

I knew Agamemnon's mood hadn't been improved by the accompanying news that his grandfather, old Catreus, had died in Crete. Obviously a family member needed to be present to ensure that a proper burial and all its attendant ceremony was carried out. Menelaus, apparently exploring a previously unsuspected spiritual side to his nature, had volunteered for the job and headed for Crete.

I wondered whether Helen had managed to coax him into taking her on this trip but suspected she'd been left behind again.

CHAPTER
FIFTEEN

W E WERE ROUSED IN THE MIDDLE of the night. Agamemnon leapt from bed, grabbing for his sword. The maid who had woken us looked terrified.

"What's the matter? You, woman, how dare you come in here and disturb your master? You'd better have a good reason."

"It's King Menelaus," was all the poor girl got out. "He is demanding to see you now. He says it's urgent."

Agamemnon grabbed a tunic and rushed out. I got up rather more slowly and slid a robe over my shoulders. It would have to be something very compelling to force Menelaus to arrive in the mid-watches of the night. The road up to our citadel was twisty, steep, and not one I would have wanted to drive by night.

It said something for his urgency that he had managed to persuade the gatekeeper to let him through. Once the city gates were closed for the night, no one was allowed in or out. Menelaus would have had to convince the guard his visit was enormously important for them to break that law.

I went into the great hall. The servants were scurrying around lighting candles, rekindling the brazier and pouring wine.

Menelaus was sitting on a bench beside Agamemnon. "She's gone," I heard him say.

"Who's gone?" I said sharply.

The men looked across at me.

"Good evening, Menelaus," I said.

His appearance was a shock. His usual amiable grin had disappeared. Beneath the fading rust colour of his hair, his face was grey and drawn.

"Who has gone?"

"Helen. Apparently she's run away," said Agamemnon. "Carry on, Menelaus. What happened?"

I sat down in a hurry. She had said she was restless and frustrated, but surely my sister wouldn't have just bolted?

"I don't know," said Menelaus. "Everything seemed fine when I went to Crete for our grandfather's funeral, but I arrived home yesterday to find Helen has decamped and gone to Troy, with Paris.

"Paris?"

"The young Trojan prince I told you about a few weeks ago. He's been staying with us as our guest while he underwent purification for killing a friend. When I left for Crete he had just about completed absolution. I don't understand. Why would Helen do such a thing? Why run away with a virtual stranger, and why would she leave Hermione?"

Agamemnon rubbed his chin. "You are sure she left willingly? I mean, are you certain she hasn't been abducted by this man?"

"I questioned the servants. They all said she walked onto his ship willingly." Menelaus rose from his seat and began to pace the floor.

"And you had no previous reason to suspect they were having an affair, or that there was an attraction between them?"

"Absolutely nothing," said Menelaus. "I would hardly have left her in the palace with him while I was away if I had thought something like this would happen. She's my wife, I can't believe she would betray me like this."

"May the goddess curse all unfaithful women," said Agamemnon. "It doesn't look good, Menelaus, having a wife cuckold you like this. Did they take anything else? Money, weapons?"

Menelaus shook his head. "I don't think so. Helen's taken her own jewellery, of course, and a couple of her slaves – the two we captured that time we rescued her from Theseus. Paris has his own ship, so transport was easy for them. He was provisioning her when I left for Crete. I still can't see why Helen would do this to me. You're right, it makes me look like an idiot, but the truth is, I have no idea why she should go."

So Helen had taken Aethra and Phisiades? I wondered at that. They had been with her so long, I suppose she felt they were friends.

"She wasn't happy," I said.

Their heads swung towards me with such a synchronised unity it would have been the envy of a trained hoplite band. I had to choke back a nervous giggle.

"What do you mean?" asked Menelaus. "She never said she was unhappy. Why would she be unhappy? She's Queen of Sparta."

"Did she say something to you, Nestra? Did she tell you she was going to do this?"

I could see Agamemnon beginning to fuel his anger. I didn't intend to be his victim, not even for Helen. "No, of course not. Of course she didn't," I said hurriedly. I turned to Menelaus. "She asked if she could go to Troy with you, and you refused her. Did she also ask if she could go to Crete?"

"Yes, but what's that got to do with anything? Are you saying she's run off with a lover because I didn't take her travelling? That's a nonsense." Menelaus was practically spluttering.

"No, maybe not. But she said she felt life had passed her by. I think she wanted to do something exciting. Travel might have given her the adventure she needed. She never indicated that she wanted a lover." I could see total incomprehension on both their faces. "Helen has always been bright and adventurous. She may have felt she wanted more from life than managing the maids and weaving tapestries."

They looked even more confused. I decided to remain quiet.

"What am I supposed to do now?" asked Menelaus. He looked so downcast my heart went out to him. I had always thought his was the nicer nature of the two brothers, although he had only half Agamemnon's intelligence. He was what he had always been, a nice man, clearly out of his depth.

Agamemnon and I returned to our bed, and the palace grew quiet around us. I lay there wondering and worrying about Helen, out somewhere on the sea. What on earth had led her to this catastrophic act? I could see no good coming from it.

What, I wondered, did Leda and Tyndareus make of her actions? I imagined them distraught. What did the people of Sparta think? And, most concerning, how was Hermione? I thought back to the sweet, golden-haired girl who had tagged around behind Iphigenia, and I grieved for her loss of childhood innocence.

I went back over the conversations Helen and I had shared during her visit. I thought I had been right in suggesting Helen had far too much spare time to overthink her dissatisfaction with life. It came to me that Helen had probably had the easiest life of us all. She had married, stayed in her childhood home and become Queen of Sparta almost by default, because Tyndareus and Leda had retired soon after her wedding to Menelaus.

She had never had the stress of leaving home or adapting to a new country and people. She did no useful work because she had never needed to. If Menelaus went away, Tyndareus kept an eye on things for him. Her life might sound desirable, but I could see how it could have been boring for an intelligent, high-spirited young woman.

Agamemnon stirred beside me. "Are you awake, Nestra?"

"I can't sleep. I'm so worried about Helen. What's going to happen when she arrives in Troy? I don't imagine the royal family are going to greet her with open arms. No one likes an adulterous woman, and Paris has betrayed his obligations as a guest."

Agamemnon's hand reached out and grasped mine. "I can't understand why she ran away. I don't believe Menelaus treated her badly, but whichever way you look, it's made him the laughing stock of Greece. Helen's supposed to be sired by Zeus. She's the most beautiful woman in the world, and Menelaus has lost her to another. You can see how that appears. It makes him look weak."

I nodded into the darkness. "I am so afraid for her. Do you think Menelaus will go after her?"

"We'll talk about it tomorrow, or rather, later today. I think he has to do something for the sake of his reputation. No man can be expected to put up with an insult like this from another sovereign country, let alone allow his wife to be so undutiful. The larger question is how involved we need to be. I can't let my brother go unsupported against Troy. It would save a lot of trouble if, when Helen arrives, they pack her onto the first ship they can and send her back to her husband."

I shuddered.

CHAPTER SIXTEEN

IPHIGENIA BURST INTO MY CHAMBER EARLY in the morning, her hair undressed and her gown barely fastened.

"Is it true? About Auntie Helen? They say she's run away and left Hermione behind."

I gathered the distraught girl to me. "It seems to be true. It's certainly what Menelaus believes."

"How could she desert Hermione like that?" she wailed. Poor Iphigenia, on the cusp of adulthood herself, trying to understand the incomprehensible.

"Oh, my darling, we haven't heard the full story. There may be an explanation that we don't know yet." Even as I spoke the soothing words, I admitted to myself the only possible excuse was divinely inspired madness. Otherwise the obvious interpretation was a tawdry betrayal of decency by both Helen and Paris.

Agamemnon had left early. He was summoning the captains of his army for a meeting with Menelaus. The men would decide what the next course of action would be.

I feared for my sister. The men would be angry and their mood punitive. Helen's beauty and semidivine reputation was unlikely to save her from an angry army bent on retaliation.

I helped Iphigenia dry her eyes and compose herself. "Your father will work out what to do for the best," I assured her, although I wondered what possible course of action could be described as 'the best'.

The palace, of course, was in an uproar. Every man, woman and child, whatever their status, had an opinion on the matter and were prepared to stand all day defending their position. I had to be quite firm with the staff to get them to return to their duties.

"I want no further gossip," I declared crossly. "We haven't got all the facts, and the warriors are working out a course of action. That's all you need to know. Now get back to work, and don't let me hear from any of you again."

Gradually they dispersed and I was able to get some work out of them. The world could fall around us but there was still food to be prepared, stores to be preserved, linen to darn and cleaning to do. When the slaves realised that standing round wringing their hands simply resulted in their workload increasing, they shut up.

I breathed a sigh of relief. I was finding it hard enough to deal with my own emotions without worrying about everyone else's.

The men's meeting carried on long into the night. Every now and then I would hear raised voices coming from the hall. I let them be. I didn't want to know what they were planning.

Agamemnon came to bed late. He was tense, wound up, overexcited and overtired.

I sat up, letting the sheet fall to my waist.

"How did it go?" I asked.

He sat on the end of the bed, sighed and ran his hands through his hair. "As you would expect, I suppose. Everyone wanted to express their own point of view, and not one of them was original. I had to sit through it all before I could get any sense out of them."

"Did you come to any consensus?"

"Not yet," he said cautiously. "But we did make progress.

Oddly enough, it was Menelaus who triggered it."

That didn't sound hopeful. Menelaus wasn't the greatest thinker or problem solver.

"What did he suggest?" I asked.

"He didn't suggest anything. But he did remind us of how he was chosen as Helen's husband. Menelaus was simply taking a trip down memory lane, but it reminded me of the oath we all swore to defend whichever husband was chosen for Helen. I think we may be able to invoke it in this case."

"Hardly," I said. "That oath is years old and was only intended to prevent the unsuccessful suitors murdering each other on the way home from the competition. I can't see what it would have to do with Helen running off with a lover."

Agamemnon smiled at me. "That's where you're wrong," he said. "There was no time limit set. The oath required us: *to stand behind whomever was selected and be ready at any time in the future to defend the favoured bridegroom against any wrong done to him in respect of the marriage.* I think this situation qualifies."

I looked at him. "Are you sure you have the wording correct? It was a long time ago."

"Oh yes," he said with confidence. "I remember very well. It's not often a man has to swear such a serious oath. I can still quote the exact form of the words."

I thought about that. I wondered if Agamemnon's recall was exact. I wouldn't put it past him to lie if it suited him, but then it would take another suitor with equally good recall to be able to refute it.

"There were dozens of suitors," I said. "If they all honour their oath and bring their warriors, it would mean an enormous army."

"I know," said Agamemnon smugly. "Just think, Nestra. This might be the chance we need to take on Troy and crush them. Imagine if we brought the entire Greek army against them? We'd have no trouble with trade routes and supplies for years after that."

"But that's got nothing to do with Helen or Paris," I protested.

"You can't start a full-scale war just because one woman's run away."

"No, but I can use it as the *excuse* to start a war, and bound by that oath, the warriors will surely unite and fight for it."

I didn't like the sound of the proposal one little bit. I was less concerned about Agamemnon's desire to fight than I was about Helen being a helpless pawn in the middle of it all.

I was opening my mouth to say so, when Agamemnon added, "Let's just hope the Trojans don't go and send the silly *porne* straight back to us. That would spoil all the fun."

The next day the warriors accepted Agamemnon's proposal. I heard the cheers ringing from the hall as they reached agreement and wondered whether Agamemnon had considered the logistics of this exercise. I hoped he wasn't planning on assembling this mass of military might on the plains outside Mycenae. How would we feed them all? The countryside would be stripped bare in days.

Any sympathy I'd felt for Helen was fading fast as the repercussions of her actions began to set in.

CHAPTER
SEVENTEEN

MESSENGERS WERE SENT OUT TO EVERY corner of Greece, reminding Helen's erstwhile suitors of their vow. It would take a few weeks for the messengers to reach their destinations and for those who took that oath to be convinced that they would have to participate in Agamemnon's grand plan.

In the meantime, Agamemnon sent urgent word to Odysseus.

He explained his actions to me over dinner one evening. "We must be seen to handle this crisis in a manner befitting our dignity and political credibility."

I rolled my eyes at his solemn mien. He couldn't fool me. I knew he wanted to go to war and was itching to have a go at the Trojans. If Helen hadn't been involved I would have been encouraging him to go. I knew as well as he that an army of bored, under-occupied warriors was a recipe for trouble in any town.

Agamemnon saw my face. "This is serious, Nestra. There must be no carping later that we were an aggressive rabble. I'm sending Odysseus and Menelaus on a mission to Troy to negotiate retrieving Helen."

"I thought that was the last thing you wanted?"

He laughed. "Menelaus I can't trust, but I guarantee I can get Odysseus to negotiate in such a manner that the Trojans kick them back to Greece empty-handed. It's the sort of game Odysseus was born to play. He'll enjoy it."

I saw them off as they started on their journey. Menelaus was a wreck. He didn't look as if he'd had any sleep in a month. Odysseus looked debonair and amused. Agamemnon was right. He would be playing to his strengths.

Still, I had overheard Odysseus tell my husband he wanted a quick resolution to the problem. Penelope had given him a son, and Odysseus wanted to be around to watch the lad grow up.

"I can't see Odysseus willingly joining your composite army," I said to Agamemnon. "He's very much a man who makes his own way. He's much too confident of his own abilities to want to be part of some mass war effort."

Agamemnon grunted. "He'll be there for the same reason the rest are. He knows he can't, in honour, break his oath. He would be seen to be forsworn before both men and gods, and Odysseus is a man to whom honour matters. He's tricky and clever, but he knows he can't renege on his given word and keep respect."

The plans for the campaign had been refined, and now the army and the fleet needed to transport it, were to assemble at Aulis. I gave fervent thanks to whoever had proposed that location. I felt sorry for the good citizens of Aulis, but I didn't want the army any nearer Mycenae.

Agamemnon had appointed himself commander of the army. There is an old saying that wherever two Greeks gather together, you will find ten differing opinions. I wondered if Agamemnon had considered his position might be challenged. I couldn't imagine Idomeneus of Crete, for one, bowing his head to an Achean, given the history of warfare between the nations.

We had heard nothing from Troy about either Helen or Paris. I just had to hope that she had arrived safely, was happy and that the fates would unravel the knots she had tied us in.

The town and our palace was suddenly a place of men. Warriors swarmed in from the surrounding countryside and kingdoms, augmenting the standing army. With them came their attendants, slaves and retinue. The town outside the citadel stretched at the seams trying to accommodate the influx. Brothels and wine shops did a roaring trade.

I passed Myrto one morning as he climbed the steps to the palace. I'd seen little of him. His role was to keep discipline in the camp that stretched out on the plain below the citadel.

"Good morning," I greeted him, noticing how tired he looked. "How is it going?"

He rolled his eyes. "I'm out of patience and very short on temper. Every little warrior, convinced he's a hero, is giving himself airs and graces. Their retinues are no better, and I'm supposed to be the voice of reason. I've spent a watch persuading a shiftless group of Argolites that it would be in everyone's best interests if they worked alongside the Acheans to dig latrine trenches. They all have to shit the same, but can they work together? No. Every petty skirmish and border wrong over the last three hundred years is trotted out to prove they can't both stick a shovel in the earth and dig a ditch together. The gods spare me from these fools."

I grimaced in sympathy.

"Agamemnon is going to have his hands full keeping this lot together. They could kill each other long before they ever see a Trojan. Each petty princeling has his own axe to grind. The sooner they leave our shores, the better."

I agreed. Life, on a purely domestic basis, was becoming frustrating.

Every tradesman and artisan was caught up in the excitement, all their efforts devoted to the war. Every smithy was turning out weapons or sharpening blades; leatherworkers were fixing horse ware and armour. It was impossible for a housewife to get a pot riveted or a pair of sandals mended, and harried workers were quite unable to say when normal service would resume.

The palace, usually a place of calm, was overrun. It seemed every room of my home was suddenly occupied with warriors having meetings about strategy, provisioning, political considerations and outcomes. The halls had turned into a de facto marketplace as traders competed for commissions on everything from provisioning ships to providing tents for the army.

The poor slaves were worked off their feet running errands for all and sundry, and the kitchens groaned with the effort of producing enough food for all who dined in the palace at night.

I kept Iphigenia well away from the public areas of the palace. Keeping control of the younger children was harder. Electra had picked up on the excitement and wanted to spend her day trailing her father; Orestes fancied himself a warrior. He had a small wooden sword with which he challenged any passing soldier. Most were happy to oblige the little boy for a few minutes, but I kept a close watch on him to see he didn't make a nuisance of himself.

Menelaus and Odysseus returned. I sat beside Agamemnon in the hall and listened.

"We were well received with all the ceremony due to ambassadors. Priam and Hector were courteous," reported Odysseus. "They allowed us to meet with Helen so we could assure ourselves she was well."

"Is she coming back?" I asked.

Menelaus shook his head sadly. "The Trojans say she made a choice to come to them, and therefore she has all the privileges of a guest. They will not return her, nor force her to leave."

"But what did Helen say?" I asked. "Is she happy?"

Menelaus and Odysseus looked at each other for a moment before Menelaus dropped his eyes.

Odysseus answered, "We understood, from what Helen said, that she was content with her life in Troy, and happy with Paris. She expressed no regret, but asked Menelaus to send her love to her daughter."

I sat back in my chair and gave an involuntary snort of disgust. I really didn't understand Helen at all.

"We picked up a story doing the rounds of the marketplace. It seems Paris was given Helen as a prize by the goddess Aphrodite," Odysseus said.

Agamemnon gave a crack of laughter. "What nonsense is this?"

Menelaus glared at his brother. "It's not funny. This is my wife they're talking about."

Agamemnon inclined his head apologetically. "Carry on, Odysseus."

"The tale is that three goddesses – Hera, Athena and Aphrodite – decided to have a beauty contest and chose Paris to be the judge. Aphrodite bribed Paris by telling him if he voted for her, she would give him the most beautiful woman in the world as his prize. Helen is reputed to be the most beautiful woman, so she became Paris's prize."

"Are you serious?" I couldn't help myself. "What a load of nonsense."

Odysseus cocked his head at me. "Nonsense maybe, but I see a process of rationalisation here. We no longer have the sordid tale of a runaway wife betraying her husband, which is the obvious way of looking at the problem. Instead, Helen is now a prize, bestowed by a goddess on Paris, and therefore on Troy. To hand her back would be discourteous to the goddess."

"Does anyone believe this?" asked Agamemnon.

Odysseus shrugged. "I very much doubt if Hector or Priam do. I got the impression they both realised Helen was a catalyst for a war which has been brewing for a while. The people in the town though, yes, I think they believe the tale, even if only because it gives them a sense of superiority over the Greeks. It may not be strictly true, but it must be metaphorically so, or else how would Helen be in Troy? The argument becomes circular."

"So, it's war," said Agamemnon with some satisfaction.

"Before you commit yourself to that course," said Odysseus, "I suggest you take the time to think this through very carefully. Agamemnon, I looked at Troy's defences and they are imposing. There is no guarantee that a Greek force could win. We would be fighting with our backs to the sea, the Scamander River on one flank, and most of all, we're against the city of Troy, which occupies the higher ground and so has a clear advantage. If we can't persuade the Trojans to leave their city and fight us in the open – and why would they? – we are going to be forced into a siege that could take years to resolve."

I saw a look of annoyance pass over Agamemnon's face, but before he could reply Menelaus interrupted. "I don't care about this. By Zeus, I want my erring wife back, that's all. Can we please remember this is what the discussion is all about?"

Agamemnon and Odysseus exchanged glances. Menelaus never was that smart.

"The sailing season for this year is over," remarked Odysseus. "You can't take an army across to Troy for the next few months anyway, even if you do assemble a force in Aulis. Agamemnon, I urge you to take time and think carefully about this matter. The Trojans will have months to prepare for conflict."

My husband shrugged. "I'll think about it." He sat, drumming his fingers on his knee.

"Thank you, Odysseus," I said. "I am grateful for the news of my sister, even if she persists in her stubbornness. Gods, I hope she is going to be all right!"

Odysseus looked at me thoughtfully for a moment before breaking into a grin. "Oh, I think your sister will do very well, Nestra. Very well indeed."

Later that afternoon, as Iphigenia and I were strolling in the gardens, we found Odysseus sitting staring into the far distance. He looked up when he saw us and smiled.

"May we join you?"

He nodded, and I sat beside him on the seat. Iphigenia sat on the balustrade across from us.

"What's the smell?" she asked, sniffing the air.

"Basil," said Odysseus. "I picked a sprig to sniff, but I've been fiddling and wrecked it." He opened his hands and let the crushed leaves fall to the floor.

"Were you thinking profound thoughts?" I asked.

"I was certainly deep in thought; I can't claim any were profound," he said smiling.

"What do you think of this proposed war with Troy?" I asked.

Odysseus gave me a guarded look. "You were there this

morning and heard what I said to Agamemnon."

"Yes, I know what you said," I replied impatiently, "but are you for the war? Do you personally support it?"

"Yes, I support it."

I frowned. "I thought you said it would be hard to win and could take a long siege. So why do you think it's a good idea? Do you really think we should fight to get Helen back?"

"You're not asking the right questions," he said. "I couldn't care less about hauling Helen back from Paris's bed. Nor am I interested in trade and whether Troy and Mycenae compete for it like dogs over a bone."

"Then why?"

Odysseus sighed. "For peace." He saw my incomprehension. "I'm ruler of a very small kingdom situated on a small island. I have a wife and a son. We have few resources, but even so, some day a bored warlord will decide that Ithaca could be a nice addition to his kingdom and will invade us. The few warriors that represent my army would be defeated in minutes and my lands conquered. There would be no independent Ithaca left for my son to inherit."

"How would war with Troy prevent that?" frowned Iphigenia.

"Because, my dear, such a war will take the combined armed forces of all our warring kingdoms and send them across the Aegean Sea. There'll be no bored armies left here preying on their neighbours. Any warriors seeking glory and plunder will be at Troy. With luck, Ithaca could have peace for another generation."

"Oh," said Iphigenia.

I mirrored her surprise, although such tortuous thinking was typical of Odysseus.

"There's one flaw in your argument," I said at last.

His eyes crinkled. "What's that?"

"You'll be one of the warriors bound for Troy. You won't get to enjoy your peaceful island with your wife and son."

He laughed and stood up. "Yes," he said, "I'm working on that problem." He grinned at us as he walked away.

"Give my love to Penelope," I called after him.

"Did he mean that?" asked Iphigenia after some minutes.

"Oh, I think so," I said. "It's really quite ingenious if you think about it."

We resumed our walk.

"It's unusual for a warrior not to want to go to war, though, isn't it?" she asked.

"It's what they spend their lives training for," I said. "They aren't much use for anything else. Your father can't even find his sandals by himself but stands there saying they're lost, until one of the slaves gets them from under the bed."

"I thought being a warrior was a good thing?" persisted my daughter.

"Of course it is," I replied. "Fighting for the honour of your king and country is the most noble and honourable thing a man can do with his life." Although Odysseus's words might bear some thinking about. They echoed those I'd heard from the townspeople.

"Then does that make Odysseus a coward?"

"I've never heard anyone accuse him of being one. I shouldn't think so." I gave a little laugh. "Odysseus has always been unusual. He's the cleverest man I know. Your father would do well to listen to his advice."

CHAPTER
EIGHTEEN

I WAS WORRIED ABOUT HELEN BUT DIDN'T care much about Troy, our trading patterns, or the glory and gain of a campaign. I did, however, respect Odysseus. If he had doubts about the wisdom of this campaign, I was prepared to listen.

Unlike my husband. Agamemnon didn't listen, of course. His mind was made up. He wanted a swipe at Troy's trade and dominance in the area, and Helen's rescue had provided the perfect excuse.

Agamemnon was everywhere: in the planning room, at trade displays, bartering with suppliers. I didn't know how effective he was. I suspected Adrastus and Amarynceus, his Achean subcommanders, quietly and efficiently did most of the work that actually got the army provisioned and ready for war. Agamemnon's constant interference and inconsistencies would have driven me to murder, but they seemed to manage. At least no one could doubt my husband's commitment and enthusiasm for the campaign.

Every evening when we'd retired to our bed, he'd vent

his frustrations about other commanders, suppliers and the inadequacy and unreliability of almost everyone else in Greece. Agamemnon could sulk better than anyone else I knew, and swing from wild enthusiasm to deep gloom. Clearly Electra inherited her father's temperament. I was heartily sick of his problems – most of which, I was convinced, were caused by his own organisational errors – and did my best to shut my ears to the constant drone of complaint.

I was also getting fed up with the beefy warriors cluttering the town, with all their attendant problems and complications. It was a relief when Agamemnon finally set the date for assembly at Aulis.

The whole town turned out to wave the troops away. Most seemed to think the campaign with Troy would be over in a couple of months and sent their men off cheerfully. I, at least, knew they could hardly leave Aulis before then, let alone reach Troy, sack the city and return. I assumed they would be gone for a year. Still, I kept quiet, and stood along with all the other women and children watching the troops depart. Beside me Iphigenia waved happily, while Electra and Orestes cried for their daddy.

It says something about our marriage that Agamemnon and I were so relaxed about being apart for such a long term. I would miss him, of course, but I had the children and the work of running Mycenae during his absence. I suspected there would be little time for pining for an absent husband.

Agamemnon had left Myrto with me to help manage affairs. We were a seasoned team now, both knowing each other's strengths and weakness. Myrto's eldest son was going with the troops. I didn't ask but suspected Myrto was pleased enough to be able to stay at home and leave dreams of glory to his son. He was a family man, through and through, torn between pride in his son and concern for his wellbeing in the campaign.

As I stood waving I was aware of the undercurrents flowing through the crowd. The storekeepers from the markets were, frankly, in mourning. They had traded more in the last four months than most had in their working lives. The troops' disappearance meant their cash flow went too. A few venturesome souls, both traders and whores, had elected to travel in the army's train and set up new businesses when they settled in Boetia for the winter.

I smiled at a woman I knew, a midwife in the town. Her husband was one of the soldiers.

"There'll be a boom in my business in nine months' time," she declared cheerfully. "After that there'll be a gap, or at least," she grinned, "there'd better be a gap until the troops come home again."

I nodded. The whores and wine shops were in for a lean winter. The farmers would be busy for months cleaning up fields the army had churned up camping on their land. They would need to get the ground ready in time for spring planting. Stock numbers were down. Many farms had been predated by hungry troops, and it would take time to restore flock numbers. Mycenae was uncharacteristically low in food reserves after provisioning boats and troops for the campaign, and feeding all the men over summer. We would need a good harvest next year.

Worst of all, labour units were down. I imagined that every farm, every little shop, every minor commercial enterprise had some young man who hoped to find adventure, fame and glory on a foreign battlefield. The young had signed up for the campaign in droves. For every warrior who hoped to be a hero, there would be ten others who provided essential services to the army.

Cooks, builders, brickmakers, blacksmiths and healers. There was a place for them all, and a certainty of use for them in the future.

We watched them march through the gates, Calchas amongst them as their official soothsayer. I climbed up the rise to the top terraces and followed the progress of the bright banners across the plain towards the sea. They turned into a smudge on the horizon as they headed for the Gulf of Saron, and I turned away. There was a lot of work to do to bring some order back into both town and countryside.

A messenger told us later that as they set sail two eagles, one black, one white, flew by on the starboard side. Then in sight of the entire fleet, they swooped on a pregnant hare and devoured both it and its unborn young. It was a complex and threatening image.

Calchas hastily interpreted this as a sign from the gods. The eagles were Menelaus and Agamemnon, and the unfortunate hare with its young was Troy, which they would capture and destroy.

With the troops gone, I relaxed my vigilance over Iphigenia and took her with me each day to see the work being undertaken to manage the town and citadel. I smiled when I remembered Leda trying to show me how to manage a household. When had I begun to turn into my mother? Iphigenia was at least interested in some of the work, which was more than I'd been. I enjoyed her company, her laughter and sometimes her common sense. She was immensely popular with the people in the town. They called her 'their golden princess' and cheered when she was around. Unselfconsciously she would wave back and smile. She had no affectations. She loved the city and her people, and they returned that fourfold.

*   *   *

Myrto marched into the room I had set aside for business with a child in tow.

"A problem," he said tersely. I looked at him, then at the child.

She was small and looked about eight or nine, ill kempt and dirty. Her hair had been cut short, her tunic even shorter. Even with her eyes cast down, she looked to me like trouble. I raised my eyebrows interrogatively.

"She's a stray, left behind by the troops. She's nowhere to go and has started stealing to survive. If I hadn't grabbed her she'd have been beaten up by the good law-abiding citizens of this town."

I rolled my eyes at him. I could recognise sarcasm. "What's your name?" I asked the child.

"Charis."

I nearly laughed. A less graceful creature would have been

hard to imagine. She'd already guessed my reaction; I could read it in her hunched shoulders and dipped head.

"Why was she with the troops?" I asked Myrto.

"Seems she's an orphan. She used to dance and sing for the men. They made a pet of her and adopted her as a sort of mascot. Spoilt her rotten for a short while before abandoning her. Now they've gone, and she's been dumped to fend for herself."

"Not much of a mascot then," I said, looking at the child. "More like an abandoned puppy. If the gods are just they'll curse men that treat a lucky mascot so casually. What do you want to do with her, Myrto?"

He looked embarrassed. "I wondered if you could do something with her. Make her a maid, maybe. If not, she'll end up in the brothels, or else murdered by some self-righteous citizen who disapproves of vagabonds."

I looked at him with a hint of exasperation. I didn't need a small child in the household. She'd have picked up all sorts of unfortunate ideas from the troops she had entertained, and judging by the independent cast of her eye, she probably had a fine idea of her own importance, which would have to be schooled out of her. The other maids and servants wouldn't be thrilled to have her dumped in their midst. I imagined endless complaints and grudges caused by this small creature.

On a moment's impulse I turned to Iphigenia. "What would you do?" I asked. I was interested in her response. I had noticed there were times when my daughter saw things in a situation that I had missed.

Iphigenia had been following the conversation keenly. I watched her assess the child.

"How old are you?" she asked.

"Thirteen."

I glanced at Myrto in surprise. I had put her as much younger.

"Have you any skills?" asked Iphigenia.

The child gave us a sly look. I shuddered at the knowingness in her eyes before she dropped them. "I can entertain," she said at last. "I dance and sing. The men liked me. I can be funny."

"How did you learn to do this?" my daughter asked. "Who

trained you?

For the first time I saw uncertainty in the girl. "I don't know who taught me," she mumbled. "I've always known these things."

"But these are real skills," pressed Iphigenia. "Someone taught you the words to the songs. Someone must have taught you the tunes, and how to dance. You must remember."

The girl dropped her head again. "I don't know. It was in the time before."

"Before what?" I asked, mystified.

"Before the warriors came and burned the village. I don't remember before."

We looked at her in silence. It was pointless to ask which warriors, what village.

I supposed I would have to take her into the household. I had daughters of my own, and the thought of this waif abandoned by the troops was disturbing.

"She could go to school," said my daughter.

I looked at Iphigenia in surprise.

"Would you like to learn?" she asked the girl. "You could serve me and attend the school. Then you would learn new skills as well as lessons in song and dance."

"You are sure of this?" I asked Iphigenia in surprise. It was one thing to ask her opinion, another to have her launch into such an ill-advised project.

"I am certain," she replied. "Just think, this may be a test. She may be a goddess in disguise asking for help. All the priests tell us these tales. We would be harshly judged if we turned her away from our door with no assistance."

I could count all the obvious problems with this idea and was about to present them when the girl said, "Yes."

I drew Iphigenia aside. "Darling, she's a street urchin. You don't know whether she'll steal from you or be trustworthy. You know nothing about her. And she knows nothing about being a lady's maid. She's going to have to learn everything – how to dress hair, look after your clothes, serve food. Everything."

Iphigenia just smiled at me.

Bother, I thought. So much for passing a decision to my daughter's judgment.

"You would have to behave," I said to the girl. "The school has the right to get rid of students who don't work and apply themselves."

The girl ignored me. She was looking at Iphigenia with adoring eyes.

"You would live with the other servants in the palace," said my daughter, "and you would be known as my maid, so that no one could throw you out or mistreat you."

The girl nodded.

It was typical of Iphigenia to take on the care of the waif. I remembered how kind she had been to her little cousin Hermione. I gave a sniff and wondered, with some amusement, what our noble families would make of the newest student at the school.

When I had arrived in Mycenae as a young bride, there had been no school for girls, a fact that had shocked me deeply. The conservative Mycenaeans saw no point in educating girls to simply end up as wives and mothers. The argument that they would grow up to be better wives and parents, with some education, held no water for them. There was little I could do to change this; it was too deeply entrenched.

As Iphigenia grew up I was determined she would enjoy the same education I had received, and ensured that suitable tutors were imported to give her lessons. Such lessons work best when there are a group of students, so I invited the daughters of a few noble families to join her. The opportunity to become a friend and playmate of a princess overcame their parents' scruples about over-educating daughters, and places on the course were fiercely prized.

It was a small step to open the classes up to other girls. The number of students was kept small, enrolment was by invitation only and, as in Sparta, no external hierarchy was allowed to influence discipline or the requirements of the curriculum. Achievement and effort were the only criteria that mattered. If a girl failed to strive, she was dismissed from the school.

It was a different exclusivity to one based purely on birth, and there were some early complaints and ill feeling from those who assumed nobility of blood would automatically guarantee them a place. In the end, the opportunity to receive an upbringing fit for a princess won over most. Iphigenia, and more latterly Electra, was growing up in a circle of friends. If there were still some nobles who were disaffected, there were many who waited hopefully for their own child's admittance.

I was pleased with the academy and saw it as a sign of progress. Iphigenia, who had nearly completed her education, was committed to the continuity of the school, and I hoped she would take what she had learned with her when she married the husband Agamemnon chose for her.

I wasn't sure how a street urchin would fit in, but I had given Iphigenia the right to this experiment and couldn't back out now.

I shrugged. The waif would either succeed or fail. Either way, I had no doubt that news of Iphigenia's latest charitable gesture would circulate and reinforce her popularity with the townspeople.

*   *   *

Altogether, the first months of the Trojan campaign were a happy and satisfying time for the family Agamemnon left behind. True, Electra sometimes asked after her daddy, but Orestes seemed happy to live in the present. Iphigenia, having a more adult appreciation of what the campaign was about, also seemed content to view it as something men were supposed to do, and left it at that.

We received regular messages about the troops' progress. Agamemnon had established a system of runners to send news to the Greek kingdoms, so we were well informed of what went on at Aulis. Agamemnon had been right – those kings who had taken the oath at Helen's betrothal did indeed honour it.

But there were those who tried to evade their obligations. Odysseus, that wily character, pretended he had lost his mind and couldn't understand the message. He was ploughing when Palamedes arrived and refused to pull over or listen to what he had to say. In frustration Palamedes eventually picked up Odysseus's toddler son and stood him right in the path of the heavy team of oxen, causing Odysseus to swerve, which put paid to his pretence of insanity.

I was amused when I heard the tale, even though I was sorry Odysseus's ploy hadn't worked.

Odysseus, narked at the exposure of his own deceit, was particularly willing to help track down Achilles. Although the boy was only sixteen, he already had a fearsome reputation as a warrior. To protect him from the draft, his mother concealed him amongst the women in Lycomedes' household. I tried to imagine the rage an adolescent male would feel, forced into this deceit, until I heard his refuge was sweetened by Lycomedes' daughter, Deidamia. Inevitably the silly girl became pregnant, about which time Odysseus arrived, disguised as a merchant, with a gift of a sumptuous suit of armour. Achilles' masculine enthusiasm and admiration for the gift betrayed his gender and soon Agamemnon's army had another conscript.

By the beginning of spring, the Greek army and fleet had assembled at Aulis. The weather grew warmer and more settled, and they waited for the winds that would blow them across the Aegean Sea to Troy. They waited, and they waited. The sun shone brightly, the sea sparkled and the wind blew from the wrong direction. Weather patterns, which should have been a given for the time of year, simply failed to eventuate.

The men had no alternative but to try and keep themselves amused until the wind changed.

The messengers brought us news of this delay.

"Still no wind."

I imagined Agamemnon's frustration and was thankful I wasn't there to share his misery. He would be worried about losing his army if disaffected warriors decided to go home.

We came to accept these regular messages as the norm.

The months passed; messengers arrived with the same dull news, and time went on. If the weather didn't change soon they would be stranded at Aulis for another winter.

Then I received an unexpected message. Agamemnon had

contracted a marriage between Iphigenia and the young warrior Achilles. I was to send her immediately to Aulis for the wedding. It would, said my husband, bring joy to the Greek army to celebrate a wedding between Mycenae's princess and the hero Achilles.

I went in search of Iphigenia.

I could hear her before I turned the corner onto the balcony. She and Charis were laughing together as they bent over a game of dice. I stopped in the doorway to watch them. Two pretty girls – one dark, one with lighter brown hair. Charis had scrubbed up surprisingly well, and an unlikely friendship had developed between the girls.

I took a deep breath and approached them. "Iphigenia, I have received word from your father."

She looked up in pleasant anticipation, seeing from my face I had something to tell her. "Have the winds changed then? They must have been getting intolerably bored."

"He has arranged a marriage for you. With Achilles," I blurted out. "He wants you to leave immediately for Aulis for the wedding celebration."

Iphigenia straightened up slowly. "Achilles? For my husband?"

I could see her assessing the news.

"Well, I've heard he's a hero," she said, "and young as well."

I tried to gather my rattled thoughts. "He's a Myrmidon. His father is King Peleus."

"So, it's a good match, my lady?" Charis had never learned that she should be seen and not heard.

"I suppose so," I said. I looked helplessly at my daughter. "I didn't think it would happen like this. I knew your father would organise a marriage, but this is so sudden."

I sat down rather hurriedly on the stone seat.

Iphigenia sat beside me, wound her arm round my waist and leant her head on my shoulder. "What do we have to do?" she asked practically.

There were, of course, endless things to do. Only a man could assume a bride could get organised, not just for a wedding, but for travel as well, in the space of two weeks.

The palace was in uproar. Seamstresses, embroiderers and every kind of skilled worker had to be called in to prepare the trousseau.

Iphigenia was massaged, oiled, her hair brushed until it fell in a fall of silk. I looked at her and realised how beautiful she had become. It wasn't just the regularity of her features; some part of her sweet nature shone out through her face. She would make a lovely bride, and Achilles would be a very lucky man.

Agamemnon had left the details around the wedding infuriatingly vague. What was to happen to Iphigenia after the ceremony? If the army was departing for Troy, they could hardly take her with them. Would she return here to Mycenae, or was the intent for her to travel to her new father-in-law's home? I could make no sense of it, and I gave Iphigenia comprehensive instructions about making sure all these details were sorted out.

I wouldn't be travelling with her. I couldn't leave Mycenae, nor could I travel with Electra and Orestes. My little girl would be going to her bridegroom on her own, without her mother beside her. My heart ached for her.

A week after the first message, a second arrived urging haste in dispatching Iphigenia to her bridegroom.

Iphigenia laughed at me when I swore at this missive.

"If my husband is looking forward to receiving me, that's a good thing, isn't it?"

I had to agree, through tight lips, that it was. I wasn't going to spoil her pleasure with my own worries and petulance. I strode off to find a negligent servant to berate instead.

Orestes was too young to have any idea of why the household was in chaos, but Electra was very excited. She followed her big sister around, watching as the maids made her beautiful, the dressmakers gowned her and the jewellers covered her in necklaces, bracelets and earrings. I found her playing brides and bridegrooms with some of her friends, trailing an old shawl over her head as a veil. How quickly they grow, I thought as I kissed her.

The night before she left, Iphigenia and I sat together in the hall. She was unusually quiet, toying with the olives and wine Charis had brought for us. Charis would be travelling with her, and I had given the girl a long list of instructions to ensure her mistress's happiness and comfort.

The baggage train was already packed, ready for an early departure on the morrow. I could think of nothing useful to do.

I put my hand on Iphigenia's. "You will make a wonderful bride," I told her.

She nodded.

"Is there anything you want to know? Anything you want to ask me?"

She smiled. "About being a wife? No, not that part." She turned her hand in mine and squeezed my fingers. "I'm just sad to be leaving here. Everything is changing so suddenly. But I'm excited as well. Father wouldn't arrange a bad marriage for me, and everything I have heard of Achilles has been good."

She was rising to this challenge as a true daughter of Sparta should. I knew how much I would miss her and tried to counter that with thoughts of how proud I was of her. Of all that had sprung from my marriage to Agamemnon, Iphigenia was the most beautiful.

I kissed her and went to bed.

They left early. The crowds lined the streets to wave and cheer their princess off on her wedding trip. She smiled and waved back, a happy, laughing girl going off on her greatest adventure. Charis, seated beside her, looked as proud as a peacock.

I watched them disappear out of sight then went to my chamber and cried like a child. Did all mothers feel like this? Grief clenched at my stomach, and terrible regret filled me. I wouldn't see her on her wedding day. She would do well, I knew. No one who met Iphigenia could do anything other than love her.

I clutched this little reassurance to me, and prayed to every god that they would care for my girl.

CHAPTER
NINETEEN

THE PALACE SEEMED NUMBINGLY EMPTY WITHOUT Iphigenia. I realised how she had become my companion, as much as a daughter. Even Myrto looked a little subdued as we worked through the usual business of the day.

I counted out the miles and days in my head. She would be at Megara; by now she must be at Thebes; perhaps today she would arrive at Aulis. I hoped Achilles was a good man and that they pleased each other. All daughters know our fate is to be married to whomever our fathers choose, but some men are wiser than others. I hoped Agamemnon had thought carefully before he contracted his daughter.

It was early evening. I said goodnight to the children. Orestes wanted to be told the story of our ancestor Perseus. Electra wanted to know about exactly what Iphigenia had worn for the wedding. She already knew every detail of her sister's wardrobe but wanted to hear it all again. We had to assume that the wedding had been celebrated by now. I couldn't wait for the messenger to arrive with the news and as many details as he could provide. I should have liked a female messenger who at least would have the sense to look at the important details. Was the bride happy? Did the groom appear to love her? Did Iphigenia look beautiful? Was her father happy? Instead I was likely to get a roll call of which heroes had attended the wedding, and an itemised list of warriors who had won fame in the hunt by providing the most meat for the feast.

The meltemi had arrived, with blustery winds that made sitting outside unpleasant. I wondered the weather was the same at Aulis. If these winds kept up there would be little possibility of Agamemnon's fleet being able to sail.

I made my way down to the dining hall. We were a small company these days with so few men amongst us. Myrto, of course, and the few men Agamemnon had left behind to guard the citadel. They were mostly experienced but elderly troopers who were enjoying their retirement on light duties.

I had reached for my wine, when there was a disturbance at the far end of the hall. The door was thrown open, and a guard strode into the room, followed by a young woman. It was dark at that end of the hall, and it took me a moment to realise the girl was Charis. She had shaved her head. My hand jerked involuntarily and I knocked my wine flying. A serving maid rushed to mop up the mess, but I barely saw her. My eyes were focused on Charis as she walked jerkily towards me. I realised the guard was supporting her as the girl seemed barely capable of independent movement.

"Charis?" I stood up in a hurry. "What's happened? Why did you leave your mistress?"

She came forwards slowly, stopped in front of me and fell to her knees.

"Charis? By all the gods, what has happened? Where's Iphigenia?" I asked sharply.

"Dead."

I hardly heard her, she spoke so softly. Or perhaps I did hear, but the gods, in their mercy, plugged up my ears for a few more minutes of peace.

There was a moment's stunned silence. I felt the blood drain from my face. All talk in the hall had ceased.

I stooped beside her and pulled her up so she had to lift her head to speak to me.

"What has happened?"

"They killed her."

I seemed to stop breathing.

"Iphigenia," I whispered.

It made no sense. How could my daughter not be alive? It must be a mistake. Fragments of thoughts jostled with each other in my brain, but I could seize none of them. Charis's words were too improbable to comprehend.

"Who killed her? Were you attacked? What happened?"

I looked at Charis. She looked terrible, her eyes wide, bruised and haunted, in a white, pinched face. The stubble on her head was ugly. She seemed to have difficulty forming the words.

"Wine," I called. "Bring Charis a drink."

Someone passed a goblet to me. I took it but found my hand shaking so badly the heavy red liquid slopped across the surface of the vessel and spilled over the sides. I thrust it back. The slave was Io. She stooped beside Charis and held it to Charis's lips.

"Have a drink, it will help steady you."

She obeyed. Maybe the wine did steady her. I passed my tongue over my dry lips.

"Carry on," I said.

"They sacrificed her," she said. "Calchas slaughtered her on the altar, like a sheep or an ox, as an offering to Artemis."

There was a horrified intake of breath from the onlookers. I felt the walls of the hall constrict round me. The people had become blurred. I couldn't control my temperature. I was hot; I was cold.

"Why?" I asked at last. "What had she done wrong? How had she offended?"

Charis was silent, as if, having told us the worst of it, she had run out of speech.

I drew her up to sit beside me at the table. The slave poured her more wine and filled my own goblet. I gripped the stem of the cup tightly to control my hands. "Start from the beginning,"

I commanded. There would be no other way of making us understand this.

Charis gave a shudder. "We arrived at Aulis. Agamemnon came to meet us, as did Achilles. Achilles didn't know they had lied to him. He thought he came to meet his bride, and he liked her. I could see he did. I think she liked him as well, and was relieved.

"They put us in a tent near to Agamemnon's so we were kept safe and separate from the main camp, and there we spent the night. Iphigenia was happy. She talked about her wedding day, and how we would have to be up early to make her look her best. She asked me if I thought Achilles was good-looking. Which he is. We giggled together about what she would be doing the next night."

Charis broke down in tears and couldn't continue for a few minutes.

I sat waiting, under the spell of what she was recounting.

"The next morning we were up early, and I dressed her in her finery. She looked so beautiful. Agamemnon came to see if we were ready then led us out to the army. I thought the men were very quiet, seeing as it was a wedding. Usually people are cheerful and a bit bawdy, if you know what I mean. But I didn't make much of it. I was more interested in Iphigenia and how lovely she looked. They walked us down a long track that led to the altar and the place of the ceremony. I could see a lot of men, officers I supposed, clustered at the far end by the altar, waiting for the bride.

"We were about two-thirds of the way towards the altar when there was this big ruction. Achilles suddenly burst through the men and ran up the track towards us, shouting at Agamemnon. 'This is wrong,' he said. 'How dare you use my name in something so dishonourable? You will not do it.'

"Iphigenia had come to a halt, not knowing what to do. A couple of the officers had followed Achilles, and I saw them trying to hold him, but he was fighting hard. 'No,' he said again. 'You will not do this. How could you all plan something so disgusting? Do you think the gods will be honoured by this travesty?'

"A priest had appeared, up by the altar. I realised it was Calchas. 'The goddess needs a sacrifice,' he cried. 'She must be appeased or she will not lift the curse.' Achilles rounded on him. 'No. This is obscene; an offence to all the gods. Give Artemis a sacrifice. Whatever you want. A deer, a sheep, a bull, maybe. I do not believe Artemis wants the blood of a young, innocent girl.'

"I heard Iphigenia give a little moan as she began to understand, and I moved up beside her to embrace her. I could feel her shaking with horror."

Charis's face was wet with tears as she spoke. I clapped my hand across my mouth, feeling sick. "Are you saying Iphigenia had been lured to Aulis to be sacrificed?" I asked.

Charis nodded, crying helplessly.

"That's what they wanted. Calchas had told them the reason they couldn't get the right wind to blow them to Troy was because Agamemnon had offended Artemis. The only way to propitiate the goddess was to sacrifice the most precious thing Agamemnon had, which was his daughter."

"And Agamemnon agreed?" I had no feeling within me. Maybe later I would begin to understand, but for now it was all words.

"Yes," said Charis bluntly. "He agreed to it. It was Agamemnon who thought to bring Iphigenia to Aulis with the promise of marriage. Most of the other officers knew but had been sworn to silence. Agamemnon knew that if the fleet couldn't sail soon, the troops would revolt, and he would lose his army. He couldn't afford that. No one had told Achilles, though. He just thought he was getting married."

I opened my mouth to speak, but no sound came out. I had to try again, to form the words, to make a noise. "Carry on."

"Achilles was so angry. I thought he would attack Calchas. It took six officers to hold him down.

"Iphigenia flung her veil back so she could see more clearly. It might have been inappropriate, but it was clear she wasn't there to be a bride. I think she decided in that moment that, whatever happened, she would look her fate directly in the eye. She looked at Calchas for a long moment. Then she turned her head and I saw she was looking at Agamemnon as if she couldn't really believe what he had done. I can't express the pure contempt on her face."

Charis swung round in her seat towards me. "Oh, lady. She was so brave. I could feel her terror, her shock and horror, but she kept her head up like a queen. I was so proud of her, and so frightened for her. This all happened so quickly. One moment she's a bride, next she's a sacrificial victim. It was too much to take in.

"So there we were, frozen in a tableau. Achilles spewing obscenities at Agamemnon, Calchas grimly waiting for his victim, and the men and the officers standing in silence around us. I think that was when Iphigenia realised that the only man there not determined to see her die was Achilles. She couldn't have escaped, however hard she tried, not even with Achilles' help.

"I felt her gather herself. She loosened my arms, put her hands either side of my face and kissed me on the forehead. 'Farewell,' she said quietly to me.

"She turned and began to walk slowly, once again, down the track to the altar. She stopped when she reached Achilles. 'Thank you for your support and your honour,' she said. 'It would have been a privilege to have been your wife.' She even managed a wavery little smile for him. He made some terrible choking noise of protest. Oh lady, it broke the heart to watch it. I could hear some of the men sniffing, though none moved to help her.

"She turned away from Achilles, and I saw her draw a deep breath as she faced the steps to the altar. I tried to run forward, but Agamemnon grabbed my arm and wouldn't let me go.

"Iphigenia climbed the steps on her own. Her tone was icy cold when she spoke to Calchas. 'How should I lie?' To do him justice, he bowed to her gravely before taking her arm and assisting her up onto the slab. She handed him her bridal veil, and he folded it and put it at her feet. He helped her lie down and arranged her skirts so that all was decent. He offered to bind her hands and feet but backed off when he saw her scorn.

"I was shouting 'no, no …' but it made no impression on the man holding me. Agamemnon could have been made of stone.

"Calchas made a short prayer to Artemis. Iphigenia never flinched or moved. Calchas lifted the curved blade over Iphigenia's throat and cut down and across. Her lifeblood flowed down over the altar and was collected in a vessel. "There was a sort of collective sigh from the troops watching. I think I screamed, because my throat was sore afterwards but I don't remember.

"After that, Calchas held the bowl of blood up and pronounced the army free of the curse. I turned and bit Agamemnon's hand so badly that he let me go, and I ran down the path to the altar.

"She was beautiful in death. Calchas hadn't marred her face, and she lay there looking so peaceful. I stood there for hours, just watching her. After a while I realised I had a companion on the vigil. Achilles had come to be with her. We stayed beside her for the rest of the day, until someone brought linen and water to clean her. I washed the blood from her neck. There was very little spilled on her dress, and it lifted easily enough when I sponged it.

"They brought a bier and laid her on it. I covered her with her veil and walked beside her to the funeral pyre. It was later I realised how prepared they'd been. They had built it before she even arrived in Aulis to be a bride. When we arrived they simply steered us away from the area so we never questioned why there was a funeral pyre waiting.

"They burned her that evening, my lady. There were few women to sing the funeral dirges, but the camp women did what they could. I sent my hair to the fire with her. It was all I had for her. The whole army came to pay their respects. Achilles couldn't bear to be near Agamemnon. I saw his hatred when he looked at him. Of them all, he was probably the only one who really grieved for Iphigenia. It would have been such a good marriage for them both."

Charis collapsed in tears, her grief raw and terrible. I sat beside her, mindlessly patting her hand, too numb to feel anything very much at all. I only half comprehended the story she'd told.

There was silence in the hall. The listeners were deep in shock. I felt their anger wind around me. They had loved their princess.

I bowed my head. This must have happened some time ago. It would have taken a few days for Charis to travel home. Maybe I had been playing with Orestes while my daughter was being murdered; perhaps I had been having lunch or an afternoon's rest. My daughter had died, far from me, with none to come to her aid.

Each minute since then I had breathed the air of a world that no longer held my daughter, and I had known nothing.

I surged to my feet. I needed to be alone and clear of the shocked faces and soft murmurs of the people round me. I couldn't bear their presence. I had no idea where I was going, just an overpowering need to be free of their curious eyes. I thrust past the guard at the door and made my way onto the terraces. The meltemi was blowing wildly. Leaves and small twigs were caught up in the gusts and twisted in little eddies of air. My hair blew out of its pins, and my gown tangled round my limbs as I stumbled along the path. I could barely see through the fog of pain that covered my eyes. My gown caught on some spiny shrub. I felt the tug as the delicate fabric ripped. I stopped and carefully untangled the material. It seemed very important to do this neatly and ensure no further damage occurred. I held the rip together with one hand but, to my distress, the wind kept the gown fluttering back towards the thorny bush. I gave a little sob as I stepped back away from it and made my way towards a seat.

It had been my intent to sit and think over Charis's words, but when I reached the seat I found the incoherence of my thoughts wouldn't let me stay still. Her words were too stunning, too shocking and too immediate. I couldn't force my brain to be calm and confront them. There was no context or greater meaning within which I could process the abomination of Iphigenia's death.

I paced restlessly up and down in front of the seat, my mind skimming through random fragments of memory, trying to force a pattern from a kaleidoscope of moments. My mind flitted backwards and forwards through the years, putting together a mosaic of incidents. The tesserae moved and shifted before forming together in the completed work of my daughter's death. Agamemnon, the children, Calchas. Small moments that now came together into a new picture of violence, betrayal and murder.

The guilt I felt was visceral. I had let this happen. I had stayed married to a man I knew to be unstable and vicious. I should have left the first time he hit me. Instead, hoping it would all work out, I had stayed. It hadn't worked out at all, and my inaction had led directly to Agamemnon's destruction of our family. I would never forgive myself. There was no offering I could make to the gods to redeem my folly.

I felt a childlike desire to throw myself down on the tiles, like Electra, to kick and scream out my rage and anguish. I needed physical pain to ease my mental torment. A sudden vision of the Queen of Mycenae sprawled on the ground, writhing in a childish tantrum, all beating fists and kicking legs, forced an unexpected burst of hysterical laughter. I startled myself with the sound.

I staggered to the bench and sat. An iron band around my chest stopped my breathing and constricted my heart. Mindless horrors pressed in on me. *Oh Iphigenia, my precious daughter.* I twisted on the seat to ease the pain, and suddenly I was crying. Tears fell from my aching eyes, and my control gave way. I heard myself uttering terrible, unstoppable groans and cries as I rocked back and forth on the seat. My arms crossed over my chest as if to hold such ugly noises in, but they failed, powerless against the force that tore the anguish from my deepest core. My voice became hoarse with the tumult of the cries but still they poured from me to be lost in the rage of the wind. I beat my hands on my knees in a wild rhythm of fury and grief. A wisp of vagrant thought reminded me that professional mourners behave in such a manner at funerals. I hadn't known they mimicked the actuality of grief.

Life was too deeply embedded to allow me to die in my anguish, much though I wished to. At last my hysterical outpouring stopped, and I was able to dry my eyes. I ached to my soul's depths. I was exhausted.

CHAPTER TWENTY

THE WORLD DID NOT STOP IN sympathy with my grief, and mundane tasks still had to be managed. Half my brain was filled with sawdust and unable to cope with, or comprehend, the hideous enormity of the crime against my daughter. I attempted to thrust my horror and grief to the back of my mind, like so much crumpled linen, and attend to my daily responsibilities.

I was surprised how calm I was, how steady my hands and voice as I dealt with my duties.

Two days later a fresh messenger arrived. He said nothing of Iphigenia's murder, but informed me cheerfully the wind was now fair for the fleet to sail to Troy.

I was aghast at his insouciance. "And how has this miraculously changed wind come about?" I asked.

Myrto was with me, and I saw him glance at me sharply. Perhaps my tone wasn't as controlled as I thought.

The messenger blenched and looked deeply uncomfortable. "A sacrifice was made to Artemis and she lifted the curse on the army. When she was appeased, the wind changed direction so that now it is in our favour."

"And that sacrifice was my daughter?"

The messenger sounded shocked. "No, lady. The goddess interceded. When she knew the army was committed to propitiating her, she changed the sacrifice at the last minute and substituted a female deer. The goddess mercifully took Iphigenia up and carried her to Tauris to serve her as a priestess."

I gaped at him in disbelief.

"Did you see the sacrifice?"

"No, lady, but I heard all about it. It was truly a miracle."

I couldn't believe the casual carelessness of his answer. I had lost my daughter and this fool prattled about miracles?

The blood rushed to my head in such a murderous rage I thrust myself from my seat and flung myself at him. My hands gripped his neck as I tried with all my strength to choke the life from him. I might be unable to reach Agamemnon, but I could kill this stupid man who made light of my daughter's death. His hands clawed at mine as he tried to escape but he was small and light, not much more than a boy. He twisted in my grip but my thumbs were pressed hard against his windpipe and his face began to turn livid. His life was saved by Myrto, who leapt on me from behind and forcibly pulled me off.

"Nestra, stop! Let him be." He dragged me to the seat, forced me into it and made me sit.

The messenger sprawled, crumpled, coughing and gasping, against the table. Papers flew to the floor and a wine flagon toppled over, its contents dripping onto the sheaves of paper below. The man's harsh panting filled the room and his hands rubbed his damaged throat. His colour slowly returned to normal, and he eyed me warily as he slowly straightened up.

"Get him out of here," I ordered Myrto.

I was shaking with reaction and suppressed violence. Did the fool actually believe the nonsense he had been saying, and was he retailing this travesty through all the royal houses of Greece? Had Agamemnon truly managed to persuade the gullible that this version of events was the truth? It was possible, I conceded. There had been enough nonsense spouted about Helen and

Pollux's birth. If we hadn't known the truth, would we ourselves have believed it?

Was this what priests called faith? Childish lies designed to appease the simpleminded? If so, the belief went deeply into us. I would have cursed Artemis myself, but a residual fear of her retaliation kept me silent. I had given her my devotion throughout the years of my girlhood only to have her betray me. I would never pray to her again. My goddess of choice now was Hera, she who had been much abused and betrayed by her husband and who understood vengeance better than any mortal.

I didn't much care what the gods did. My rage was focused on Agamemnon. If there was any to spare it could encompass Calchas, but I had no doubt whose weakness had led to my daughter's death. Agamemnon had lied to me, entrapped his daughter and allowed the army to use her life as a tool for their stupid war. Agamemnon had given in to pressure. I had always known him to be weak. I hated him with an intensity that threatened to make me ill or send me over the edge towards insanity. I remembered Leda's words about the Atreus line and their cursed deeds. I willed to destroy it forever.

Myrto returned from escorting the messenger out. He brought a slave and a fresh flagon of wine. The slave mopped and tidied up.

The killing rage was ebbing and I started to shake.

"Lady," Myrto said quietly as he passed me a filled cup.

I swallowed, forcing the liquid down through a sudden constriction in my throat.

He reached out and gently squeezed my shoulder. The quiet support and kindness nearly undid me.

"Thank you," I whispered.

*   *   *

I took to lacing my wine at night with a concoction Chryseis brewed for me. I didn't ask what was in it; all I wanted was that it let me sleep through the night, otherwise there were wings and shadows in the bedchamber and low mutterings of anger in the dark watches of the night. The Furies were searching for Agamemnon. I could feel them gathering round, looking for their prey. They'd have to move to Troy if they wanted him. They couldn't want him more than I, and I didn't intend to rely on them for justice.

Sane or insane, the intensity of my rage kept me purposeful. I lay in bed and planned my vengeance. Time after time I destroyed my husband in an endless series of excruciatingly cruel deaths. I gouged, burned, ripped and maimed him, destroying his mind and his flesh as I took my revenge. I prayed to every god and goddess I could name that if he died in Troy it would be a slow, agonising death. If he returned to Mycenae alive, I would kill Agamemnon myself.

I stood in the sanctuary of the temple, in front of the altar of Hera. I had brought a calf, and I watched while the priest dispatched it for me and offered it to the goddess. The sickly smell of blood spilt on the altar lingered after he had taken the creature's life. I thought of Charis's description of Iphigenia's sacrifice and shuddered as I waved the priest away.

We stood as a close group of women – Charis, Io, Chryseis and I. Io was trembling, Chryseis more composed. I could read the cold anger in Charis's eyes. I had no doubt she would plant a dagger just as effectively as I to avenge Iphigenia.

I had wondered whether to include Myrto in the group but eventually decided it would put him in a difficult position. He served Agamemnon, and to ask him to change loyalties would have been unkind.

I moved forward to the altar and put my hand out in a plea to the goddess.

"I swear by Hera, and by all gods and goddesses, making them my witnesses, that I will fulfil, according to my ability, this oath and this covenant, though it may take my lifetime to achieve it. I will avenge my daughter's honour and her memory. I will oppose those who conspired to bring her to her death in any way I can, and I will repay Iphigenia's death by the death of her father who ordered the wicked deed carried out. I will take upon myself such punishment the gods may deem just for this act. May I fulfil this oath and not violate it."

I had never before prayed with such intensity. I needed those who heard to understand the depth of my rage and my need to exact revenge.

After, I stepped back, well pleased. Let the gods chew on that, I thought with some satisfaction.

The women shadowed me as we walked back to the palace. Passers-by dipped their heads in recognition and respect. The whole city mourned the loss of their princess. Myrto had issued a statement to the people, giving them the bare facts of her death and making Agamemnon's responsibility clear. The version the messenger had tried to peddle was also in circulation. There would be some confused citizens.

We reached the steps at the foot of the palace. They were slowly being covered with laurel and other evergreen wreaths, placed there in mourning by the citizenry. I bent to look closer at them. Some were already drying out in the late summer heat. They were such small symbols to celebrate my daughter's life, but the thought behind them was kindly meant.

"We will need to work out how to dispose of them," said Myrto. "We can't just sweep them up and throw them out. It would be disrespectful."

"They can be taken to the temple of Artemis at the end of the week," I said, "and burned there as an offering. We'll make the occasion a memorial service to Iphigenia. The people have not had a chance to participate in any ritual for her, so it will be an opportunity for us all to mourn."

I liked the idea of having our own funeral pyre for Iphigenia.

Myrto nodded. "I'll make all the arrangements."

* * *

I went to see the children. I realised how quickly Orestes was growing when I saw how short his tunic had become. He wasn't my baby any more but a wriggly toddler who was learning new words to say every day. I picked him up and cuddled him. I loved the smell of him and rested my nose in the crease of his neck, inhaling his essence. He squirmed in my arms, impatient to be set down again. He looked more like Agamemnon every day, with the same colouring and the same stocky body; but his nature was very different. He shared Iphigenia's essential sweetness. He was an easy little boy to love.

Electra was playing with a rag doll, fiercely concentrating on her toy and shutting the rest of us out. I could hear her telling herself some involved story.

Charis sat on the floor near her, ready to play with either child. Her act of mourning had been to take on the role of big sister to Iphigenia's siblings, providing them with a continuity of support and protection.

"I love them for Iphigenia's sake," she had said, simply. "When I am with them, I can feel her presence. She would have wanted them to be protected and loved."

I nodded at her. I had told the children their big sister wasn't coming back, and that their father had been responsible for sacrificing her for his army's gain. Orestes grew sad and quiet for a while. I doubt he understood much of what was said.

Electra was full of questions. "But why, Mummy?" she asked as I explained the idea that her sister had been sacrificed to appease an angry goddess.

"I don't know, darling," I said sadly. "Calchas told your father the goddess wanted Iphigenia as a sacrifice."

"But how did Calchas know?"

"Maybe he made it up. I don't know. I'm sure no goddess would have wanted a young woman murdered."

But an unpleasant, rancid man might have been happy to kill in her name. It demonstrated his power over Agamemnon and, by default, over the whole Greek army. I wondered whether Iphigenia had really been a sacrifice to Calchas's ambitions.

"Daddy loved Iphigenia," said Electra. Her bottom lip was trembling.

"Not enough," I said sharply. "When he had to choose between a fair wind for sailing and her life, he chose to kill his own daughter."

How do you tell a six-year-old ugly truths? Could I say to her, as I so wished, 'Your thrice-cursed abomination of a father murdered your sister'? Or worse, because it was closest to my truth, 'Your father is no sort of man at all. Yes, even now somewhere there is a fool of a poet writing an ode in his honour, or elsewhere some sculptor is chipping away at a lump of marble trying to immortalise his face and form, but the truth is, this man couldn't get through the simplest of day-to-day living without abusing others and making them carry the blame for his actions. Now he's murdered your sister. Be grateful; it could have been you.'

I could see Electra trying to reconcile the brutal facts with her love of her father. I suppose I could have been kinder, but I wanted her to realise just what sort of man he was. I just didn't have the courage to tell her so in a realistically brutal way.

The wreath-burning ceremony was simple and poignant. I think the whole town must have assembled to see the floral tributes put to the torch in Iphigenia's honour. I watched the smoke rise and wondered where her spirit was. I prayed she was at peace. Was there a place in Elysium for a gentle young woman?

The crowd watched silently. I saw many with tears in their eyes.

"She was too young to die," I heard one crone mumble.

"She was too perfect for this world," replied another.

"The gods take the young and beautiful for their own," said yet another.

The crowd's palpable sorrow soothed my own. I stood with the children, watching until the last ashes fell inwards to the fire.

It was done.

* * *

Days became months, seasons became years. As Odysseus had predicted, there was no easy victory for the Greek army. Occasional messengers brought news from Troy. The army was laying siege, camped around the town. There were occasional skirmishes but no real progress in the war. I wondered bitterly who else Agamemnon would be prepared to sacrifice to break the impasse.

Mycenae, like all the other kingdoms of Greece, was quiet. We had adapted to the men's absence. Women performed work that men traditionally did, whether on the farms or in the town itself. The few men who had been left behind were growing older, but there was a new crop of youngsters growing up. Those who had been too young for conscription were now young men and ready for citizenship.

I saw Myrto watching a group of these youngsters.

"Are you looking for potential trouble?" I asked.

He looked startled then gave me his slow smile. "No. I'm just wondering what my boy looks like now. They've been gone five years. He won't be a boy at all but a fully grown man. My wife misses him – and the grandchildren he could be giving us."

I heard the wistfulness in his voice and nodded. Similar conversations could occur anywhere in Greece. The war against Troy, which was supposed to be over in a couple of months, had split families. There were many parents who would never see their boys again.

Traders still called and brought their goods to the town, but their numbers were down. With Troy blocked as a trading post, many brought their goods directly to Mycenae, so at last we had first pick of their wares. Agamemnon had achieved one of his goals at least.

"There's no profit in it any more," one of the merchants said to me. "We used to be able to sell goods in Troy, then pick up fresh supplies as we went from kingdom to kingdom. Now there simply isn't enough new product for us to make up our stock. We are having to look to other markets."

I nodded, but I was concerned. Much of Mycenae's wealth depended on the traders and the taxes and levies they paid to the city.

The man shrugged. "Still, we bring what we can to Mycenae, if only for the sake of your beautiful face, my lady."

I snorted. For a merchant, flattery is his stock in trade, but I was the queen and didn't like impertinence.

Then the merchants brought something else. Disease.

The first deaths went unnoticed, part of the usual pattern of life and death, but others followed in short succession. Soon it seemed every family in Mycenae had at least one sick member. The onset of symptoms was sudden, with burning fever, headache, coughs and sore throats. Death occurred within hours, and very few of the sick survived.

The disease moved swiftly through the city putting additional stress on a town already operating at full stretch with all the men away. Maintaining a basic civil infrastructure became a daily nightmare, and Myrto and I were worked off our feet. Those who recovered had a protracted convalescence that lasted weeks. Most disturbingly, the disease was at its most lethal in vigorous young adults, those you would have thought least likely to succumb.

The healers worked round the clock caring for the afflicted. Bodies had to be buried in a mass grave; there was no time for the usual ceremonial funerals. I was terrified that Electra or Orestes would be affected.

Chryseis worked tirelessly, brewing tonics and soothing syrups. She separated herself from the household to avoid bringing the disease to the palace. "We don't know where it came from, or how it spreads," she said sadly. "Only that it kills so ferociously. It could be a curse from the gods, it could be caused by an evil miasma or foul water. Who knows?"

"When Helen was last here, she mentioned they had suffered a plague in Sparta. Do you think it's the same?"

"Maybe," replied Chryseis. "But if I remember, the cure for Sparta's plague was for Menelaus to travel to Troy. I don't think we can do that now. There's no one left to send, and Troy is under attack from our own people."

"Just be careful of yourself," I exhorted her.

Myrto became ill the next day.

"Go home," I said. "You can do no good here. Let your wife nurse you."

"My wife already has it," he coughed.

I looked at his flushed face and strained eyes. "Then you need to be with your wife so you can both look after each other." I put my hand out and grasped his arm. I could feel the abnormal heat of his skin. "I need you too much to allow you to take a risk," I said gently. Then, when he looked to argue, "Go to bed. You look wretched."

He gave me an exhausted smile but went gratefully.

Chryseis brought word later that he and his wife died that night.

"I called by to see them and check they were all right. They were both cold. His wife must have died first, for she was in his arms. I am so sorry, Clytemnestra."

I went out on the balcony, sat on the balustrade and looked over the town. Io arrived with some stuffed peppers, olives and wine. She poured for me, but I sat with my hands useless in my lap.

I hadn't loved Myrto as one would a lover, but he had been a close friend and support for many years. I thought of the son, far away in Troy, who would never again see his parents. Myrto and I had worked together for Mycenae, and though we discussed our personal lives little, I had come to know him as an honourable, loving man for whom family was the core of his world.

Mycenae was a poorer place tonight for his loss.

I felt a terrible depression creep over me. What was the point of carrying on when it seemed everything I cared about was taken from me? I wondered whether Helen, who had chosen a life of passion and adventure, was happier than me. I had tried to do my duty, and a grim choice that had been. I bent my head and wept.

Charis and Electra found me.

"Why are you crying, Mother?" asked Electra.

I dried my eyes hastily. "Myrto and his wife died today, darling. He is a terrible loss."

Electra looked at me with cool eyes. "He wasn't family, though, was he? Not really your friend either. Just a sort of palace servant."

I gasped at her lack of respect.

"He was much more than that. I relied on him for so much," I said.

Electra gave a little shrug and turned away. I stared at her back. Had I once been as callous? I tried hard to remember how young she was, that she couldn't yet know the reality of adult pain.

"He was a good man," said Charis softly. "I am sorry, Clytemnestra."

"Thank you, my dear. Yes, he was a good man."

CHAPTER
TWENTY ONE

T HERE WOULD BE A STRANGER IN the hall for dinner. Actus, who had become my principal assistant, warned me early. I sighed. We were short of rations, short of serving staff and most certainly short of the appropriate spirit of joy a stranger is supposed to inspire in us. Still, the rituals must be observed, the rites honoured, and guests were sacred to us.

I was at the head table with my family. None disputed my absolute right to be there. No one ever would. This much Agamemnon's absence had given me – the undisputed rule of Mycenae. We were a small group gathered that evening. The plague, whatever its cause or name, had left many places at our tables empty. I could look down the scarred wood where once high nobles and warriors had sat. Now their places were taken by servants, mostly women. Mycenae had become a ghost town.

Our guest entered formally, and I rose to give the greeting. He was a tall man and well favoured, although I had supposed myself past noticing such things. He wasn't young. I placed him between forty and fifty years of age. It may have been more, but his physical form carried the years lightly. Tall, well muscled and with long legs, he was a man to command attention. His hair was cropped short; clearly it had once been dark but was now well peppered with grey. It suited him. His skin was ruddy, indicating an active, outdoor life. I looked again at those long thigh muscles. This was a man in his prime, physically fit and strong. I wondered how he had avoided the call of the army that was still encamped outside Troy. Most men of his age wasted their lives away on the barren plains of Ilium.

I used the ritual phrases, welcoming the guest into our home and offering him the assistance granted to such a visitor. "Come, friend, and give us something. Do you have news, or a story you can share with us? You appear to be noble. May I know whom I address?" I finished with a query. So far there had been no indication of who he was or why he had come to Mycenae.

He rose slowly to his feet. I noticed his moves were careful and well balanced. I imagined he did training drills regularly. He raised his goblet to me. "All thanks to the lady of these halls. I come as a guest, seeking your hospitality, which you have already provided so generously."

I raised my goblet to mirror his and waited.

"I claim kin with you, lady, and my joy in this meeting is unrivalled. You are beautiful, gracious and a most generous host. Your kindness pleases Zeus who watches over us all."

He raised the goblet again and drank a toast.

I was irritated. Kin? I couldn't place who he could be. No relation of mine, I was certain. If he was related to my husband, then I was sure I had never met him.

"Your piety is exemplary, sir. May I know whom I address?" I was bored with games. The man was attractive, but Orestes needed to get to bed, and Electra too, if her yawns had been any indication. I didn't have the time to waste on pretentious civility.

He lowered his head and bowed before me. "I am Aegisthus, lady. Your cousin."

Zeus! I knew that name. This was the other contender for the throne of Mycenae. As I understood it, Agamemnon had driven him out, after killing his father Thyestes.

Strictly speaking, he was Agamemnon's cousin, not mine, although marriage eliminated that distinction. Most certainly he was Agamemnon's enemy; by extension, of course, he should be mine. I stared at him until it became clearly unmannerly to do so.

"That is a name I didn't expect to hear in these halls." It wasn't the most inspired speech I had ever managed, but the man had caught me off balance.

Suddenly his face was alive with life and laughter. "No, lady. You probably didn't expect to hear my name." He gave a laugh. "May I say I am glad to meet you? Your safety is sacrosanct. You need have no fear about my presence. I am Mycenaean, born and bred, and I have been in exile for too long. I claim a kinsman's right to return to the place of my birth and visit my kin."

I couldn't help but respond to his vitality. How long, I wondered, had it been since a face in these halls had been alight with laughter, enthusiasm or desire? Then, immediately, and in equal measure, I felt my folly. I was no longer young or desirable. Two days ago I had held out my arms and seen the sagging skin beneath. My face, in the mirror, had lines I had never noticed. It was enough to stiffen my spine. Had I been younger I would have been yearning for his bed. Recognising my unattractiveness, I could maintain a calm demeanour.

"You are, naturally, most welcome as my kinsman. You know I cannot protect you against those who would use history to discredit you or cause you harm. Still, may you sleep well tonight in the safety of my protection. Tomorrow we will talk again."

I turned away. Orestes had become a convenient alibi. I hauled him to his feet, tersely ordered Electra to follow us, and left the hall.

That night, needless to say, I couldn't sleep. Surely I had noticed before that I was a woman of breeding years without the comfort of a husband in my bed at nights? Certainly I had, but my choices were constrained. I never wished to share anything with Agamemnon again, but I was, nevertheless, a queen. I couldn't take a commoner to my bed, even had I found one I desired. And I hadn't. The remaining representatives of our noble families were at least twenty years older than me, if a day. None were a tempting prospect.

By default, I had developed some considerable skill with my own right hand. It was safe, private and probably more satisfying than an ungenerous lover. Had I been prepared to reinstate my husband, he would have had trouble nowadays competing with the satisfaction I gave myself.

I made generous use of my talents that night. I decided I needed to arm myself against any charm offensive from this unknown cousin, and the best way to do so was to preempt such physical needs as I might have. That night I almost raped myself in my determination to retain control over my emotions.

While Myrto was alive I had allowed nothing to come between me and my duty, but now I made sure family duties constrained me the next day and eliminated the chance of encountering our disturbing guest.

I wasn't sure how to respond to Aegisthus. His physical charms were only one issue. Did his presence meant he was intending an overarching claim to power in Mycenae? So far, and in Agamemnon's absence, I had managed to cling on to power in his name. A large part of that success lay in two camps: there were so few men left to challenge me, and Myrto's support had given me security. I didn't have that any more. Decisions made from now on were made without that support. I was certain Aegisthus knew that already. He was a vitally attractive man, but there was more at work here than sexual tension and a family reunion.

I couldn't avoid him that evening in the hall. I had taken some pains to organise things in my favour. Aegisthus was given the honoured seat – as he was a close relative of my husband's, I could do no less. As might be expected, no etiquette I knew instructed me how to deal with a scion of a family my husband had tried to destroy, regardless of blood ties. If you went further back into the Atreus family's bloody history I had absolutely no clue who was right or wrong. They seemed to have murdered each other with equal fervour. Leda's lessons in decorum were not going to work here.

It was simple enough to talk to Aegisthus that night. I said the most prosaic words in my mind. "Tell me your story …"

Had I never realised the power in those words? Aegisthus could spin a yarn for hours out of that invitation, and most of them were amusing.

I had never met a warrior so little concerned with his dignity. "Are you saying you acted as a servant in the court of King Lycidias?" I asked in amazement.

Aegisthus laughed, his deep and throaty laugh. "Most certainly, and may I tell you that being his servant involved several expectations which a nice Greek boy was unable to satisfy."

"You mean …?"

"Yes, I mean that in every way you can think of. You have no idea how degenerate some of these little kings can be. I was deeply shocked."

I suspected it took a lot to shock Aegisthus. He seemed to have no shame. He was equally comfortable claiming he had spent time working in a smithy, as having adorned the courts of kings.

I took his stories lightly, as entertainment confections. Aegisthus hid his truths in stories, which may or may not have been fact.

When we parted that evening I had been well entertained but was little wiser about the man and his intentions in Mycenae. I thought about that as Io brushed out my hair.

Since Agamemnon left, I had been maintaining control of his kingdom, ostensibly on his behalf, until he returned to retake his throne. Stupidly I hadn't considered the full implications of what I was doing. I intended to execute Agamemnon as soon as he returned, so I wasn't ruling Mycenae on his behalf at all. I was doing so because it pleased me, it was my responsibility as queen and because I was protecting Orestes' birthright. If Agamemnon and his opinions were removed from the equation, then whatever Aegisthus's purpose in Mycenae, I could approach the matter purely on the basis of how it would affect Orestes. With Myrto gone, it might be timely for me to reconsider my alliances. Sooner or later some ambitious princeling would eye up the kingdom. A new generation had grown to adulthood and were itching to prove themselves as warriors. It was likely our time of peace was over.

I fell asleep turning contingency plans over in my head.

*　　*　　*

Two months later, Aegisthus was still with us, and I was no nearer to understanding the purpose of his visit, nor much about the man himself. His easy charm made him popular, and I enjoyed the evenings in his company. He had a fine tenor voice and a vast store of songs and tales to entertain us. I wondered if he had ever been a professional bard, but he denied it.

"I'm only a gifted amateur. *'This price the gods demand for song, that we become what we sing'*," he quoted. "I was never that dedicated, I'm afraid."

For many years I had kept up the habit of taking a morning walk around the town. It allowed the citizens to approach with their concerns, and it gave me the opportunity to sense the mood on the streets. Myrto had usually accompanied me, partly as escort, and partly to share the news of the morning.

After a couple of weeks, Aegisthus took to joining me. "I need the exercise," he joked when I asked him his purpose.

I looked at him levelly. "Why?"

"Don't you trust me? I won't crowd you or get in the way."

"I don't know if I trust you," I said honestly. "Trust is earned, and you haven't been here long. You still haven't said exactly why you've returned to Mycenae. I don't think there are many people left who remember you."

He shrugged. "Most of the warriors I knew are at Troy, and half the townsfolk died in the epidemic, so no."

"Then why have you come back?"

"Does an exile need a reason to want to see his native land?"

"Does the exile's return have something to do with his enemy being away overseas?"

He laughed. "Well, of course. I wouldn't be walking down the road with his wife if Agamemnon were here, now would I? He'd have had me cut down the moment I put my nose through the door."

I walked for a while in silence. I noticed the gutter was blocked at the end of the road. We would need to get it cleared before the next rain.

"Do you miss your husband?" The question was casually asked.

I flicked a look at Aegisthus. "He murdered my daughter. What do you think?" I said.

"Ahh," he said thoughtfully. "So you won't be greeting him with open arms when he arrives home?"

I said nothing. My oath burned in me like an old scar every time I thought of Agamemnon returning.

"'*My enemy's enemy is my friend,*'" he quoted softly.

I turned to face him. "Are you saying that makes us friends?"

He was watching me carefully, his eyes very steady. "It could be. That would be your decision of course."

"Of course," I agreed and took a deep breath. "Then let's not make that decision today. Friendship takes time."

"But attraction can be instantaneous, don't you find?"

I looked up at him. His eyes were warm and laughing again. I felt flustered. He was getting beneath my skin. I would need to be very careful around him.

I gave a rather prim nod, and we continued our walk.

A few nights later, Charis was helping me with my hair before dinner. "He's nice, isn't he?" she asked.

"Who?" I said cautiously, not wanting to be drawn.

"Aegisthus, of course," she said as she brushed my hair off my face. "He seems to have a nice way with everyone." She secured a twist of hair into place with pins. "Do you like him?"

I looked at her in surprise. "Well, yes, I suppose I do. Remember we don't know him very well."

"He's a man who likes women," she said.

I glanced at her sharply. "Is he making a pest of himself with the maids?"

"No, nothing like that," she said. "I mean he likes women as people. He talks to them as if they were equals."

I thought about that. "I suppose he does."

"Plenty of men say they like women, but they just mean they like to bed them. They don't really care for females at all otherwise. Aegisthus is different."

"Do you mean you think he's effeminate?" I hadn't thought so myself, but sometimes it was hard to tell.

Charis giggled. "No, I most certainly don't think he's effeminate. Quite the opposite."

I grinned at her. "You had me worried for a minute."

"That's why I asked whether you liked him," she said. "He could be good for you. Maybe make a good lover." She wriggled her eyebrows suggestively.

I stared at her in astonishment. "My dear girl, I'm old enough to be your mother. You can't say things like that to me. It's not proper."

She laughed at my shock. "It's just girl talk. You need a nice man in your life. You've slept alone for too long."

I felt myself beginning to blush. "Really, Charis, this isn't a suitable matter for discussion."

She pinned the last bit of hair into place. "You will think about it, though, won't you?" she asked.

I picked up my brush to throw at her, and she laughed at me as she scurried out the door.

"Wretched girl," I muttered as I gathered myself together and headed for the hall.

CHAPTER
TWENTY TWO

AEGISTHUS WAS BEGINNING TO EARN HIS keep. He took hunting groups into the hills behind the citadel and killed enough game to supplement our supplies. The youngsters with him enjoyed the trip, and the camaraderie. It brought back to me again the cost of having a generation of men rotting on the plains of Troy. The uncles, fathers and brothers who should have been here with their sons, teaching them men's ways, were effectively lost to us. In a sense it didn't matter if they survived the Trojan campaign or not. The damage to the next generation had been done.

Orestes had taken to following him round like a small puppy. I fretted that he had chosen Aegisthus as a role model, but I could hardly fault his need for male company. I missed Myrto, but he had been an older man and hadn't captured Orestes imagination. I began to think every conversation I had with Orestes now started with 'Aegisthus thinks …' or 'Aegisthus says …'.

I laughed a little at my son's hero worship but didn't interfere. We all need someone to look up to.

I now avoided Aegisthus as much as I could. Charis's

Helen Had a Sister | 163

comments had alarmed me and made me self-conscious. Did everyone think the same? Were they all waiting for me to bed the man?

When I encountered him I was curt to the point of rudeness. I saw him raise his eyebrows at one particularly churlish comment, but he said nothing. I hated myself for the childishness of my behaviour, but Aegisthus largely ignored it. He accompanied me on my walks each morning, and I appreciated his company as we walked through the town streets.

The early morning zephyr was cool on my skin. I loved this time of day the best. Each morning seemed to bring fresh possibilities in a newly created world.

Aegisthus seemed on first-name terms with a large number of people. Stallholders called to him as we passed through the market, children waved from their play at the side of the road.

"How is it everyone seems to know you?" I asked.

"Don't know," he shrugged. "They're just people I talk to."

"You must talk a lot then," I said tartly.

"You're very scratchy these days," he said.

I turned to glare at him. He was getting far too familiar with his comments.

"Some would say it was a sign that you like me."

I gasped. "How dare you? You must have the most overwhelming conceit to think such a thing. As it happens, I dislike cocky men."

He laughed at that.

"Cocky, am I? You've a great talent for one-word descriptions. How would you describe yourself?"

"I wouldn't," I snapped.

"Come on," he teased. "Are you afraid? Or do you want me to find a description for you?"

I opened my mouth to say something cutting but found I was distracted by the easy way he laughed at me. I lost my words and stopped still on the pavement while traffic manoeuvred round us.

"All right," I said eventually. "How would you describe me?"

The bright laughter faded from his face, although his eyes remained warm. "Most of the words I could use would be compliments, and you wouldn't believe me."

I shrugged. "So you can't describe me?"

"I didn't say that. There is one word that fits."

"And?" I asked.

"Lonely. If there is one word that encompasses you, it would be 'lonely'."

I stared at him, quite disconcerted. "Is that what you think?"

"I know it to be the truth," he said gently.

I gathered myself together, and we began walking again. I was silent. Only habit made me respond to the waves and comments of the citizens we passed.

He broke the silence as we climbed the steps leading into the palace. "Have I offended you?" he asked in a quiet voice.

"No. I don't know. Is that how I seem to you? Someone pathetic?"

He stopped and spun towards me. "Never," he said. "Brave, of course, resilient, and competent. Never pathetic." He gave a little laugh. "Don't you know your citizens are torn between loving you and terror that you will find them out in some error?"

I sniffed at that, but it made me smile. "How should I solve my loneliness then?" I couldn't believe the words that had just fallen from my mouth. Was I flirting? Even to my own ears, I sounded coy.

"Very easily. You need to allow a friend to get close enough to get past your armour." He was smiling down at me with a look that was turning me to jelly.

"And how do I find such a friend? I'm the queen. Queens don't have friends."

"Then maybe you need a relation. Queens can be friends with their cousins."

He still held my gaze. We had crossed several boundaries, and there would be no going back.

Eventually I broke eye contact and was able to smile at him. We walked into the palace together. Charis had been right. I did need a nice man in my life.

We became lovers a few nights later. I was nervous and tried to hide it beneath a sort of brusque efficiency.

"What are you doing?" he asked.

I had moved towards the bed in a no-nonsense fashion and was starting to shed my clothes.

He didn't let me. "Come here." He pulled me to him. There was a glint of amusement in his eyes as if he knew very well what I was feeling. "This is where we take our time. I want to seduce every layer of your garments off you, one at a time. Then I'm going to let your hair down your back." His hands were gentle as he pulled me into a kiss.

I let my lips open beneath his and allowed him entry. He kissed me long and leisurely.

"That's better," he said at last, with satisfaction, as I began to relax against him. "You needed a good kiss." His lips moved down my throat until they reached the sensitive area at my collarbone.

I moaned as I felt his mouth move on my skin.

I barely noticed as my tunic fell. I was lost in sensation. His hands moved over me, learning the curve and shape of my breasts, the sensitivity of my nipples. I nearly cried out as he tugged gently on them.

I thrust my hands to his groin and tried to reach for him, but he stopped me.

"Later," he growled. "Have some patience."

"I want to touch you," I begged.

"You will, but just now, I'm in control. Your turn will come."

My breast band had long since disappeared, along with my under-tunic. He stroked my slit with knowledgeable fingers while I writhed against him.

Suddenly he scooped me up and carried me to the bed. He pulled his own tunic over his head and sat down, with me on his lap.

I felt his fingers move through my hair, removing the pins. The weight of hair tumbled down onto my shoulders. He pressed his face against it. "You smell beautiful, like flowers."

I smiled.

Then he kissed me and pulled me down beside him.

He was tall, and the lines of his muscles were long and lean. Now he let me explore the length of his body and stroke his penis as he watched me lazily. I laid my head on his hard chest as I stroked him, finding my way through the responses of his body. He had very little hair on his chest, just a few greying curls.

I stroked between his legs and trailed my fingers over a white scar high on his thigh. "How did you get this?"

"Fighting your husband."

"Oh. How fortunate it wasn't higher."

He reached out for my hand and shifted it. "This can work a little higher, though," he said, placing my hand over his groin.

A few minutes later he groaned softly in pleasure and rolled towards me. "I think this is going to be exceptional," he said as he moved on top of me.

I laughed up at him in joy as we moved together in rhythm.

Our lovemaking was easy. Aegisthus had a light touch of humour that eased any tension between us. As we discovered each other and learned to trust, we became progressively more passionate and intensely carnal. By the end of the night I was wrung out, sated with a surfeit of sexuality.

I woke to find him leaning on his elbow, looking at me.

"What are you doing?" I asked drowsily.

"Watching you sleep. You looked all soft and relaxed in your dreams."

"I hate being looked at," I said, embarrassed. "Anyway, I feel soft and relaxed."

He grinned at me. "So do I. I'm relying on you to change that condition."

I gave a little laugh. "You mean again? I won't be able to walk."

"That's fine then; we've got a nice bed to lie in so neither of us has to walk."

He kissed me, very gently. And we made quiet, morning-time love, as sweet as warm summer honey.

Afterwards, he kissed my eyelids. "Such beautiful eyes. You shut them when you make love and hide what you are feeling from me."

I looked at him in surprise. "I hadn't realised, but I want to concentrate on the sensations. Vision distracts me from feeling. I'm not trying to hide."

"It wasn't a criticism," he smiled.

It was such a warm, loving smile it brought an echoing one to my face and stayed with me for the rest of the day.

CHAPTER
TWENTY THREE

W E ENJOYED A HALCYON PERIOD. I was more in love with Aegisthus each day I spent with him. Perhaps it was to be expected. As a middle-aged woman who'd been without a man for many years, Aegisthus's attentions couldn't help but flatter me and put new energy into me. I could feel the new spring in my step, and it wasn't just because of the night-time interludes, although they were wonderful. Aegisthus was proving to be my equal. He didn't try to usurp my rule in Mycenae as I had half feared. Instead he helped me, much as Myrto had. I felt disloyal to the shade of my old friend, but Aegisthus, younger and infinitely more charismatic than Myrto, was energetic and effective.

I was pleased to see he took an active role in supervising the training of the boys at school. Orestes, now rising eight, was very proud to be able to spar with his hero, and he wasn't the only boy to idolise Aegisthus.

"I can't move in the training grounds," he complained. "I don't know how many young boys there are in Mycenae, but they all seem to be at the gym with me at the same time."

"It's deliberate. They plan to be there when you are. They all think you're a hero."

He looked at me quizzically. "Now that's a strange thing to think. All the heroes are supposed to be at Troy."

"You're the only one they have here, so I suppose you've got to expect their admiration."

He came and sat beside me. It was natural for him to reach his arm out and draw me against his shoulder. "I'm no hero," he said soberly. "That's a term for a different sort of man. I was bred by my father for one purpose only, and that was to kill Atreus and avenge my dead older brothers. I was trained exclusively for that role, and when we succeeded, and Thyestes and I took the throne of Mycenae, I had achieved the purpose I was born for."

"Is that the truth? What a burden to place on a child," I exclaimed. I thought of Orestes, running around with his friends, fighting play battles and imaginary monsters. What would it be like to grow up knowing your only purpose was to be a tool? I reached out and stroked his thigh. "How old were you when you took the throne?"

"Twelve. I had to grow up fast."

I winced.

Aegisthus read my face. "It wasn't that bad. At least I learned a high level of skill at arms."

"Was your father proud of you?"

"No." His tone was curt. "I was an inadequate replacement for my murdered brothers. I was simply a weapon."

I could have wept for him. "What a messy family," I said. "Every generation carrying on its own blood feud, no one breaking free." I sighed. "I told you that Agamemnon murdered our daughter?"

"I know," he said. "You've never spoken of her to me. It must have been terrible for you." The grave sympathy in his voice gave me the courage to tell him the rest.

I nodded. "I've sworn to kill him." I raised my eyes to his. "I took an oath at the temple of Hera. If Agamemnon returns I will murder him."

He looked at me steadily. I wondered if he would be disgusted by such an unwomanly revenge.

He put his hand out to cover mine where it rested on his thigh. "Then if I can, I will help you," he said.

We moved on to lighter topics and less serious banter, but the conversation marked another phase in our relationship. We trusted each other enough now to share our deepest secrets.

Charis rolled her eyes when she first discovered we were lovers.

"I told you so," she murmured as she dressed my hair.

I smiled happily at her. "You're a very cheeky girl, you know that?"

She just grinned and carried on pinning my hair up. "You've just won me a coral necklace, wagered in the servants' quarters."

I gaped at her. "The servants were betting on whether I would take Aegisthus as a lover?"

Charis nodded. "They are all very happy for you," she said cheerily.

I felt shocked. I wasn't ashamed of my actions, but equally I had thought them a private matter. To realise I had been talked about before I had even considered the possibility of having an affair was unnerving.

"Well, I'm glad they're happy," I said. "Let's hope everyone else is happy for me. I don't want a scandal."

I went to inspect the frescoes on the walls of the south terrace. A blocked gutter had caused rainwater to back up and flood the decorated wall. I ordered the slaves to check other downpipes or gutters then knelt to study the damage. Large flakes of plaster had lifted off the wall, and the delicate painting was ruined.

Aegisthus came in, followed by his faithful shadow Orestes. He grimaced at the mess. "It doesn't look pretty," he commented.

"I don't even know where to get the sort of artist who can repair it," I said. "It's fine work, and I'm pretty sure we don't have anyone in the town up to this quality."

"I would think it's Minoan work," he said. "Probably done by some slave captured when we conquered Crete. I'll spread the word that we are looking for an artist."

I nodded, standing up and stretching my back. "Maybe talk to the traders. They might know of someone."

I looked at Orestes standing beside Aegisthus. Now was as good a time as any to tell him about Aegisthus and myself. Charis had made me aware the children should hear the news from me first. What did you explain to an eight-year-old?

"Thank you, Aegisthus," I said. "What would we do without him, Orestes?"

Orestes gave an awkward shrug, embarrassed to be asked an opinion in front of his hero.

"Aegisthus has become my best friend, and I love him very much," I said to the boy. "You may hear comments from others about this."

Out of the corner of my eye I saw Aegisthus grin.

"We're all one family," I added. Had I said enough? Orestes didn't seem interested, and I didn't want to give him inappropriate information.

I looked at Aegisthus.

He moved beside me and put his arm round me, giving me a hug. "All one happy family," he echoed and gave me a quick peck on the forehead.

"Come on, Orestes, time to get down to the training grounds. See you later, Nestra." It was man talk, casual and short in front of a woman.

They left together. I heard Orestes chattering as they walked away.

It would be far trickier to talk to Electra. We had never had an easy rapport. She was eleven and displaying early symptoms of pubescence, not just the fat pads growing into breasts on her chest, but in mood swings and general contrariness. I decided to stage-manage some quality mother/daughter time in the bathhouse, reasoning that intimate confidences could more easily be shared if we were relaxed in warm water.

I rehearsed the words I needed to say. Nothing too personal or sexual in nature, just a statement of my love-affirming, life-affirming, relationship with Aegisthus. It was important I present this as a joyous situation. Electra would soon be old enough to be developing her own relationships with men. I wanted her to approach her sexuality with confidence.

She burst through the doorway, slamming the door behind her. I looked up, startled, from my work, and my heart sank. She had a thunderous scowl on her face, which didn't bode well. Of all my children, she was the most like her father, given to bad moods and tantrums. If anything, these were getting worse as she approached menarche.

"Hello, darling," I said cautiously. "I was just going to send for you to see if you wanted to come to the baths with me for a massage."

"You're having an affair with him, aren't you? I overheard the maids. They say you're sleeping with Aegisthus."

"Yes," I said, as calmly as I could. "Aegisthus and I are lovers. I'm sorry you heard it from the maids because I wanted to tell you, which is why I was going to say, come to the baths with me and I could tell you there."

"How can you do it?" she exclaimed. "How can you betray my father? He's your husband. How can you cheat on him like this?"

I hadn't expected this approach, that she would try and support the murdering bastard who had sired her.

"Electra, you do realise that your father organised the murder of your sister, don't you? I know you were young at the time, so perhaps you didn't understand."

"She was a sacrifice," said Electra dismissively. "Anyway, everyone knows she was saved at the last minute by the goddess."

I stared at her. Surely she didn't think that was the truth?

"Iphigenia had her throat cut on an altar at Aulis. Agamemnon deliberately deceived me and lured her to that death. It wasn't an accident, darling. Your sister was killed because the wind wasn't blowing from the right direction, and remember, it could just as easily have been you in her place. So don't talk to me about betrayal. Agamemnon sundered any obligations I had to him when he killed my daughter. He's a murderer, and I owe him nothing."

"My father is not a murderer. He didn't murder Iphigenia. It's all a lie that you've made up so you can have an affair."

Her eyes had gone dark and slitty with anger, her face flushed and ugly. I cautioned myself to hold on to my temper. She was only a child, after all.

"One thing you should know, Electra, is I don't lie. I don't need to. You mustn't believe the stories that circulate the markets. You know that. If we listened to every fabrication, we'd have to believe that your granny mated with a swan, or that Auntie Helen is a god's daughter. These are just made-up tales, darling. Iphigenia was murdered. If you don't believe me, talk to Charis. She was there."

"Charis is just a slave. She'd say anything you told her to," said my daughter.

I sighed. "Charis hasn't lied either. You were too young to remember the state she was in when she returned from Aulis. You couldn't doubt her story. She watched your sister burn on the funeral pyre."

"It's not true!" she shouted. "And you do lie, and you are cheating on your husband. It's disgusting that a woman as old as you should have a lover. You're acting like a whore. A nasty, cheap, slutty whore."

I pulled my hand back, and, before I could think, struck her hard across the face.

She pressed a hand to her abused cheek, and we stared at each other, both shocked to the core. I regretted the action immediately; I had never struck my children. But I couldn't back down now.

"I am not only your mother, but your queen," I said coldly. "You will treat me with respect on both counts. I won't tolerate that attitude from anyone. Least of all from my daughter. You will mind both your manners and your language around me."

I watched her face crumple, childish temper tantrum transmuting into impotent rage. "I hate you, I hate you!" she shouted, as she turned and fled the room.

"So that went well," I said sourly to Aegisthus some hours later.

"At least Orestes didn't seem to care," he said consolingly.

"But I've lost Electra forever," I said, feeling sad. We'd never had the warm affection I'd had with Iphigenia, or now with Orestes. I couldn't claim this as a mother/daughter problem. Iphigenia and I had been close and affectionate. But I had failed with Electra. Was it her, was it me? She was a child, so the responsibility was obviously mine.

Orestes was different. I liked to think, after thinking it through, that Orestes might talk to me if he had concerns. He'd always visited me daily to talk about his schooling, or his ambitions as a warrior. I had been able to share so much of his boyhood that the bond between us was close and strong. I believed it unbreakable. I loved his hunger for success, his quick intelligence, and I admired his persistence and diligence when things went wrong. I had tried hard not to burden him with my anger at Agamemnon. Instead, when a bard sang an appropriate poem in the hall, I would try to focus his attention on kings and princes who behaved well. On justice and honour, and the behaviour the gods expected. A boy's father is important. Orestes would carry Agamemnon's name for the rest of his life, and I wasn't going to shame my son with slurs on it. Sufficient if I could provide a moral compass for him based on mythical heroes.

I turned towards Aegisthus, wretched that I couldn't spend our lives in that perfect privacy we'd enjoyed for a few short weeks.

He hugged me close.

"I'm sorry I've caused grief for you," he whispered.

I shook my head. "It's not you. It's just the reality of being in the world." But I clung to the warmth his body offered.

I was cradled in his arms later that night. If he wasn't asleep, he was very close to it. My thoughts ran free. I felt Aegisthus was my own private miracle. He had opened my shuttered life and poured sunlight into areas I had ignored and abandoned.

I realised I had been turning away from Agamemnon imperceptibly for years before his murder of Iphigenia. Probably the first blow he laid on me began it, and each subsequent episode of childish intemperance heightened my contempt. I appeared a loyal wife, but I had begun to conceal myself from my husband years ago. I can't claim it as deliberate deceit. It was a protective shell to shield me from endless childish tantrums, those tedious, meaningless scenes, and of course the occasional violence. I had shuttered myself so well I hadn't noticed the circumscribed life I had permitted myself.

Aegisthus stirred beside me. "Are you all right? What troubles you?" he asked, reaching for my hand.

I struggled to express the way I felt. "I've realised you've 'opened' me up. I was rigid until you refused to see my boundaries, and I'm very grateful you forced your way through them."

He was silent for a while. "Do you want to tell me now about life with your husband?" His voice was blessedly anonymous in the darkness, otherwise I doubt I could have replied.

"It was … he wasn't …" My voice frayed at the thought of describing our marriage.

"Take your time," he said calmly, "but you should tell me."

And I did. From my childish memories of two fugitive brothers, through to our wedding and all that came after. I spared neither of us. Two people make a marriage, after all.

He listened quietly, not saying anything. At the end he just pulled me closer into his arms and held me.

"What about you?" I asked eventually. "Did you never marry?"

"No," he said. "I had nothing to offer a wife. Apart from the few years when Thyestes and I took back Mycenae, I've always been a refugee of sorts."

"Have you ever been in love?" I asked.

"Well, I've met my share of friendly girls over the years."

I saw the flash of white teeth in the dark as he grinned.

"Is that what you wanted to know?"

"No." I shoved him hard. "I meant serious stuff, like a real relationship with a woman."

"A couple I suppose you could call serious, but the problem has always been I've had to move on. When you earn your keep as a mercenary, there's not much place for a permanent relationship."

I recalled Agamemnon had said something similar years ago.

I wanted to ask the next obvious question, 'what about now?' but stopped myself. It was enough that he was here. The future could look after itself.

News from Troy was intermittent. It was easy to pretend Agamemnon and the problems he represented were irrelevant.

CHAPTER
TWENTY FOUR

FIVE YEARS LATER WE CELEBRATED THE summer solstice with the games. In the early years of the war, we had cancelled this annual event. There simply weren't enough men of appropriate age and status left to compete. But those troops had been gone ten years, and the young they left behind had now reached their own manhood. Mycenae of course didn't share the Spartan tradition of allowing their girls to compete.

"I've put extra troops on duty," remarked Aegisthus. "Some of those temporary wine shops are about as shifty as you can get. I've found one is simply a cover for a fencing operation. They make more money dealing in stolen goods than they ever do selling their rotgut brew. And it is rotgut, I tasted it."

I nodded, although I was distracted. I'd started that morning with a report detailing the failings of the public latrines dotted throughout the games. They were proving inadequate for the crowds in the temporary games camp, and in the summer heat the stench was overwhelming. I'd organised a detail to deal with it, only to be faced with a string of other problems, from unlicensed brothels to missing children.

I thought wistfully of my couch on the shaded terrace and a chilled drink, but I wouldn't be able to relax for hours yet.

Aegisthus read my frown. "Bear up, lady. Remember, it can only get better."

I gave him as toxic a look as I could manage, which caused him to grin and reach for me. We were interrupted by a messenger being announced from Troy. I sighed. There never was any useful news from Troy. It was a massive waste of time, manpower and resources. I wondered how my errant sister – the cause of this debacle – was doing. I hoped one day to be able to wring her neck personally. Then I thought how, indirectly, she had brought me Aegisthus, and wanted to kiss her.

I gestured to the messenger to speak.

"The Greek army is in disarray," he reported. "A quarrel has arisen between Achilles and Agamemnon, and Achilles now refuses to take the field at all. The demoralising effect this is having on the rest of the army is incalculable, and the Trojans are taking full advantage. For the first time the balance between the two armies has shifted entirely towards Troy."

I drew a startled breath and sat down on the bench beside the table. We had become so used to the Troy situation being static that any change was dramatic. I pondered the ramifications if Troy won. I wanted my husband dead, but I was quite prepared to do that myself. The more happily wed wives and families of Mycenae would be devastated to hear this news. I wondered if it would wreck our games.

"What reason is given for the quarrel between Agamemnon and Achilles?" asked Aegisthus.

The messenger paused, giving me an uneasy look. "It concerns a slave girl, Briseis. Agamemnon forced Achilles to hand her over to him, although she was Achilles' prize. Agamemnon lost his own woman when he was forced to return her to her priestly father. In retaliation he ordered Achilles to give Briseis to him. The quarrel has split the army, as most agree Agamemnon overreached himself with the demand. Morale has slumped to an all-time low, and Achilles is threatening to sail for home with his men and urges the other forces to sail with him."

I gave a vulgar snort. Nothing was more likely than that Agamemnon would behave unreasonably and alienate his officers. It sounded just like him, and I wondered how it had taken ten years for his men to realise the calibre of the man who claimed to be their chief commander.

The messenger was clearly concerned he'd hurt me by disclosing my husband's sexual practices and found it hard to meet my eye for the rest of the briefing. We let him go, with instructions to the maids to feed him and give him a bed for the night. He would be working his way east and south. I asked him to pay my respects to my parents when he called at Sparta.

As I expected, the news from Troy dwarfed all other concerns as the information spread. There wouldn't be a family at the games who were not affected by the campaign. Many might wish it over, but none wanted us to be on the losing side. I had other concerns. If Troy won, or the war ended, hundreds of men would return to their cities and their farms. The shortage of male labour that had made every task difficult would suddenly be reversed. I tried to imagine a surfeit of unemployed, under-occupied and aggressive men loosed on the city, and grimaced. Why was nothing ever easy?

*   *   *

As the season rolled on, messengers became more frequent. Each time they visited, the news from the battlefield more dramatic. Names we had become familiar with fell in battle. Patroclus, trying to rally the army and stand in for Achilles, was killed. Hector, heir to Troy and with a reputation second to none for honour, courage and fighting skill, had been killed by Achilles, and then his body despoiled by being dragged around the walls of Troy three times. Most shocking of all, the great Achilles himself fallen. His fury at Patroclus's death caused him to abandon his feud with Agamemnon and go back on the battlefield, only to be slain by an arrow. Finally, Paris himself, the infamous seducer and direct cause of the war, was dead.

I wondered how Helen was. With Paris dead, she would be in a uniquely difficult situation immured in war-weary Troy.

The war would end and soon. I could feel it. There was new energy in the citadel. Conversations seemed more urgent, merchants at the markets were inclined to stop and chat with their clients. Everyone wanted to feel part of the coming climax, whether for good or ill.

I avoided any speculation about Agamemnon's return. I would do what I had to when that day arrived. I attended the temple more frequently, praying for skill, strength and divine help in fulfilling my vow. In private I began a regime of training. Common sense told me I needed to be physically hard and fit to have any hope of killing a man who'd spent ten years at war. His skills would be honed with hours of battlefield experience.

I remembered the fierce, fit girl I once was and grimaced. Time had softened me. Living with Aegisthus had softened me in other ways. Happiness had robbed me of my abrasiveness. I wanted, with all my heart, to be able to live with the man I loved, peacefully, for the rest of my life.

Electra was waiting at the foot of the steps when I came down from my chamber. She was fifteen now. Shorter than Iphigenia at a similar age, she was a diminutive female version of Agamemnon. Her stocky build was starting to lose its puppy fat, and if she could ever bring herself to smile she would be pretty enough, with her dark, curling hair and dark eyes. Unfortunately her default expression was sulky, which gave a heavy cast to her face.

I smiled at her, receiving her usual scowl in reply. We had never healed the breach between us, and she usually avoided me unless forced into my company. Since the day I hit her, she had remained formally polite with me, never volunteering any intimacy. I told Aegisthus I felt I'd lost a daughter but gained a citizen. Electra never allowed me to forget her anger.

"Good morning," I said as I approached. "You're up early this morning."

"Is it true?" she asked. "Are the ships coming back from Troy soon?"

"I haven't heard that yet. But we have heard the war has intensified, so hopefully it will end soon, and then, yes, they'll come back."

I saw malice written on her face.

"Then what will you do, Mother, when they all come home?" she sneered. "My father will hear all about you and Aegisthus. What will you do then?"

"What your parents do is none of your business, Electra," I said sharply. "I will continue to do what I have always done. I'm Queen of Mycenae, and nothing's going to change that." I tried to keep calm. Let the girl say what she wanted, it would change nothing.

"My father won't let you be queen any more. Not once he knows about all the things you've been up to. He'll fix you then," she taunted.

I saw the pleasure that causing pain gave her. So like her father, I thought sadly.

"Well, it's still none of your business, Electra." I walked past her. I would not rise to her challenge.

"I'll tell him," she threatened from behind me, still trying to get a reaction.

"I'll tell him myself," I replied.

I walked away. I could hardly wait to be free of the palace and my sour daughter. She was old enough to be thinking about marriage, love and romance. Instead, here she was, twisted up with malice and resentment.

How had I gone so wrong with this daughter?

Aegisthus had been away on a hunting trip for a few days. The palace relied on the game the hunting band brought back as an important part of our food supply. The winter rains would start in a few weeks, prohibiting these excursions, and our diet would necessarily become centred on fish until the following spring. I didn't dislike fish, but it became monotonous when served every mealtime.

We lay in bed later.

"What's wrong?" he asked.

I looked at him in surprise. "Was something wrong for you? I enjoyed it."

"Not with that," he smiled into the darkness, "but you're unusually tense."

"Ahh." I told him about my run-in with Electra.

He rolled over to face me. "We've been avoiding any discussion about what happens when Agamemnon gets home. We've got to talk, Nestra. You've got to tell me your plans and let me help. We work together, remember?"

"It's my fight," I mumbled. "I don't want to involve anyone else."

He gave a snort of exasperation. "It's my fight as well. The man killed my father, and his father murdered my older brothers, if you remember. You aren't the only one with a blood feud, Nestra, however personal you feel this is. I have just as much a desire to kill the bastard as you do. You could make me your champion and let me do the job for you. You would have fulfilled your vow."

"I took an oath," I said stubbornly. "I have to carry it out myself or the gods will destroy me."

"All right, I understand that. But you can't kill Agamemnon without some planning or help. What are you planning to do? Challenge him to a duel? You'd be dead in thirty seconds."

"Do you have a better idea?" I resented him making me deal with the awful reality, but I was grateful for his support.

"Whether you like it or not, you are going to have to be a bit tricky about this. If he thinks he's in danger from you, he'll dispose of you before you get a chance to hurt him. You are going to have to convince him you aren't a danger, so he allows you close enough to kill him. You won't achieve it any other way. He must be aware you will be angry at Iphigenia's death, so he may be very wary of you."

I thought of the number of times Agamemnon had hurt me then expected to be taken back as if nothing had happened.

"Knowing my husband, it probably won't occur to him I'd do anything other than welcome him back with open arms," I said tartly. "He's not the most self-aware man. Look at the mess he's made at Troy."

"Hmm."

I looked at him suspiciously. "You've been thinking about this, haven't you?"

"I barely think of anything else these days," he sighed. "So far my thought is, the only way to get close enough to him is by you taking him to bed and killing him while he sleeps. And I really don't want you to do that."

I shuddered beside him. "I honestly don't think I could do that convincingly. The thought repels me so. Even thinking about it makes me sick. He'd know, any man would, that I didn't desire him." I lay there thinking. "How do whores manage, do you think? They must encounter this all the time."

"Don't get distracted," Aegisthus said severely. "This is serious. If we both agree you can't go to bed with him, then how else are you going to be able to get close enough to him at a time when he doesn't have a weapon handy?"

"Hide under the bed while he has it off with a slave girl, then jump out when they've dropped off to sleep?" I was beginning to feel more cheerful. Any plot I thought of veered rapidly into farce.

"Grr." He reached over and swatted my bottom lightly. "I love you to pieces, but you're the most irritating woman I know. All right, we'll talk about this again later, but you keep thinking. Time will run out on us soon enough, and we need to have a workable plan."

CHAPTER
TWENTY FIVE

NEWS CAME SOON ENOUGH THAT TROY had fallen. The messenger who came was white-faced and exhausted. We'd known this messenger for some years. Usually a fresh-faced young man, he had spent the last few years reporting nothing more exciting than an occasional raid on some hapless Trojan fishing village. The real brutality of war had shocked him deeply.

"The sack of the city was still going on when I left. It was terrible. There was fire everywhere, and troops were running riot in the city." He gulped in his distress. "The women and children were … " He stopped abruptly.

"Sit down," I said.

Charis poured him wine, and I watched him slug it down like water.

"Pour him more," I said.

Eventually he calmed down.

"Have you heard anything about Helen? What has happened to her?" I asked.

"She was captured, along with the other royal women,

although she was kept apart from them. Menelaus killed her husband."

"Husband?" This was news, Paris having died some months earlier.

"After Paris was killed they married her to Deiphobus, Paris's brother. Priam didn't want her to be single and unprotected."

So, once again she had survived. I wondered what she looked like now. She would be in her mid-forties. Surely even the most beautiful woman in the world would be starting to look her age?

He filled us in with some of the details. In the end it took deceit to destroy Troy. Odysseus had come up with a plan to make it look as if the Greek army was going home. The troops boarded their ships, ostensibly ready for departure, leaving the plains of Ilium empty for the first time in a decade. As an offering for Poseidon, the Greeks left a large, wooden statue of a horse on the beach as an apparent request for fair winds on the journey home. Concealed in the horse were some elite Greek warriors. I suppose they were lucky the Trojans didn't simply consign the statue to the fire at the first opportunity. Instead, the poor, gullible citizens of Troy hauled the thing into their city in celebration. The Greeks exited the horse that night and opened the city gates to the waiting army. The rest was inevitable.

Odysseus's reputation for wily intelligence was reinforced. No one seemed to find such tactics dishonourable, or against the Hero's Code warriors prided themselves on living by. I thought again of Aegisthus's instructions to me. It would take deceit to enable me to kill Agamemnon.

"Have we word on when the army will return?" asked Aegisthus.

"No. Troy was burning when I left, and the looting could go on for a week or more. After that they'll sail, I suppose."

Aegisthus looked at me.

We had no more than a couple of months. The time for action was getting close.

I stood in the stands at the training grounds and watched Orestes march with the rest of the troops. Aegisthus had increased their training. He told them he wanted them to impress their fathers and uncles when they returned from Troy. I knew he was getting them ready, under his command, for any potential trouble that might follow Agamemnon's death.

I loved watching my son. He was twelve, still at school, but proud to be part of Aegisthus's army. The young boys trained as I had as a child. Fighting, dance and music – the three pillars of our culture. They wheeled and turned in hoplite formation, shield to shield as they presented an unbreachable wall to any enemy.

Afterwards he came and sat beside me.

"All is well?" I asked.

He grinned. "Very well. Aegisthus said he'll take me out on the next action. I bested Cantor in fair fight yesterday. He let me manoeuvre him until the sun was in his eyes. Then he couldn't see enough to fight effectively, so it was easy."

I knew Cantor. He was one of the older boys, so I understood Orestes pride.

"Well done. I'm not surprised Aegisthus was pleased."

Orestes and I had always enjoyed a relaxed camaraderie. I found it easy to talk to him, and the same must have been true for him as he shared his stories of school and the gymnasium. He probably took it for granted, but I cherished our conversations.

"Aegisthus says every warrior must think when they fight. Strategy wins battles, not just strength."

I smiled. Five years on, and he still prefaced half his conversations with *Aegisthus says*.

"Sounds good to me." I smiled and let him run off to the other boys. Love works in strange ways. Why had it been so easy to love Iphigenia and now Orestes? Why had I never felt that surge of affection for poor Electra?

Orestes was everything a Spartan mother could want in a son. Bold, brave and turning into a skilled warrior. Fortunately he was also intelligent, affectionate, moral and sweet-natured. I was overwhelmed with the pride and love I felt for him.

"There will be trouble, one way or another," Aegisthus said as we changed for dinner. "Agamemnon's death is going to pose a whole heap of problems for us."

I carried on dressing, letting his words roll over me. I had spent a wonderful afternoon in the bathhouse and felt more relaxed than I had in weeks. There's nothing like a salt scrub, followed by a really good massage, to get the blood flowing and the skin feeling silky. Chryseis had found a young slave girl and trained her up with the skills of masseuse, beautician and therapist. The girl was now available for casual assignments, and I had used her services that afternoon. I applauded Chryseis on her business acumen.

"I don't know how I can go wrong," she had said to me. "The women of this town are prepared to spend a fortune maintaining themselves. The money pours from their husbands' coffers into mine. Best of all, it doesn't involve dealing with the dead, dying, plague-ridden, or anything else nasty or brutish. Beauty makes everyone feel better, male or female."

"Men as well?" I had asked, surprised.

"Oh yes," Chryseis giggled. "Our tough men love luxury, once they're introduced to it. The hardest part," she scowled, "is to get them to understand that Nerissa isn't part of the deal, that sex is not part of the package."

"And do they understand that?" I asked, my curiosity raised. I had seen Nerissa, and she was a lovely girl any man would fancy.

"I got her out of a brothel to which she'd been sold when she was eight years old. Do you really imagine she'd tolerate any man trying it on now? If they do attempt anything she'd skewer them herself, but I find it easier to keep a bodyguard to do the job. I don't want my best girl up on a charge."

I let her words sink in and opened my eyes wide.

"Best girl?" I grinned at Chryseis. "I'd wondered, of course. Congratulations."

I was still smiling at the thought several hours later.

"You're not listening to me," complained Aegisthus.

"Yes and no," I replied. Then, as casually as I could, I said, "I've worked out how to get Agamemnon naked and defenceless."

Aegisthus whipped his head round. His eyes narrowed as he

looked at me. "How?"

"When he arrives I'll meet him at the doors of the palace and escort him for a ritual cleansing in the bathhouse. I will let him know that he must be rid of the dust, dirt and death of Troy before he enters the palace proper to retake his place as its monarch. I think, if we make it sufficiently ceremonial, Agamemnon will accept it as part of the formalities he will be expecting. Can you source me long lengths of carpet, preferably purple? He must feel he is being treated like a king."

Aegisthus gave a grunt of amusement. "Please tell me there's an actual link between your sudden need for carpet and the death of your husband?"

So I explained. "Where else are we all stark naked without thinking about it but in the bathhouse? We expect to be scraped and oiled and scrubbed, and you don't have that done fully dressed with your armour on, now do you?"

"True." Aegisthus was working his way through the plan.

"I can have him escorted to the baths by fifty virgins, all dressed in white, singing his praises and wearing wreaths, if that makes the difference. Anything to make him think it's a celebration in his honour. The details don't matter so much at this point; we can work on them. But are you in agreement?"

I watched the smile grow, the laughter lines round his eyes deepening as a rumble of pleasure burst from his lips.

"Inspired," he said at last. "Completely inspired." He laughed. "Consider yourself the owner of however many costly lengths of carpet it takes. You'd better get the distance measured. We don't want to run short at a critical time."

He kissed me thoroughly, and we ended up entering the hall rather late for our meal.

The basic plan established, everything else was, as I had declared, simply detail. We were like actors setting a scene for an audience. In this case, an audience of one man.

I didn't share with Aegisthus the nights I lay awake worrying. I was ashamed to discover that though I might hate Agamemnon and be vowed to destroy him, I was afraid I would also destroy that which so recently I had come to value. Orestes, my beautiful son. My lover, who was a partner in every way I could have wished for. I avoided all thought of Electra. I wanted a continuation of the present, not the uncertainty of a future that rested on my ability to carry out a murder successfully. Truly, love makes cowards of us. I was being carried forward on a tidal wave of expectation, which a small, fearful part of me dreaded. In a sense, Aegisthus carried me on. I had said what I wanted, and he would provide the means to achieve it.

And then a craven voice in my head asked, 'What if you fail?'

I rolled over restlessly.

In the darkness Aegisthus reached out and held my hand. "What is it?" he asked.

"Just night worries," I answered.

His grip tightened. "Don't over-think this, Nestra. All you have to do is act when the time comes."

"But ..."

"Shh," he said. "Don't you think every warrior feels like that on the eve of battle? You will be fine when the moment arrives."

I went to sleep comforted by his warmth and confidence.

Aegisthus obtained the carpet, at an exorbitant cost. I shuddered at the drain on the Treasury but decided the investment was worth the outcome.

Mycenae's virgins were indeed co-opted into the procession. Fifty young maidens needed gowns and wreaths. They had to be rehearsed again and again so no detail was out of place. The girls had been selected by drawing lots. I'd had a terrible fear Electra would manage to end up in the processional, but the gods averted that disaster.

Aegisthus, I knew, was more concerned at the damage the returning army could do to the town and countryside when they realised their commander was dead.

"I'm picking that the townspeople themselves and the local forces I have trained will support you. They know about Iphigenia's death; they saw your grief. From what you told me, they all attended the service for her, and I think they will understand. It might be different for the returning soldiers. I don't know whether to put them up close to the town where I can keep an eye on them, or billet them somewhere in the countryside where they can't do much harm."

I bowed my head. There would be consequences, I knew. For every action there is a price to be paid. The gods grant I could take my vengeance first.

"How will you kill him?" Aegisthus, ever the pragmatist, asked.

I stared at him blankly.

"Well, you've got a killer glare when you're in a temper, but that's hardly going to fell a hero of Troy, now is it?"

I snarled back at him. I hated being pinned to the wall like this, but I knew it was part of Aegisthus's planning, and it was why he was successful. Orestes had expressed it well: it took thought and strategy to overcome an enemy.

"Years ago, before I was a bride, one of my suitors gave me a labrys. I had thought to use that. It's a dangerous weapon but will give a killing stroke for relatively little effort on my part. I am afraid that with a dagger or sword I might not be strong enough – or fast enough – to kill cleanly." My unspoken fear was of an unclean stroke that left Agamemnon wounded but still capable of fighting me.

Aegisthus said. "All right, that would do it. When was the last time you practised with the axe?"

I knew perfectly well I hadn't practised with it at all; not since before my wedding, when I had twirled it around and shocked my mother.

I said nothing, but Aegisthus knew me intimately.

"You haven't practised with it, have you?"

I had to admit, no, I hadn't got that far yet.

He gave a sigh. "Nestra ..."

From then on I trained with him at some impossible time each morning. We wanted privacy, naturally, and the terraces of the palace are unattended at five in the morning. Even the sun had barely climbed high enough to give us light.

Aegisthus made me train, and train, and then train some more.

The muscles in my arms shrieked, my back hurt from the weight of the axe, and I had no technique at all. I had never learned how to use an axe. Spartans use javelins, swords and daggers. The axe is a northern weapon.

Somewhere in his travels Aegisthus had learned the basics, and he imparted these to me, quite brutally, in three weeks of intense activity. If I hadn't loved him, I would have hated him then. As it was, I made him bear my physical misery and complaints every evening.

He laughed a little at me, but not too much. He was sympathetic to my aches and pains but unyielding as a trainer. "I have never sent a warrior into a fight unprepared," he said calmly. "Those I train don't fail, and neither will you. But you will work, my darling, so don't even bother with that pout."

I bared my teeth at him. I was in pain and miserable. He laughed, not unsympathetically, rolled me onto my stomach and proceeded to massage my shoulders. I felt the knots ease as he worked on them.

"Did I tell you that your new figure is sexually alluring?" he murmured provocatively.

"What?" I woke from the stupor his hands had induced.

"You've lost a lot of weight, your body is firmer, and you look wonderful."

I glared at him. I wasn't so far gone that I couldn't recognise blatant flattery. But the next morning, once he had left, I checked my reflection. He was right. I was looking good and with his appreciation evident, I started to feel good.

Unspoken had been the fear Agamemnon would see me as an aged crone, of no use or consequence, and refuse to have me near him. Aegisthus had restored my confidence in myself. I preened in front of the mirror for a while before remembering I was running late for the latest round of axe training. Aegisthus was not known for leniency towards tardy trainees. I sighed, but ran to the terrace anyway.

CHAPTER
TWENTY SIX

T HE SMOKE WAS A FAINT SMUDGE on the horizon, barely visible in the flat, early-morning light.

"Can you see it?" Aegisthus stood beside me.

I nodded.

The guard who had summoned us pointed further to the right. "That's where the next beacon along is, but it's not alight yet. They're set an hour's travel apart."

I followed the line of beacons across the plain. "So they'll be here in about three hours?"

"Yes, lady. About that."

Aegisthus dismissed the guard.

We looked at each other, and I assayed a small smile.

"Ready?" he asked.

I nodded, then decided the occasion demanded something more assertive.

"I'm ready," I said firmly.

I dressed in my best new gown. Chryseis sat and watched Charis as she wound my hair up. I hadn't discussed my plans with them, nor had they asked. It was probable that Chryseis had worked out why the bathhouse and Nerissa featured as the day's highlight, but she said nothing.

Smells of baking bread wafted in through the open shutters. The kitchens would be busy today. They had been preparing food since the early hours of the morning. Outside, in the square, trestles were being set up ready for the feast that evening, and spit roasts were already turning. The whole town would celebrate the return of their men.

The palace hall, large as it was, couldn't accommodate the whole army, so we would eat with the townsfolk and their men in the town square tonight.

Aegisthus had left to get his troops ready for the chores of the day. They would start by erecting trestles and end by maintaining the peace. Whatever the outcome, Mycenae would need law and order.

I stood straight and proud to wish him goodbye.

"Two things," he reminded me. "Don't over-think, and don't be tempted to make a speech to Agamemnon telling him why he must die. Just kill him. You can make a speech to his shade once he is dead."

He saw me start to protest. "You *will* be tempted, Nestra. Many a man has gone to his death because he forgot to act first, speak afterwards." He had kissed me hard. "You will be all right," he said, and gripped my shoulders and left.

When Charis finished she knelt beside me and kissed my hand. "The gods be with you, lady."

Chryseis nodded. "May fortune favour you," she said quietly.

I smiled my thanks and they left.

I picked up a pile of linen I had prepared to conceal the labrys in and made my way down to the bathhouse. Nerissa was already there setting up.

She nodded to me as I entered, then ignored me as she carried on preparing for the day. I could smell the spices she was grinding into the salt as a rub.

I hid the axe behind a tapestry and checked, then double-checked, I could remove it from its hiding place both quickly and quietly.

I smiled at Nerissa as I departed.

A runner announced that one chariot had broken away from the army and was racing ahead towards the town. I smiled grimly. Agamemnon had always been impatient.

I positioned myself just inside the palace doors, waiting until his chariot appeared at the foot of the steps below, when I would emerge to welcome Agamemnon home. I had seen the townspeople lining the streets, waiting for their men. There would be many sorts of welcome in the town tonight.

The chariot pulled up at the steps. I had anticipated a wave of cheers following Agamemnon's progress up from the gate, giving us advance warning. Instead there was an eerie silence.

I ordered the palace doors flung open, and I walked through them to the top of the stairs.

A groom had run up to grab the horses' heads.

Two people were in the chariot. I walked down the steps, on the carpet we'd laid at such expense, to stand in front of it. I raised my arms and made a silent plea to Hera.

"Hail and welcome, Agamemnon, High King of the Greeks and Hero of Troy," I said formally. I don't know where I had summoned it from, but as I welcomed Iphigenia's murderer, I had a bright smile on my face.

Agamemnon raised his hand in greeting. "Nestra!"

I could barely recognise him. He hadn't aged well. He'd lost the thick, curly hair that had defined him, and I saw a squat, bald, aging man with a paunch. I hadn't expected that.

My eyes moved to his companion.

"This is Cassandra," he announced. "Once, Princess Cassandra of Troy." He smirked at me. "Now she's Agamemnon's slave Cassandra." He gave an evil grin. "The spoils of war."

I nodded, afraid to say anything in case the words betrayed me. The girl was very young, younger than Electra. She was thin and pale with dark, bruised circles under her eyes. Her arms were like fragile little sticks. I couldn't imagine the horrors she would have borne in the last weeks.

I focused on Agamemnon instead. "We have prepared a welcome for you," I said cheerfully. "If it would please you to walk with me to the bathhouse for a ritual cleansing, then after, we will enter the palace where we can celebrate your safe return."

I held my hand out to help him from the chariot. He looked at the purple carpet stretching up the steps. "What's the purpose of this?"

"To honour you and celebrate your success. Only the best and noblest can walk on carpet of this colour."

Surprisingly he hesitated, staring at the fine carpet in front of him.

"Surely only the gods should step on something so fine. Suppose I anger them by hubris?"

I hadn't thought of that. Never had it occurred to me that Agamemnon would feel humility.

I smiled reassuringly. "This won't anger the gods," I assured him. "They like to honour their favourite mortals. This night is set aside to pay homage you and your deeds in the victorious sack of Troy. There is no hubris in that."

He glanced briefly at Cassandra before accepting my hand and stepping on to the carpet.

I raised my eyebrows at the girl, indicating she should join us, but she turned away. I saw the little head drooping on her long neck and left her in peace.

I led my husband up the steps. We made some sort of conversation, but I don't recall the subject.

The bathhouse was full of the warm scent of spices. I introduced Agamemnon to Nerissa and watched him run his eyes over her.

Dirty old man, I thought.

"Let me be your maid, my husband," I coaxed. Soon my acting would qualify me to join a troupe of players. "I will remove your cloak."

He consented, and gradually I peeled the layers away. Tunic and sword belt, dagger and greaves. I placed the weapons on a convenient bench some distance from him.

I had been right. He had a paunch, and his flesh had turned flabby. His buttocks hung loose and flat. I wondered how often over the last ten years he'd actually been in combat, and how much time he'd spent ordering others around. Once his muscled, stocky frame had looked strong and powerful. Now it just looked old.

I hung his clothes up on the pegs.

"Nerissa will look after you," I assured him as I went to sit on a stool on the far side of the room.

She indicated the long bench to him and he lay down on his stomach.

She rubbed him with oil then scraped the sweat and dirt off. I watched as he grew progressively more relaxed under her hands.

"Roll over," she asked.

He turned on to his back. I looked at the body that had fathered my children and realised I felt nothing. Not even regret.

My attack was planned for the next phase, the salt rub, when I anticipated any resistance or caution on Agamemnon's part would have abandoned him completely. I tried to control my breathing. I knew it was too fast. I could feel my heart thumping in my chest. As the moment for action drew near I knew myself to be terrified.

I waited, counting down the seconds, forcing myself to stay still, when the peace of the bathhouse was broken by appalling screams from outside.

I leapt to my feet. "What in Hades is that?" I asked, preparing to rush out.

Agamemnon grunted. "Don't worry, sit down. It's just that silly Cassandra. She's a seer or something; supposed to be able to tell the future. I've never yet heard anything sensible from her."

The noise stopped and I sat down again. I was seriously rattled, my hands shaking and my breathing ragged. The calm I had imposed on myself was completely gone, but Agamemnon seemed as unconcerned and relaxed as ever.

"She's woken me at night screaming like that," he said sleepily. "I beat her the last time she did it; I thought it would teach her a lesson."

I looked at him in amazement then glanced up to see Nerissa's eyes on me. We shared a look. One other person who wouldn't grieve for him, I noted.

Nerissa turned him back on to his stomach and began to apply the rub to his back and arms.

I stood quietly, retrieved the labrys and stepped beside him. Nerissa, her eyes opening wide, obligingly continued holding his arm as she rubbed and polished his skin.

"For Iphigenia," I said loudly in defiance of Aegisthus's advice, before bringing the axe down hard on his skull.

He must have heard me and realised my intent in the second before the axe connected because he had started to turn his head. Consequently the axe sliced deeply in a line between brow and temple rather than into the back of his head. I had swung so savagely it was hard to pull the axe back out. I felt like a woodsman struggling with a knotted piece of wood before it came free.

I stood looking down at him.

"He's dead," said Nerissa calmly.

I looked at her in amazement.

"It was a clean blow. You don't have to do anything more."

I looked back at the heap of flesh that had been Agamemnon and agreed. He was definitely dead, I could see through the skull to his brain. There was very little blood, I thought. I only had a small drop on my gown. Hardly visible.

I was shaking with reaction. Nerissa went and got his clothes from the hook. She handed me his dagger.

"I'll roll him over," she said. Then if you would feel safer, you can stab him as well, just to be certain."

I held the dagger, but shook my head. "No," I said. "You're right. He's dead. There's no need."

"I'll roll him over anyway and cover him with a sheet. That way he'll look decent when they carry him out."

I stood, uselessly watching her. My task accomplished, I had run out of ideas. She was right. Laid on his back and fully covered he did indeed look decently like any other corpse.

There was another episode of screaming from outside, the bathhouse door burst open and Cassandra came running in. I turned to stop her before she saw the body; I was still holding the forgotten dagger. I will never know whether it was an accident, or whether she impaled herself deliberately, but she ran straight on to the blade.

For a moment she stood straight in front of me, like a butterfly on a pin.

I gave a gasp of horror and released my grip on the dagger. Without the support she slowly sagged and fell, crumpling at my feet like a discarded garment.

"On no!" I moaned. I fell to my knees beside her to give her aid, but from the spread of blood on her gown I could see the wound was fatal. The dagger stuck out from her chest like an obscenity, and I pulled it from her.

Nerissa ripped the dress from Cassandra's shoulders, and we stared at the ugly gash beneath her small left breast. This killing had resulted in blood, a lot of blood. It was on my hands and my gown.

"I didn't mean to kill her," I said in grief. "I wouldn't have hurt her for the world. I felt so sorry for her. And now she's dead at my hand."

"It wasn't your fault," said Nerissa quietly. "She either didn't see the blade, or she ran onto it deliberately." She reached out and closed Cassandra's eyes. "I've heard of this girl. They say she could see the future but was cursed by Apollo, so no one would believe what she told them."

"She was just a child," I said, mustering all the bitterness I felt. "A poor, abused little girl. She'd lost her family, her home, was probably raped multiple times in the sack of Troy, and was then forced to be a concubine for Agamemnon. Now I'm responsible for her death. It's horrible." I felt the full weight and guilt of Iphigenia's death once again.

Another beautiful young woman destroyed for no good reason. I felt sick with remorse.

"It still wasn't your fault." Nerissa straightened Cassandra's limbs and folded her arms across her chest, hiding the wound.

There was no hiding the blood.

I stroked her hair. It was soft and warm beneath my fingers. I bowed my head and tried to find some words that were appropriate. None came.

All I could do was repeat, "I'm sorry, I'm sorry, I'm sorry."

Nerissa pulled me to my feet. "Lady, you cannot stay here. You must call for help, or tell the people what has happened. You must not fall to pieces now. There is work for you to do. It is very important that you act now as Queen of Mycenae."

I stared at her blankly. Shock had robbed my head of intelligent thought, and it took some minutes for her meaning to penetrate.

Reaction was setting in. My legs felt wobbly and my hands shook. A fog of disbelief had invaded my head. Cassandra's death had been no part of the plan.

She shook me gently. "Lady, you must leave here and be a queen."

She reached for a cloth and wiped my hands clean, holding them firmly to steady their shakes. There wasn't much she could do for the gown. I stood as she cleaned me up, mindless beneath her ministrations. I just wanted the dark to swallow me.

She clucked at me in frustration. Eventually she pushed a phial of some foul-smelling substance beneath my nostrils. The harsh ammoniac smell woke me. I choked and coughed. It burned in my nostrils and refused to allow me to slip into unconsciousness. For a moment I thought I would vomit, then the urge passed.

I took a breath and realised I was alive and my vow accomplished. Aegisthus, I thought with some urgency. I must let him know.

"Thank you, Nerissa," I said at last. "You are right. I must go."

I walked to the door and put my hand on it. I turned back for a look at the carnage I had wrought. Agamemnon's corpse lay tidily beneath the sheet, and Nerissa was busying herself with the small body of Cassandra. There were bloodstains on the tiles. I froze, sick to my heart. Then Nerissa raised her head, looked at me and waved me impatiently on my way.

It took more courage than I'd known I'd had, to push through it and emerge on the other side in front of the crowd.

Aegisthus and I had agreed there should be nothing hidden about Agamemnon's death, nothing to allow a rumour to grow that his murder was a shameful crime.

"You'll have to let everyone know," he'd said, "that this is execution, not assassination."

The quiet muttering ceased when the crowd caught sight of me. I saw their faces lifted towards me. Silently they watched, as I walked down the steps, seeing the blood on my gown and assessing its meaning. Halfway down the flight I stopped. Out of the corner of my eye I could see Aegisthus close by and his troops a short distance away, ready to dispel trouble.

"People of Mycenae," I called. I had their attention, even though my voice on its own could not have penetrated far into the crowd.

"People of Mycenae," I cried again, as loudly as I could. "Agamemnon is dead. The oath I made before the gods is fulfilled. Iphigenia's murder has been avenged. Her innocent blood has cried for ten years and at last she can rest in peace. I have executed Agamemnon. The blood debt is paid."

I could hear the surge in noise now as word was spread from person to person down the road. I let it run for a few minutes, wondering all the while if someone would challenge me over the killing. None did. I remembered the sinister silence as Agamemnon had entered the town. Others had remembered my daughter's killing and wondered what I would do. I'd never spoken of my vow, but it was probably common knowledge. The temple priest would have talked.

At last I continued. "I regret that Cassandra, the princess of Troy whom Agamemnon brought with him, accidentally ran onto his dagger and is also dead. I grieve for her loss."

The volume from the crowd rose as this news was passed on.

I waited a few moments for any response, then turned and began the climb back up the steps.

There was a shriek and a sudden rush of feet above me as Electra came pounding down towards me. "You murdered him!" she cried. "You murdered my father!" She was crazed with rage and horror and her clawed hands sought to scratch my face. I tried to hold her, but she spun in my grip and sank to the ground, screaming like a mad woman.

Aegisthus reached me, picked Electra up, slung her over his shoulder and carried her back into the palace. The noise of her screaming cut off as the palace doors closed behind them. I shut my eyes briefly and breathed heavily. My mouth tasted foul, and I ran my tongue over dry lips.

I turned back to the crowd. "Agamemnon was justly executed for his crimes," I cried. "He was not fit to return to this city, nor to rule again. A daughter's grief for her father is understandable but will pass. Justice has been done before the gods. My oath has been discharged."

I turned and followed Aegisthus into the palace. Let the crowd do what they would, I was too exhausted to care.

An hour later the troops from Troy arrived. Aegisthus, tireless in this emergency, had gone back to his men and organised the newcomers into a camp outside the city. I left the management to him. That evening they would parade into the city and be united with their families. I heard later the army's arrival was peaceful, the troops more concerned with their own personal reunions than worried about Agamemnon's fate. He hadn't been popular, particularly since his stupidity with Briseis had nearly cost the Greeks their victory at Troy.

I let Charis bathe me, change my gown and pour me wine. She bathed my face with cool lavender water, and I felt some of the tension ease. I looked up to see her smiling.

"You did it, Nestra. You fulfilled your oath." Her eyes shone with pride and admiration. "Iphigenia is avenged."

I nodded – a mistake, as my head ached. "I've felt such rage for so long, and now it's over. I can let it go. I just wish I could feel more excited about it. Instead I feel exhausted."

Charis laughed softly. "I'm not surprised. But you can feel very proud of yourself."

I clutched at her fingers. "I fulfilled my oath, Charis, but Electra will never forgive me."

Charis shrugged. "She's a difficult girl, and she's always championed her father, probably because she knew it annoyed you. There's not much you can do about it. You had no choice, and really, I don't think anyone else will question what you did. All Mycenae knows Iphigenia died because of Agamemnon, and they loved their princess. I don't think you have any need to worry. They respect and love their queen. Your people will be loyal to you."

Charis was wrong. There was one other person who cared about Agamemnon's fate.

I entered the square that evening, with my maids behind me, to sit at the official table and welcome the troops home. There was a spirit of celebration in the air. The men paraded briefly before being engulfed by families welcoming them back. Old folk, relieved their sons had returned, lonely wives and fatherless children all rejoiced. The problems of readjusting to each other would start tomorrow. Tonight the town and its men were happy to celebrate, eat the roasted meats and drink the brew the kitchens had been preparing for weeks. There was music playing, and dancing had started in the square. My maids were in the midst of it, revelling with the rest. I saw Charis laughing up at a young warrior. There were many young women in the town who would be happy to have so many eligible men return.

Aegisthus had been with me at the start of the ceremony, but left to supervise his men. Night fell and the torches were lit. I was still sitting on the raised dais, a smile of welcome painted on my face, waving at happy couples stepping past and wondering how soon, in all decency, I could leave proceedings and go home to bed. The headache that had been niggling all day had settled in, and my head was throbbing. I was having difficulty concentrating. I needed time and space around me to come to terms with my actions that morning. Instead I was surrounded by people. I had rarely felt so claustrophobic.

Orestes approached. I smiled at him, then thought I had never seen him look so ill. I stood up in concern and reached for him. "Darling, are you all right? You look terrible."

He avoided my arms. "Mother," he stammered.

"What's wrong? Are you ill?"

"Mother," he began again, "they say you killed Agamemnon. They say you murdered my father?"

I felt the colour rise to my cheeks as my heart rate sped up. I hadn't considered Orestes. I wondered where he'd been standing that morning; well away from the palace I hoped. I took a deep breath. "No," I said firmly. "I took vengeance on a murderer. Agamemnon killed my daughter, your sister, for no good reason. I was the only one who could make him pay for his blood guilt, so I did."

Trying to make him understand, I continued, "He has paid for his crime, and Iphigenia is avenged."

"Oh gods!" he cried. "How could you do that? Don't you see what you've done?"

"I have done what I had to do," I said. "When Agamemnon killed Iphigenia, I took an oath before the gods to avenge her. I have honoured my oath, before gods and men."

"He was my father," he said.

I was getting angry. "He was a murderous father. He killed his child. You never knew him."

"That's hardly the point."

I felt the cold force of his judgment.

Orestes and I had never quarrelled. It had never occurred to me that we could. "Orestes …"

He gave a choking sob and overrode me. He was struggling so hard with emotion he could barely get the words out, but eventually cried, "Don't you see what you've done? You killed my father. Now I, his son, have to avenge his death. It's my duty. Do you know what that means? It means I am going to have to kill you in retribution. How could you force this bloodguilt on me? How could you do this to us? I loved you, Mother, and you have made me your murderer."

I felt I'd been kicked in the stomach and blenched. I sat down in a hurry as my brain absorbed his shocking words. I stared at him in appalled horror.

Before Agamemnon's death I'd been worried about Electra,

worried about the troops returned from Troy, worried about the reaction from the townspeople. This was a complication I hadn't considered. Orestes couldn't possibly remember Agamemnon, nor mourn for him as a man does his father. I hadn't thought such a theoretical grief would undo him. He had always treated Aegisthus as a father. I was shaken to the core. Too late I remembered his rectitude. Orestes had always had a firm moral code, young though he was.

"Orestes," I pleaded, trying to regain control. "You are twelve years old. Give yourself time. Trust me. Things will look different in a few days and weeks as you have time to think things through. You are not in any way responsible for avenging Agamemnon. I had to take vengeance for Iphigenia. She was defenceless against his ambitions and had no one to speak for her or avenge her murder. That episode is now finished. You must see that. The gods are satisfied with my oath."

"That doesn't change what I will have to do, though, does it?" he said.

I could see the despair in his face and reached to him. "Darling …" My cry was desperate with pain. "It doesn't have to be like this. Please don't forget how much I love you. Don't forget you love me."

He twisted away from me. "That can't be allowed to matter," he cried.

"Orestes!" I was frantic. "Don't try to make this into some quarrel between us, because it isn't. The house of Atreus has enough blood on its hands already from your father and his brother. Don't carry blood feuds on to a new generation, please. Let it go," I said urgently.

"You shouldn't have done it, Mother." His eyes were as blank and inhuman as a statue of the gods as he wrenched away from my reaching hands.

He disappeared into the darkness, and I sat there with my heart hammering, wondering whether to go after him. I decided both of us were so distraught I'd only make the situation worse.

Electra had always positioned herself as loyal to her father, and nothing would change that. But Orestes had been *my* child.

Heart and mind, he had been mine. We had an easy camaraderie, shared jokes, tastes and dreams. Orestes was my pride and joy, and now he hated me. Hated me for a father he couldn't remember and wouldn't have liked if he'd known him.

Agamemnon was still causing grief from beyond the grave.

I sat, feeling waves of sick hopelessness wash over me. I loved Orestes with all my heart. If I listed what I valued in my life, my son would be its first item. I was less concerned with the threat he'd made to me, than distressed by his pain. If I could spare him hurt, heal his grief and make the world a perfect playground for his enjoyment, I would gladly do so. I think most mothers secretly feel the same. To see Orestes in such anguish tore my heart apart; to be the direct cause of his agony was intolerable.

I reached for the wine goblet in front of me and drank its contents in one gulp. The liquid hit my stomach's curdled mess disastrously. Feeling a violent desire to vomit, I pushed back from the table and rose to my feet. I looked round, but the maids were still dancing. I would make my way home alone.

As I walked the dark, deserted streets back to the palace I wondered, *what is the point of it all?* I had been so proud that I had honoured my oath; so certain of my rectitude. Now the son I loved thought of me as a monster. This time yesterday I'd had a son who loved me and a husband I hated. Tonight, such a few hours later, I had neither.

CHAPTER
TWENTY SEVEN

“YOU'LL NEVER UNDERSTAND THAT RIGHT FROM the start you've been used by Aegisthus, will you?” yelled Electra.

We were sitting in her room overlooking the gardens. It was a lovely spot. I had gone to try and make peace with her but was failing.

“He's got exactly what he wanted,” she said. “He rules Mycenae. Agamemnon's dead, and Aegisthus didn't even have to lift a finger. You did it all for him. You murdered my father for your lover. What's he going to do now? Murder Orestes so he can wipe out my father's line completely?”

“Don't be silly, Electra,” I said. “Aegisthus has always been like a father to Orestes. You're just talking hysterical nonsense.”

“It's not nonsense,” she sobbed. “You just don't want to see it. Aegisthus has won back his kingdom, and all by sleeping with you. Now he's going to want to keep it. If you can't give him an heir, he'll probably get rid of you too.”

My hand itched to slap her again. I held myself together with an effort.

"Electra, please try and be pleasant. Being rude to me, or insulting Aegisthus, isn't going to help. I took Agamemnon's life to avenge your sister's. That's all. There's nothing sinister going on, no plots or attempts to get rid of Orestes. All this is in your imagination. And you'll make yourself sick if you can't come to terms with reality."

"It's you who can't see the truth, Mother," she shouted. "It's plain and clear for everyone else to see."

I gave up and left her to her tantrum. The sooner I found a husband for her the better. There'd be no peace while she remained in Mycenae. Now that the men were back from Troy there was bound to be some king or princeling looking for a bride. Preferably one from a far-distant part of Greece.

Agamemnon and Cassandra were buried in state. The townspeople lined the route to the cemetery and watched as we laid them in their graves. Electra managed to take full advantage of the opportunity for drama – wailing, draping herself in sackcloth and tearing at her hair. I saw Orestes, but he avoided me, which hurt. I hadn't managed to speak to him since the night of Agamemnon's death, and I hoped he was all right.

I had refused to allow Cassandra to lie in the shaft grave beside my husband, so she rested in another tomb. I thought it the least I could do for her memory. She had been so abused in life. I doubted she would want to sleep beside Agamemnon.

Over several days I went through a purification ritual to be cleansed of his death. The priests were respectful and pious as they made their sacrifices and prayers. I'd had no qualms about honouring my oath, but I appreciated the ritual and being able to put the whole terrible episode behind me.

Calchas hadn't re-entered Mycenae with the troops, although he'd travelled back from Troy with them. He had decamped when he'd heard Agamemnon had been killed.

"He must have realised just how short his lifespan would be once you got hold of him," said Aegisthus.

"I would love to have been able to execute him," I said wistfully.

"Then it's just as well he didn't return. Like him or not, he's a priest and a seer. You'd probably offend the gods if you killed their servant."

I thought back to the first time I met Calchas. Had he known then what would happen?

"If he's such a great seer and can really read the future, you'd think he would have refused to sacrifice Iphigenia. That's what started it all," I said crossly.

Aegisthus smiled. "'What started it all' depends who's telling the story. You could argue the curse on our house started back with old Atreus, or even with Tantalus before him, and the rest of us have just been swept up in it. Are we responsible for our actions, or are we part of fate working itself out?"

"That's very profound," I said, startled.

He gave me a smug grin. "I'm a very profound man."

I smiled. At least our relationship was still strong, even though I was now a murderer. I reached a hand out towards him, and he squeezed it gently.

"I haven't seen him in days." Charis was helping me dress. "Last time I saw Orestes was at the funeral." She fastened the brooch at my shoulder and stood back. "That looks good."

"I haven't seen him since the funeral either, and I'm worried about him. He was so angry and upset with me. I wanted to talk to him, but I think he's been avoiding me."

"He'll turn up," she said cheerfully.

I asked Aegisthus whether he'd sent Orestes out on patrol, but he hadn't seen him either. The influx of returned warriors crowding the town meant Aegisthus had been busy. Those troops who had been able to return to their homes, farms and families were fine, but there was a core with no home to go to. Mycenae had no need of a large standing army, and Aegisthus was working to find ways to assimilate these men into civilian life. The army camp that had hastily been established was beyond the city walls, and there was a constant coming and going between the town and the camp. The usual tight controls at the gates to the city had been relaxed. Orestes had disappeared amongst the chaos.

Seriously worried, I organised a search throughout the city for him. His messmates knew nothing, simply that he had gone. He wasn't in the palace, nor could he be found in the town or barracks. Eventually I had to accept he'd left Mycenae.

Some days later Charis arrived in the room I used as my office, dragging Electra behind her.

I was trying to tally the food stores required for the town now the troops were home. I just hoped we had enough for the coming winter, so I wasn't pleased with the interruption.

"She knows," said Charis abruptly, rather out of breath.

My daughter wrenched her arm free and glared at Charis.

"She knows what?" I asked.

"She knows what's happened to Orestes," said Charis. "She was laughing about it with Selena."

"Electra?"

She looked at the floor, avoiding eye contact with me. I felt a surge of exasperation with this surly girl. "What were you discussing with the slave girl? Do you know where Orestes is? You must tell me."

She stared stubbornly at the floor.

"Electra, you have got to talk. This isn't a child's game."

She raised her head then and looked at me. A very unchildlike expression crossed her face. "You want to know where he's gone? I'll tell you. He's left Mycenae. I sent him away for his safety. You won't find him."

"Have you gone mad?" I said. "For what possible reason would you do that? What threatens him?"

"Do you think I'd let you kill the last heir to Agamemnon's throne? You murdered my father; well, you won't kill my brother." She had her head up now, her chin raised as she declaimed her lines, for all the world like a poor actor in the marketplace.

I heard Charis give a snort of disgust.

"For the gods' sake, Electra. Stop talking such drivel. You know perfectly well Orestes isn't in any danger. How dare you accuse me of wanting to kill him? Where is he?"

My scorn jolted her from her dramatic pose. Now she was all malice. "Where you can't find him. He can grow to manhood safe from you and your lover's plans. Don't bother looking for him because he won't return. He hates you now." I saw the satisfaction in her eyes.

"Is that what this is about?" I said slowly. "You've been jealous of Orestes' affection for me? And of mine for him?"

"It's nothing like that. I want him safe and out of the danger you and Aegisthus pose." The sulky look was back. "When he returns, he can avenge our father and deal with you both."

I looked at her, realising for the first time how deep her enmity was. This was no petulant adolescent but a fully fledged adversary intent on the kill.

"When Agamemnon came home, it gave you satisfaction that he'd probably avenge himself on me and Aegisthus. Now you want Orestes to do the same? Is that all that drives you, Electra? A puny need to inflict pain, although no one has harmed you? A need to assign blame?" I took a deep breath. "One thing I can say for you, you take after your father in both looks and character, and believe me, that's not a compliment. You're a poor excuse for a woman. Go away."

I turned away from her to Charis. "Where is Selena?"

"I'll get her for you. You can whip any information you want out of her. I doubt she'd hold out long. She's another nasty piece of work. None of the other maids like her, she's too sly and spiteful."

Electra stood there, looking suddenly uncertain, as Charis left the room.

"You have been given leave to go, Electra," I said coldly. "I've no time for you."

Suddenly her eyes brimmed over with tears, she whirled and fled the room.

I gazed blindly out from the window. How had I gone so terribly wrong? I had tried to be a good mother to Electra, even if I'd never found her an easy child. How had I caused such malice and hatred? In spite of my anger, I hadn't missed the tears as she fled. Somewhere in that horrid girl was a hurt child, but how I could unlock it, or eliminate the danger her malice posed, I had no idea.

Charis brought Selena in. From somewhere she had obtained a rather nasty looking little whip which she'd waved in front of Selena's face all the way as she marched her up from the kitchens. The wretched maid had no resistance. I imagine Charis had told her terrible things I could do to her.

Selena collapsed to her knees in front of me in a blubbery mass of tears. "I didn't do anything," she wailed. "It wasn't my fault the young master fled." She threw herself forward, her face to the ground in front of me.

I took a deep breath and looked down at her whimpering form. I had a nasty fear she might forget herself and wipe her nose on my feet.

"Zeus defend me," I muttered. "Hand me the whip, Charis."

Charis passed it over.

"Now," I said to the wretch, "I want to know where Orestes is and who he is staying with. If you tell me this freely, I will let you go. Do you understand?"

There was no reply from the girl, just more mindless wailing. I gave her a few moments to settle, then tried again. "Selena, can you hear me? Answer yes or no."

There was no further attempt at an answer; instead she started rocking her body back and forth as an accompaniment to the keening.

"All right," I said, exasperated. "Have it your way." I uncoiled the whip and brought it down over her buttocks with a short, satisfactory snap. Immediately the wails were cut short by a squeal. She sprang back on her knees and threw herself sideways. Her eyes, wide with horror, met mine.

I held the whip behind my back and waited for her to settle again.

"Get up."

She scrambled to her feet, away from me. She looked a wreck, but at least the wailing had stopped. I blessed the sudden silence, even as she collapsed to her knees again. "I mean you no harm," I said again, "but I will have answers to my questions. Where is my son Orestes?"

"He's gone to Phocis, my lady."

At least she'd regained her wits, even if she did kneel there wringing her hands.

"Do you mean he's gone to Delphi?"

It wasn't an unreasonable question. Many kings and princes sought advice from the oracle at Delphi. Had Orestes gone there to seek answers to the moral questions Agamemnon's death had raised?

She looked at me blankly. Her mouth drooped open unattractively. I fancied I detected moisture at the corners of the slack mouth.

"Well?"

"No, my lady. He's gone to the King of Phocis. He wants to live there."

I exhaled deeply. I would have to ask Aegisthus about Phocis; I knew next to nothing about the place.

"Who is the king? Has he gone there?"

Apparently I had exhausted her store of knowledge because she began to shake her head, a low moaning sound seeping from her lips. I battened down my desire to smash her to the ground in frustration.

"Is there anything else you can tell me? Has Orestes arrived safely at Phocis?"

The girl flinched, showing the whites of her eyes, for all the world like a flighty chariot pony.

"Did Orestes arrive safely?" I repeated.

This girl was so stupid there really was no point in browbeating her, she would only get hysterical again. As long as she stayed reasonably able to answer questions she had nothing to fear from me.

"I think so, my lady. Please, I don't know any more." She sank onto her knees again. Everything about the girl was saggy, sloppy and vacant-minded, but she had probably told me all she knew.

I glanced across at Charis. Her face mirrored my contempt.

"Take her away, Charis," I said wearily.

They left. Once I'd heard them walk away down the corridor, I dropped the whip in disgust. Where had the days gone when I made clean moral judgments? I had prided myself on not losing my temper, on not abusing servants. I had once prided myself on being a good mother. I tasted shame and ashes. My life was turning into a wasteland of time and effort. A story of pointless toil, ambition, pride and pain.

It seemed that Agamemnon alive had been less dangerous than Agamemnon dead. I simply couldn't fathom how he had got away with his own daughter's murder without losing his other children's respect, yet I received nothing but grief and calumny for avenging that murder.

Aegisthus and I talked long into the night. He had visited the court at Phocis during the years of his exile, and declared its king, Epistrophus, to be a decent and honourable man.

I wanted Orestes back in Mycenae, but Aegisthus cautioned prudence. "Orestes left because he wanted to, Nestra. Forcing him back isn't a good idea."

"He left because Electra filled his head with a load of nonsense. If he doesn't come back and learn she's wrong, those ideas will just set in his head and become immovable," I countered. "Besides which, he is prince of Mycenae. He needs to grow up among his own people."

Aegisthus gave me a funny look.

"What?" I said.

"Name one Atreides who's managed that? Every generation of us have been exiles for part of our childhood."

I thought about that. "It's very different to the way my brothers and my sister and I were brought up," I said eventually.

"You were lucky, Nestra. You had parents who got on with each other and who gave you all a place to grow up safely. It's different in Mycenae. Children here have to grow up fast just to survive."

"I thought all our troubles would be over when Agamemnon died," I said sadly.

Aegisthus shook his head. "No, that only got rid of one

problem. There are always others. I felt the same way when we killed Atreus. He'd been such a monster figure all my childhood, I thought the nightmare would end when we got rid of him. But Atreus's death only meant Agamemnon and Menelaus became our enemies. The Hydra has many heads, and they all grow back, lop them as you will. Feuds never finish."

I sat beside him and he put his arm round my shoulder for comfort.

"If you want my advice, for what it's worth, let Orestes stay where he is. Epistrophus will make a good foster father. We can send to him, requesting he gives Orestes hospitality and full fostering at his court. Orestes can grow up away from whatever intrigue Electra and others stir up. If he is in Mycenae, there will always be factions tearing at him, wanting his support for their own political ends. Let him grow up in peace."

"Oh Aegisthus," I cried, "I love him so much. It breaks my heart to have him so angry and distant with me. I never thought that would happen."

He hugged me to him and kissed the top of my hair. "I know, Nestra. I know," he said soothingly.

"All right," I agreed at last, reluctantly. "Orestes stays in Phocis." I shut my eyes against the press of sudden tears. What was the point of crying anyway?

After a while Aegisthus said, "Electra needs a husband. We can't put that off any more, even if she is still young. She's neither pretty, nor sweet-natured, but someone must want her as a wife, if only for her status as princess of Mycenae. If she stays in the palace here she will sit and fester, and that will spread to others. She has to go."

I nodded. "I know that as well." I sighed. "I feel such a failure," I said sadly. "How is it possible to have everything you want and yet lose everything you want at the same time?"

"The gods' influence maybe, or perhaps our fate," he said. "Who knows what decides our lives?"

"What do you want, Aegisthus?" I asked eventually. "Everyone else wants something. What is your ambition?"

He rubbed his chin, in the way I knew meant he was

embarrassed, and looked at me shamefacedly. "I have everything I ever wanted and worked for, Nestra."

I made a 'pfffffd' noise of contempt, at the clumsy compliment.

"No," he said, reading my thought correctly. "I'm not trying to flatter you." He shifted uncomfortably. "I am lucky enough to share your bed, that's true, and it's something I value greatly. But others will point out I've won back the kingdom I lost to Agamemnon, without any fighting, simply by bedding his wife. My adversary is dead, again without effort on my part. The heir apparent has decamped voluntarily. Any dream I had of regaining my kingdom, of living in peace with my subjects, of a happy domestic life – these have all been achieved by the simple master stroke of sleeping with you."

I looked at him steadily, and his eyes dropped in embarrassment. I had heard this before from Electra and wondered whether it was the view the whole world took of my behaviour.

He raised his head and looked back at me.

"Nestra, I swear that when we met and loved, this was not a plan of mine. I wasn't trying to use you. But you must also see our lust has been very convenient for me." I was surprised at the bitterness in his tone.

I stood, and moved away from him.

"Do you regret it then?" I tried to keep the hurt from my voice, but I couldn't blind myself to the facts he was laying before me. A desolation I hadn't anticipated filled me. Had I been so stupid I couldn't see the only reason a man like Aegisthus would desire me was for the political gain I could bring?

He rose as well and came close to me. I stiffened, expecting his embrace. Instead he stood in front of me, not touching, but urgent in his manner. "Nestra, I swear by all I hold sacred, I have loved you from the day we met. You are my home, my family and my lover. But there are others saying what I have just laid out to you. Others are judging me in ways that offend my honour and dignity. We have had five years together to learn about each other. I trust you to know and respect me for what I am, as I respect you. I trust you, and I ask you to trust me. It is impossible to stop these comments being made. You asked me what I wanted, and I said I had everything I had ever wanted or worked for. I have more than I ever dreamt possible, thanks to you."

I looked full at him and tried to read deceit and deception in his eyes. I'm not good at interpreting men, I reminded myself. Yet all I saw was Aegisthus, for better or worse, the man I loved. If he had deceived me, or used me, I had lent myself willingly to his goals. Perhaps he had lent himself to mine. His presence in Mycenae had been useful since Myrto's death. His assistance and support had allowed me to fulfil my vow and take revenge on Agamemnon. Orestes had loved him. Who was I to judge his motives when my own were so complicated? I had used him equally, in every sense of the word.

That thought made me smile wryly and, watching my face, he caught the change of expression. I saw the mirroring leap of excitement in his eyes as he pulled me towards him.

"You are my woman, Nestra, and I love you. I want your love as well. Let nothing else change that, whatever else gets thrown at us. You are my strength, as I hope I am yours."

He kissed me so brutally hard I felt his cheekbone bruise my face as his lips crushed mine. I moaned beneath his fingers, not so much from pain, as from an excess of emotion. I felt him give a stifled laugh of triumph as he scooped me up, dumped me on the bed and proceeded to demonstrate the strength of his devotion.

Had we resolved the problems? No, of course we hadn't. But he was part of my life, as I was part of his.

By the end of the night we'd proved we didn't intend to change that.

CHAPTER
TWENTY EIGHT

❝WE HAVE A PROBLEM," HE SAID.

I glanced at him and he gave me a significant look, one that said he needed to speak to me alone.

I stood up and stretched. I had been taking a turn at the loom with the maids. It never failed to amaze me how much cloth the household used. In spite of five household slaves whose sole function was to keep the shuttles moving, we never had enough material. I saw it as my duty to lend a hand occasionally when I had the time. There was something soothing about the rhythmic backwards and forwards slap of the shuttle through the threads.

I gave the slaves a smile as I eased my back. "Good work," I said encouragingly.

They smiled shyly back at me, probably relieved I was going to leave them to it.

I walked out into the gardens with Aegisthus. The afternoon sun was warm, and the air rang with the noise of cicadas in the trees.

"What's the matter?" I asked.

"Electra," he said shortly.

I looked at him. Aegisthus was rarely rattled, his ability to absorb and deflect stress one of his most comfortable characteristics. Today he was tight-lipped and pinch-nosed with anger. I could feel the fury rolling off him.

I sank down onto the stone bench at the end of the path. "Tell me," I said.

"One of the messengers came to me. Electra had given him a message to take to Sparta, urging their army to come to her aid, invade Mycenae and rescue her. She intends to depose you and me and avenge her father." Aegisthus was breathing hard.

"To Sparta? You mean to Menelaus?"

When the Greek army returned from Troy Menelaus had peacefully resumed the rule of Sparta. Rather more surprisingly he had brought Helen back with him. Their marriage reconciled, she was once again Queen of Sparta. My sister had a cat-like ability to survive any catastrophe. We had received no word from either of them, although the news of Agamemnon's death must have reached them.

I pulled my mind back to Aegisthus.

"If it hadn't been a messenger we've known and dealt with for years, the message might have got through. Not every man is so honest and loyal," he said.

"Or else he weighed up the possible outcomes and decided which had the most chance of success," I said cynically. "I assume you've rewarded him well?"

"Very well. He's a much wealthier man today than he was yesterday. Still, this is treason, Nestra. Electra is deliberately setting out to destroy Mycenae's independence, to usurp your throne and allow a foreign kingdom to invade her own. She has to be stopped now – and permanently. You can't keep a viper like this around as a pet. One way or another she has to be crushed."

"I know." I thought unhappily of what we might have to do to stop her. She was still my daughter. I didn't like the thought of having to imprison her, let alone execute her for treason, but left unconstrained, she was dangerous.

We had sent out messengers to the royal houses of Greece

telling them Electra was ready for marriage but had received no interest from prospective suitors. I had hoped that Penelope's son, Telemachus, might be interested. He must be of an age with Electra, and I had made a point of requesting the messenger to visit Ithaca. He reported back that Telemachus was too busy dealing with his own problems to be interested in marriage. His father Odysseus had survived Troy but hadn't been seen since the fleet sailed for home. There had been no word of what had happened to him, and Penelope and Telemachus were in limbo. There was great pressure on Penelope to marry again, but she was refusing all offers. In such a climate, Telemachus sent his regrets, but he couldn't contemplate marriage himself.

I thought back to when it was my turn for wooing and the number of applicants who had applied for my hand. The number of Helen's suitors, of course, could have populated a small village. Poor Electra was paying the price of belonging to a family with an unfortunate matrimonial record. Even if that hadn't been an issue, the war with Troy had depleted the resources. Few kingdoms had enough to court foreign princesses. They were too busy trying to rebuild their shattered economies. Wooing royalty took a substantial investment.

"If only we could get her married," I said sadly. "I hoped a husband would solve the problem, particularly if he gave her children to keep her occupied. What else can we do? If we send her into exile she would be an ever-present danger, stirring up trouble wherever she goes. Surely some prince will want her eventually."

Aegisthus sat beside me. A leaf fluttered down into his lap from the wisteria shading the bower. He picked it up and began shredding it. "I don't think we have the luxury of time. The bitch has to be dealt with now."

I nodded my head glumly. He was right. Whatever he thought, Aegisthus had never before criticised my children, let alone used a term like 'bitch' to refer to Electra. Perhaps he knew it was a line no lover could ever safely cross. It said a lot that he was now prepared to. I rested my head against his shoulder.

"Do you have any bright ideas?"

He continued demolishing the leaf. "Not ones that you'd like," he said eventually.

"Anything's got to be better than nothing," I said. "I can't think clearly, I'm so shaken up with what you've told me."

He dropped the leaf and turned to me. "Nestra, whenever we've talked about Electra's marriage there's been an underlying assumption that we would only consider royal suitors for her hand. That hasn't worked, so what if we spread the net wider?"

"You mean a noble?" I considered the option. "Well, it's a possibility, I suppose, but it could disturb the balance of power in Mycenae and cause all sorts of upheaval. Given Electra's attitudes and ambitions, we'd be handing a very powerful weapon to any one of the noble families. Once she was married we wouldn't be able to control her. I think it would be dangerous."

Aegisthus shook what remained of the unfortunate leaf onto the ground. "I didn't mean a noble family," he said shortly.

"Pardon?" I looked at him in surprise. "What do you mean?"

He was gazing across the garden towards the far horizon. "Nobles aren't the only men available in Mycenae," he said harshly. "There are merchants, tradesmen, farmers, warriors, slaves."

I think my mouth may have opened I was so startled.

"You can't be serious? Marry a princess of Mycenae to a peasant? That's unthinkable." In spite of myself I was shocked.

Aegisthus wouldn't meet my eyes. "I didn't mean that we should marry her to a slave. I'm not lost to all sense, but there are decent and successful men who aren't nobles, Nestra. The one I'm thinking of could probably buy and sell most of our noble families. He's a merchant who owns a fleet of trading ships that work round the Mediterranean and bring Mycenae its wealth. He's a self-made man, and no prince or warrior, but what of it? Electra would have a good, comfortable life with a man who could provide her with luxury. I believe him to be decent and honourable, and in his house she'd have no outlet for her treachery or political ambition. Marriage to an ordinary citizen would automatically stop her being a beacon to any ambitious kingling who wants to threaten us."

I tried to swallow my outrage. Electra was heir to two royal lines – Mycenae and Sparta. How could I force this marriage on her? It would be so demeaning. I could only imagine her reaction to the loss of standing she would suffer. Any children she had would automatically be commoners. I hadn't realised I was so proud of my royal blood, but there it was. It had been bred into me, and I had no doubt Electra would feel the same.

"She'd hate it," I said. "I couldn't make her do it. She'd hate her husband for lowering her so. It would be a nightmare."

"Then what's your solution?" he asked. "I don't imagine you want her locked up in a cell for the rest of her life, and the other alternative is to execute her for treason. We can't leave her free to cause trouble, so, what bright ideas have you got?"

I was silenced. In my heart I knew Aegisthus was right. He might not like Electra; she'd never given him any reason to, but he wasn't petty or malicious. If I weren't the girl's mother, would I see things more clearly? I sighed. Years of ruling a great city state and I still couldn't manage one unruly daughter.

"Who is he?" My throat was tight and it made my words harsh. I cleared my throat and tried again. "I'm not saying I agree, you understand, but what's the man's name?"

Aegisthus smiled. "You know him well. Eumenides."

"Ahh." I did indeed know him. As Aegisthus said, he was a young man of good reputation and standing in Mycenae. He was also one of our wealthiest citizens, known for his generosity, giving to charity and supporting the local infirmary. We had met on many occasions, and I had always found him civil, intelligent and supportive.

I tried to think clearly and analytically. All those lessons in logic we had learned at school had to be useful for something. Although I thought of Eumenides as being very young, I realised he was probably thirty or thereabouts. He might seem young to me, but to sixteen-year-old Electra he was likely to come across as terribly old. That might not be a bad thing if it gave him some authority over her. I knew nothing to his discredit. Quite the contrary; he had a fine reputation as an honest, hard-working man. If you ignored the issue of his class, it would be a reasonable match. It would also keep Electra close to home where Aegisthus and I could keep a discreet eye on any trouble she tried to cause.

Reluctantly I nodded.

"Have you spoken to Eumenides about such a possibility?"

"Only obliquely," he replied. "I couldn't proceed without your permission. The match has advantages for him, of course. He allies himself with a royal patron and his children will have royal blood and a position in society far above any he could achieve purely by being a trader."

"And what for her?" I asked.

"She gets to keep her life," said Aegisthus brutally. "And she'll prefer being the lady of a household rather than kept as a prisoner at the bottom of a mineshaft for the rest of her life."

He stood up and turned to me. The sun was behind him, which made it difficult for me to look up into his face, but I absorbed the intensity in his tone.

"Electra may not like this solution, Nestra, but she was attempting high treason against her sovereign state. This isn't a little girl's naughtiness that can be dealt with by a smacking. Under different circumstances it could well have cost her her life. If she feels she is being punished, then I've no qualms about that. She needs to be punished severely for her treachery, and if her disparagement hurts her pride, so much the better. She's been arrogant, self-centred and childishly stupid for as long as I've known her. I very much hope this shocks her into good behaviour."

I couldn't deny what he was saying was correct, even if I didn't like it.

"Do you think Eumenides will be kind to her?" I asked.

"I imagine he'll spoil her rotten," he said. "Make no mistake, Nestra. If she accepts Eumenides and this marriage with a positive attitude, she'll be in clover for the rest of her life. Yes, I think she needs some chastisement, but you know I wouldn't be deliberately cruel. We aren't marrying her to a brute."

The details were agreed between the men. Orestes was absent, and in any case still too young to be Electra's formal guardian. Aegisthus was her nearest male relative, so I left the contract to him.

I summoned my daughter to my chamber, making sure Chryseis and Io were present in case she resorted to violence.

She entered with her usual sulky slouch.

"I have news for you," I said cheerfully, and congratulated her on the betrothal contracted for her.

I have seen a wine bladder collapse when stabbed. As if her legs no longer held her, Electra sagged the same way and collapsed onto the footstool.

I saw her try to speak, and fail.

She ran a tongue over her lips. "You can't," she croaked. "You can't do this to me."

"It's a good match," I said. I was determined to present everything that was positive about this wedding. "Eumenides is a lovely man, he has wealth, intelligence and a fine reputation. He'll make you a kind and wise husband."

"He's a peasant," Electra spat at me. "You can't wed a princess to a peasant, you stupid woman. You're just trying to ruin me."

"He's not a peasant at all," I said, trying to keep my voice light. "He's a successful trader and a good man. I'm sure you'll be very happy together."

"I won't do it," she declared, suddenly getting a rush of courage. She stood and faced me. I could see the fear and panic in her eyes and pitied her, but I had sworn to stay firm.

"You will do it, Electra," I said coldly. "It is a good match, and you will find him a kind man to be married to. No, don't," I added quickly as I saw her rage building, "don't tell me what you will or won't do. Whether you want to believe it or not, Aegisthus and I have your best interests at heart."

This time Electra actually spat at me. She missed and spattered the tiles.

I stepped back. Io rushed over with a cloth and wiped the globule off the floor.

"Be very careful, Electra," I warned. "We know of your

attempted treachery with Sparta. If you weren't my daughter and a princess of Mycenae, you would have been executed for your crime. Fortunately for you, I have the power to exercise clemency and condemn you to a life of imprisonment. That can still be your fate if you refuse this match. You won't see sunlight again."

I saw her pale. "That's a lie," she said. "Who accuses me of treachery?"

She hadn't expected the messenger to betray her. I thought about that.

"What did you bribe the messenger with?" I asked. "What idiocy made you attempt such treason and think you could get away with it? The messenger came straight to Aegisthus."

She gave a frightened little moan. "He couldn't have," she whispered.

"What did you promise him, Electra?" I asked again.

"I said I'd marry him," she blurted out. "I said he could be my husband when Mycenae was free."

My jaw dropped. "You promised a messenger you'd marry him? Just so he could deliver a message?" I gave a startled little laugh. "Well, at least the disparity in station and class between yourself and Eumenides obviously won't be a problem for you. You've already crossed that line, and Eumenides is several strata higher on the social scale than a messenger boy."

"Don't make me do this," she begged. "I didn't do anything. It was just a message to my Uncle Menelaus. It wasn't wrong."

"Don't lie, daughter, I've had enough of your nonsense. You marry Eumenides, and you will make him a good, true and loyal wife. Do you understand?" I turned to walk away.

"Please, no," she begged. "My brother won't allow it."

That stopped me. I turned back to her. "Your brother isn't here, and even if he were, he's not your guardian. Aegisthus is."

She swore at me, so I repeated Aegisthus's words about the need for her to receive punishment.

"If this stings you, Electra, then you've brought it on yourself. Actions have consequences. You choose to condemn me because I executed your father, and yet you try to do the same thing to your mother and betray me for much lesser cause than I had. Believe me, Mycenae won't be grateful if they hear you invited Sparta in. Make the best of it, Electra. Marry Eumenides and try to be happy for a change. I promise, you wed, or you spend the rest of your life in a cell."

"Take her out," I instructed Io. Electra's misery tore at me so, I could hardly bear to look at her.

Io took Electra by the arm and pulled the limp, sobbing girl from the room.

I collapsed onto the foot of my bed, utterly drained by the exchange.

Chryseis knelt on the bed behind me and began to work on the tight muscles in my shoulders.

"We need Nerissa," I said.

"She'll come to you later," promised Chryseis. "In the meantime, we need you to relax."

I gave a half-sob. "That wretched girl. She winds me up tighter than anyone else can. Pity help Eumenides. He'll have his work cut out."

Chryseis gave a sniff I interpreted as agreement but said nothing, her hands working and kneading the tension away.

CHAPTER
TWENTY NINE

W E WERE ALONE! WELL, DISCOUNTING SERVANTS, slaves and the other hangers-on that plagued and enhanced our lives.

Aegisthus swung me into his arms and danced a few steps across the terrace. I gave an embarrassingly girlish squeal as I demanded he put me down. He grinned, dropped his head and kissed me thoroughly. It was a short step from the terrace to the bedroom.

Was it wrong of me to feel this deep welling of joy? Electra's wedding had freed us. For the first time in years, Aegisthus and I were able to live the life we wanted, without considering the sensitivities of my children or the problems posed by my erstwhile husband. We were giddy with the simple joy of being lovers – with no tensions, duty or obligations.

The mornings disappeared as we lay in bed. We could be talking, reading or making love. There was little difference; it all enhanced our intimacy.

I looked at him one evening, fresh from the bathhouse. His hair, a grey and white patchwork when we met, was now snowy white. My own had long since lost colour. My waist had thickened, although I still prided myself on my figure. Viewed from a distance, through the dimness and smoke of the dining hall, I looked all right. I refused to discuss with anyone the hairs I pulled out on a daily basis from my chin. My menses had ceased some years back, so I was officially a crone, although Aegisthus and I coupled with all the enthusiasm of the young, but in rather less athletic positions.

"Have I become tame?" I asked Aegisthus one evening.

"Tame? As in a 'tamed wolf'?" He laughed. "You won't ever be tamed, my darling. Gentled, maybe. Wiser, kinder and more tolerant, most certainly. You aren't the brittle, scratchy creature I met all those years ago."

I was hurt and tried to hide it. "If I was that bad, why did you stay?" I asked as casually as I could.

He rolled over and faced me. His free hand stroked my breast, wandered over my nipple and gave it a light squeeze. "Because you were the most wonderful woman I had ever seen," he said. "Not the kindest, not the most holy and virtuous, not even the prettiest. You were beyond all those silly adjectives. You were the most completely authentic woman I'd ever known. You were a deep lake a man could bathe in and be refreshed; you were a Sphinx in your wisdom, and yet you had kindness." He gave an apologetic grin. "You taught me so much. I didn't know a woman could be strong, and yet so vulnerable. So brave, and have so many fears." His hand continued roving. "I didn't mean to love you."

I lay still, trying to work out whether this was a good or bad thing.

He gave a little sigh. "If I die, I will have been the better for the years I spent with you. Without you, I was a lost man. You made me whole."

My body stilled. I was a deer confronting a hunter. The extravagance of his words silenced me. I wanted to look at him, to assess his honesty.

He buried his face in my neck so I couldn't see it.

"Do you mean that?" I asked. "I think that's the nicest thing you, or anyone, has ever said to me."

"Of course I mean it," he said indignantly, raising his head from my neck. He rolled onto his back. "Just think. I was little more than a boy when Agamemnon ousted my father from the throne, then I spent years as an exile from my own country. I did anything I had to, just to get by. I had no family, no home." He gave a little laugh. "I must be the only warrior of my generation who didn't go rushing off to Troy to become a hero."

I hadn't thought about that before, but I supposed it was true.

"Did you really want to go to Troy?" I asked, intrigued. I hadn't imagined Aegisthus being interested.

"I wanted to go all right. I wanted to be part of the adventure, part of that masculine world of battle and conquest. It's a man's nature. We are reared to be warriors, and without a decent war, what are we? But I couldn't go. Who would I have served under? What kingdom was I part of? I couldn't have sailed with Agamemnon's ships."

I lay beside him. "So when you came here …?"

"I came because Agamemnon wasn't here. I wanted to see my native land, and it was my opportunity. Then, I met you, and everything changed."

"I thought you were such a dashing, romantic figure when you first arrived," I said. "The mysterious stranger; the homeless wanderer who went from place to place having exotic adventures."

Aegisthus chuckled into the dark beside me. "In truth, I was just another vagrant, until I met my queen." He reached over and pulled me to him.

"I'm glad you came to Mycenae," I said drowsily. "It must have been meant."

"Let's agree to live today," he said. "Not in the past, not in the future, but today when we can choose joy and happiness."

I sleepily agreed.

Neither of us spoke of the future. Electra's malice may have been contained within Eumenides' household, but both Aegisthus and I knew that, far off in Phocis, a more potent danger lay. If Orestes meant us well he would have returned home by now. We could only assume him poisoned by Electra's bitterness. I mourned his loss, mourned the years of his growing I would never see. His absence was a small but persistent pain I kept in my heart.

I saw Eumenides from time to time, in the market, or at trade delegations to the palace. He was always courteous in his dealings with Aegisthus and myself and made no remarks about anything Electra may have said. Equally, he made no criticism of her. I couldn't establish whether the marriage was happy or not. I asked, with mindless frequency, about the possibility of her being pregnant but received no satisfactory answer. If she was in the family way, then he wasn't going to tell me. If not, and they were having problems, it was clear my intervention wasn't wanted.

I closed my mind to the worries of parenthood. Electra didn't need or want me, and Orestes was beyond any help I could give. Aegisthus was right. We had to live in the present, and for each other.

Times were good. I could feel excitement and optimism when I walked through the markets. Trade had improved. The men returned from the wars were being assimilated, and their labour and productivity were lifting our trade figures. Mycenae was exporting its grain, horses and natural resources in the form of ores. We were importing luxury goods from Asia. For the first time in many years we were showing a healthy surplus that wasn't eroded by the needs of the army at Troy.

Life was good. In the evenings, we toasted each night to 'the gods and the blessings they bestow'. Each libation we poured carried a prayer for continued safety and prosperity.

CHAPTER THIRTY

CHRYSEIS, IO, NERISSA AND I SAT under the lime tree. The garden was full of the noise of cicadas, and bees lazily making their way through the flowers. The afternoon heat was heavy, but it was pleasant in the shade. I was idly winding spun wool into a ball from Io's outstretched hands. The heavy scent of lanolin from the wool clung to my fingers.

"At least my hands will be well moisturised," I remarked, looking at the age spot that had appeared on the back of my right hand. I supposed it was to be expected. I was fifty-three years old, a fair age for a woman, and although the thought of the years didn't trouble me, the changes in my body could catch me unaware. I used to pride myself on the fineness and elegance of my hands, I thought ruefully.

Charis was lounging on cushions in the sunlight, playing the flute. The fierce light burnished her dark hair with red glints. She broke into a light country dance, the trills and syncopation recalling celebrations from years before. I felt a pleasant nostalgia.

"What time are you expecting her?" Nerissa's voice broke

into my thoughts.

"Oh, soon. She said early afternoon."

In spite of myself I was nervous. Electra's visit would be the first contact of a private nature we had shared in many years. I had seen her occasionally with her husband, but she had always chosen to ignore me.

Yesterday I had received a message requesting I allow her to visit me. She wanted, she said, to present her new baby to its grandmother. I was beside myself with excitement, both because of the child, but also with hope that now, as a mother herself, Electra would be more open to my advances. Age can mellow us, and there is nothing like a child of one's own to make us reassess our relationship with our mothers.

It would be so good if we could let the past go and enjoy the present. I prayed the gods would let it be so.

Charis laid down her flute and stretched forward for the jug of chilled wine. As she started to fill her mug, there was a sudden scream from within the palace. Charis dropped her drink, spilling the wine over the cushions.

The scream was followed by shouts and voices raised in panic. I could hear the sound of people running.

Charis jumped to her feet.

"I'll go and see what's happened," and she was off, running towards the door.

"It's probably only the cook burning the dinner," said Chryseis calmly as she started to mop the wine up from the cushions. I glanced at her, but her eyes were focused on the door where Charis had disappeared.

"I hope so," I murmured, putting down the wool and wiping my hands, "but a scream like that seems a bit excessive."

Charis came running through the door a few minutes later, saw me and checked her pace. I saw her urgency vanish as she looked at me, and I knew the news was bad. I stood to hear it.

"My lady," she gasped. "I don't know what to say." She looked at me helplessly, and I could see the tears start in her eyes.

"Go on," I said impatiently. "Whatever it is, you can't break it to me gently. Just tell me."

"Aegisthus is dead," she blurted. "He's been stabbed. His body lies in the great hall."

I started running. It was dark inside the palace after the bright light, and I nearly tripped on the threshold in my haste. I could hear the rising noise of chatter from the servants as I ran towards the hall. They saw me enter and stood back, leaving a clear space for me to walk forward.

Aegisthus must have been killed instantly. His body was crumpled on the floor. A tide of blood flowed from the left side of his chest and spread a stain beneath his body. I knelt beside him, pulled back the cloth of his tunic and examined the wound. Whoever killed him had stabbed him with one powerful thrust. There was only one point of entry.

From memories of my school days, I remembered our drill sergeant telling us how difficult it can be to negotiate the ribs in such a cut, but this had been done neatly and effectively. There was no evidence the killer had met with resistance. Aegisthus must have had no suspicion of the danger.

I stroked his face. It was still warm. Impossible that his eyes wouldn't twinkle as he sat up and told me it was a joke. I gave a ragged sob and gently closed his eyes. It felt like turning out a lantern. I took his hand and knelt beside him as the grief hit me with full force.

I stayed beside him a long time while my heart and mind struggled with a world that had no Aegisthus in it. He had been my lodestone, my north star, my anchor.

At last I raised my head and looked around me at the frightened faces. "What happened?" I asked. "Who did this thing?"

There was some mumbling, but no one spoke up. I heard the shuffle of feet and saw eyes slide from my face so nobody had to answer me.

I turned my head back to look at my dead love. I raised his hand to my lips, straightened my spine and knelt back on my heels looking at the group around me. "Well?" I said. "Someone must be able to tell me."

It seemed no one was brave enough to say, and I was becoming impatient with the evasion. Then, like the best theatre troupe in the land, the mass of people parted as she walked through them. I looked up into the animated face of my daughter, read the malice and triumph in her smile and realised there had been no reconciliation, no new baby, no hope for the future. Her visit had been a ruse to ensure easy entry to the palace for the assassin.

I knew the answer to my question then, before she opened her mouth.

"Orestes," she declaimed loudly. "Orestes has come to avenge the murder of our father."

Again there was a shuffling and muttering among the onlookers.

There was nothing for me to say, so I didn't try. I turned my back on Electra and returned my attention to Aegisthus. I could hear the crowd's chatter. They would be deciding which side to back.

Nerissa and Chryseis had come to kneel beside me.

I drew a shuddering breath and tried to take leave of the man who had given me so much. All older couples carry death's shadow on them. Neither discussed nor acknowledged, we know it's there. Our mortality is implicit in our wrinkles and the aches in our joints. We look at our lover and read the same signs. One will die first – the other will have to live on alone. We become tolerant of this foreshadowing as we age, even while we deny we are old.

I should be able to say goodbye to my love with dignity and acceptance. Instead the pain and pity of his murder was a dagger in my breast. I saw his poor, abused flesh, and grief swept me.

"Chryseis," I started, then found my throat was too blocked to speak and I couldn't get any sound out.

I tried again. "Chryseis." At least this time a whisper emerged.

"Stay with him, please. Make sure he is prepared for his funeral. I don't want him left alone."

Her hand squeezed my shoulder. "Of course not," she said. "Nerissa and I will prepare him with honour."

I looked up at the group surrounding us, ignoring Electra. I could see the captain of the guard hovering at the edge of the crowd. He looked distraught, as well he might.

"Lift Aegisthus up, and take him to where Chryseis directs," I said. "Let all be done with dignity."

He nodded. "Lady, I am so sorry. Electra vouched for them. I am so sorry." Poor man, he was virtually wringing his hands.

"The fault is not yours," I said curtly as I turned away to Aegisthus.

I kissed his hand once again, before laying it carefully on his chest. I stood up and took my last look at his flesh.

"Wait for me," I whispered to his shade. "It won't be long and I will join you. Wait so we can make the journey together."

I returned to the garden.

Charis put her arm round my shoulders, lead me to a seat in the sun and thrust a mug of wine into my hands. "Drink," she urged. "It will help steady you."

I slugged back the wine, and she refilled the mug. I had started to shiver in spite of the sun's heat, and she threw a stole over my shoulders.

"It's just shock," I said.

She gave a grim chuckle. "I know it's shock. Even so, the wine and the warmth will help the body's reaction."

I sat quietly, letting my thoughts drift. Implicit in Aegisthus's death was the certainty of my own, and soon. I tried the thought out and found I didn't care much. I wondered if it would hurt, whether Aegisthus had suffered when the sword cut him. I couldn't summon up the urge to be afraid. Fear depends on having something to care about, and I had nothing left. That knowledge framed my grief for my dead love. I wouldn't be alive to mourn him long; I needed to endure the pain of his passing for only a short period before I joined him. I comforted myself with the thought, although I couldn't control the surges of grief that possessed me. Aegisthus's death seemed so wasteful. I moaned at the pity of it all.

"I wonder where he is," I said eventually. "Orestes, I mean. He must still be in the palace, but where?"

"Do you want us to find out?" asked Io. "Should we call out the guard?"

I shook my head. "No. This is an accounting I hoped would

never happen, for his sake more than for mine. But the die is cast, and Orestes is here for revenge. Let it be."

They both cried out at that, but I shook my head. I felt so very weary, so tired my head didn't seem to want to work properly.

I sat for a long time, my head bowed, my hands clasped uselessly in front of me. Eventually the sun's warmth became uncomfortable, and I went from intense cold to sweatily hot and had to move.

I looked at my companions as I stood up. We had been together for so many years we were more than mistress and slaves. They were my friends, and they both looked stricken. I gave them a shaky smile. "He died quickly," I said. "He must have known very little." I wondered if Aegisthus even had time to recognise Orestes. The boy he had known would now be a man.

"I want to go inside," I said. "Io, could you go and help Nerissa and Chryseis with the laying out? Charis, come with me. I need to prepare."

I didn't elaborate on what my preparations were for, and Charis seemed surprised when I required her to wash my hands, change the dress stained with Aegisthus's blood and dress my hair. Perhaps she thought I would be issuing a call to arms for the guard, but she didn't question me.

I was grateful for her silence.

When she had finished, she brought me more wine and some olives. I thanked her and dismissed her. She started to protest, but I waved her away.

"Thank you, Charis, but I need to be alone now."

She left reluctantly.

I looked at my reflected image, trying to understand what Orestes would see when he came to me. If he had changed, then so had I. I looked every one of my years.

Was I afraid to die? I probed that thought again, as you would a missing tooth, and found no pain. I would welcome death if it meant I could join Aegisthus.

"Wait for me," I said again.

I tried to compose my mind for prayer and contemplation, to ready myself for the afterlife, but such thoughts require a quiet mind, and mine was seething with swirling emotions. There was grief, of course, in its many facets, for Aegisthus, for Orestes and even for Electra. I tried to envisage a tomorrow without me in it but lacked the imagination. I wondered what Mycenae's fate would be without Aegisthus or me to protect and guard her. Had Orestes returned for the throne as well as for vengeance? Did he intend to rule? I wasn't native born but I had given my life to serving this city I had come to as a bride. I would like Mycenae to have a good ruler.

I thought bleakly that Electra's judgment was the one that would be accepted by history. I didn't suppose I would be remembered as a great queen and custodian. I would be remembered as the queen who murdered her husband and was, in turn, murdered by her son. Our priests teach that our fate in the afterlife depends on being remembered and honoured by the living. By such measure, I was unlikely to reach Elysium, regardless of how well I had honoured the gods during my life, or however many sacrifices I had offered. I just hoped the gods judged us by our good intentions, otherwise I was likely to be sentenced to Tartarus.

I didn't care. I just wanted to be with Aegisthus, wherever we were sent.

I took the wine and went outside to the terrace to look over the city. The view was beautiful, and in the far distance I could see the sea.

It was pleasantly cool but the balustrade and pillars held the warmth of the day's sun and pressed comfortably against my back as I sat on the railing in the twilight. Beyond, in the shrubbery, I could hear the susurrations of little night creatures starting to go about their business. The scent of jasmine hung in the still air and it was magically beautiful. Moonrise would be early tonight. Last night it was full and lit my room with its silver light.

It was as good as anywhere to wait. I shut my eyes and leaned back against the pillar and let the long minutes pass.

CHAPTER
THIRTY ONE

'We can and must pray to the gods that our sojourn on earth will continue happy beyond the grave. This is my prayer, and may it come to pass.'

Plato: The Death of Socrates

I HAD THE ADVANTAGE, MY EYES HAVING been long adjusted to the dark. He came onto the terrace silhouetted against the flickering lights inside the palace. He paused and advanced cautiously. He knew I was there, but seated in the moon shadow of the pillar, I was invisible. I watched him in silence for some minutes, trying to take his measure. What sort of man had he become? Was there anything left of the loving, laughing boy I had cherished?

At last I moved slightly. He was quick. I saw him swing towards me, then stop some five paces off. We looked at each other warily.

I broke the silence.

"Good evening, Orestes." I cursed myself for such a banal greeting, but truly, what else was there to say? Sometimes courtesy is the only defence.

I heard the quick intake of his breath. He said nothing, but shifted his weight. Something in his motion tore at my heart. He still had some of the awkwardness of a boy about him. I looked at him, searching for family similarities. His early resemblance to his father had gone. He was taller and slighter than Agamemnon. Where his father had been built like a wrestler with short, bulky musculature, Orestes was of finer build, with long, lean muscles. He looked like a runner.

Unconsciously my head tipped sideways as I assessed him. If anything, I thought, he looked most like my own father Tyndareus. I could see the resemblance in the shape of the eyes and nose.

He gave a sort of growl. "Stop staring at me, Mother."

I gasped. His voice was deep.

"Sorry," I said. "You look like your grandfather Tyndareus."

He turned awkwardly, shaking his head as if to ward off the comment. "I'm here to avenge my father," he said roughly.

The words fell like stones between us.

"I know," I replied.

The words said, he seemed at a loss to know how to proceed.

"Come and sit beside me," I invited. "Talk for a while."

I saw anger in his face. "You won't sway me by sweet talk. I have a duty to perform."

"I wasn't trying to stop you," I said tartly. "You're the one with the sword in your hand, which you can use anytime you want."

Aegisthus's words came back to me. *Don't talk to your victim, just kill them.* Now I understood his meaning. Talk weakens a killer.

Orestes looked embarrassed. I could almost feel sorry for him.

I marvelled at my calm. "I haven't seen you in seven years," I said more softly. "Can you not satisfy my curiosity for a few moments? We loved each other once."

"What do you want to know?"

Everything. What sort of a man have you become? Have you a woman? Are you happy? Have you had a good life?

I shook my head and didn't ask any of them.

"Promise me you will rule Mycenae wisely."

He looked startled. Perhaps he'd never considered his responsibilities to the kingdom.

"It's your inheritance. You are the last heir."

"I don't know. I've not thought about it."

Silence fell between us.

"I have missed you terribly," I said. "There has never been a day when your absence hasn't grieved me." I found I needed him to know that, and with that need came others, as if my heart had come back to life. "I want you to know I have always loved you," I said. It would be terrible to die and not have told him. It was terrible to die and never regain the love we had lost. Regret pierced me for all that could have been but wasn't.

"Will you grant me your forgiveness for what I have to do?"

I stared at him in amazement. Old habits resurfaced: the reactions of a mother, eager to please her son. I was almost tempted to agree, before common sense reasserted itself.

"No. You know I cannot do that," I said sadly. "You killed Aegisthus, a man unfailingly kind to you. There was no justice in that death. It was murder. And as for my death, matricide offends all gods. There is not a female god in all Olympus who will not curse you for the act."

He bowed his head. "I must do my duty," he muttered.

Against my will my body betrayed me and I began to shake. I hated that he would see it, know that at the end I was afraid.

He hesitated then, and my nerves and patience wore thin. I could see his anguish, and it dragged at my heart. I hurt him by living, I hurt him by dying, this son I loved with all my being.

I took a wobbly breath. Better to get it over with. There was no easy way to go through this, and the knowledge made me rough with him. "Oh, never mind," I said curtly. "Get on with it then. I only ask that you give Aegisthus and me a decent burial with proper funeral rites. There is no need to shame us in death."

I lowered my feet to the ground and stood, readying myself for the blow. I could barely force myself to stand upright, my knees were shaking so hard. I couldn't have taken a step forward.

"Make it quick and clean," I asked. I was ashamed that my

voice wobbled.

"I don't want to do this, but I must," he said. The words were wrung from him. I saw the pain in his eyes."

"So be it," I replied. We stood still for a moment. There was nothing left to say.

I was watching his eyes and saw them change. He reached for my arm and spun me quickly so I staggered back against his shoulder. I saw the sword lift to my throat, felt it penetrate my flesh. I heard rather than felt the skin tear, but there was little pain. I tasted the metallic taste of my own blood in my mouth as he made the cut. The world spun and for a moment it became dark.

And then I stepped free.

I watched as Orestes slowly lowered my discarded flesh to the ground, and winced at the terrible groan of grief he made.

I turned to the shade that stood at my shoulder and smiled. Aegisthus was with me, as I had known he would be. I looked behind once more at my son, now prostrate and crying beside the body I had left. Then, still smiling, I turned to walk beside Aegisthus, together on that dark road.

AUTHOR'S
NOTE

Aftermath

IN AESCHYLUS'S DRAMATIC TRILOGY, *THE ORESTEIA*, prior to confronting Clytemnestra, Orestes had visited the oracle at Delphi to ask the god Apollo what he should do to avenge his father. The oracle replied that Orestes must kill his mother and her lover. Matricide, however, is a terrible sin. Following Clytemnestra's death, the Furies, spirits of justice and vengeance, were enraged by his bloodguilt and pursued Orestes, tormenting him and driving him mad.

Orestes fled to Delphi, but Apollo was powerless to help him against the Furies. Eventually the oracle instructed Orestes to go to Athens and present his case to the Areopagus, the ancient court of the elders. During the trial that followed, Orestes was supported both by Apollo and Athena, goddess of Athens. The jury was divided equally on their verdict, and Athena cast the deciding vote for acquittal. The Furies were eventually placated and given a cult in which they were called the Eumenides (the Kindly Ones).

Orestes returned to Mycenae where he became ruler and eventually married Hermione, the daughter of Menelaus and Helen.

*   *   *

Clytemnestra's story has fascinated people from Classical Greece through to contemporary times. This retelling of her life is an attempt to see and honour the woman behind the myth. Her motive for murdering her husband is usually presented as a political plot to bring her lover Aegisthus to power, or alternatively as jealous rage because Agamemnon brings Cassandra back from Troy with him. The more obvious motive, at least to my mind, of vengeance for Iphigenia's murder, is largely ignored or treated as a relatively minor subtext by the ancient playwrights.

Writing this novel has posed several problems. Many modern readers may only be familiar with Homer's *Illiad* by way of the 2004 film *Troy*, a rather loose interpretation of Homer's story which focussed exclusively on the Trojan war. In that adaptation the story of Clytemnestra had no part. Other readers may be familiar with her story through the plays of Aeschylus and Euripides, although the myths and themes on which the plays are based come from much earlier sources, and there are several different and sometimes contradictory versions of events.

One tradition has it that Clytemnestra's first husband was Tantalus, King of Pisa. Agamemnon kills both Tantalus and their young son before making Clytemnestra his wife.

Other variants are that Artemis substituted a young doe for Iphigenia on the altar at Aulis, whisking the girl away to serve in her temple at Tauris. Subsequent to his trial, Apollo orders Orestes to go to Tauris and bring back the statue of Artemis. There the siblings recognise each other and escape together, taking the statue with them.

For the purpose of writing this novel, I have relied largely on Homer's telling of the story and elected to use the most straightforward sequence of events as the narrative, although where possible I have mentioned such variants as serve to enrich the plot.

Until the mid-nineteenth century, the Trojan War was considered to be non-historical, but the German archaeologist Heinrich Schliemann was convinced that Troy was at Hissarlik in Turkey, and he took over the excavations on the site from its previous owner. This identification is now largely accepted by scholars. Whether the Trojan War actually occurred as Homer described is a harder question to answer. Those who believe the stories are true point to archaeological evidence of a catastrophic burning of Troy apparent at one level of the excavated ruins. If true, the war is generally dated between 1260 and 1240 BC, at the end of the Mycenaean period.

As Homer didn't compose *The Iliad* and *The Odyssey* until the 8th or 7th century BC, several centuries after the events, it is reasonable to assume his stories are a fusion of tales circulating around ancient sieges and expeditions by the Mycenaeans during the Bronze Age.

I have simplified place names and certain terminology. Greece, of course, did not exist as a unified country until 1830, but I refer to 'the Greek army' as a simple collective to cover the myriad of kings and kingdoms involved in the Trojan conflict.

Perhaps the hardest part of writing this book has been evoking a culture where patricide, matricide and fratricide are acceptable as tools to fulfil oaths of vengeance. The culture of war, violence and blood feud is a very different ethos to modern Western sensibilities, although it is not hard to find instances of it even today in our news media. I have elected a *plus ça change, plus c'est la même chose* approach, where I posit that human nature and motivations have changed little over the centuries, although cultural expressions of dangerous emotions may have altered as society has developed. We enjoy Shakespeare's plays, or the Classical Greek tragedies precisely because we can still understand what drives the protagonists in these dramas.

Please continue reading for a bonus excerpt from Penelope Haines's first novel in the *Claire Hardcastle* Series –

DEATH ON D'URVILLE

PROLOGUE

THE BODY SLUMPED IN THE SAND. An abandoned shell of lifeless flesh, incontrovertibly dead. *Dead, dead, dead.*

The words rang in the head and twined into a chain. A necklace of finality that could be grasped and wound round the fist like a talisman; a rosary of the joyful mysteries; a protection against the evil this man had tried to spread.

But his words weren't dead. He was a writer and they would still live on in his computer.

They must be destroyed.

It was a short step to the house. A quick glance around to see if there were watchers, but the landscape was empty. The house was unlocked. Who locked their home here, when the total population of the bay only grew to around twenty, and that in high summer?

The laptop sat on the table. A tea towel wrapped round the hand to prevent fingerprints. Fumbling to find the keys through the cloth, but it was easy to identify and erase the file.

It would have been useful to have time to search the place, but that would have to wait. For now it was enough to know the man and his words had been wiped out.

CHAPTER
ONE

I FELT THE WHEELS TOUCH ON GRAVEL and let the aircraft roll forward down the strip. I gave a sigh of completely unadulterated pleasure. (I was alone and entitled to do so.) God, but I loved my job, and on a day like that when the sky was clear, the wind calm and the surroundings so breathtakingly beautiful, I couldn't believe my good fortune. My office was my plane. It didn't come much closer to heaven than that.

I turned the aircraft and taxied back, pulling off the strip in the space beside the barn. It was the only area wide enough for me to park without obstructing the runway. Another aircraft was already there in the shade of the dunes. I took a look and gave a snort of recognition. I knew that plane, knew it really well. ZK-FOG was registered to Paraparaumu Aviation, and I had watched Roger sign her out to a pair of foreign pilots a week ago. The little Piper Cub was supposed to be miles to the east of us, somewhere in the vicinity of Kaikoura.

How it had ended up on the strip at D'Urville Island I couldn't imagine. I thought Roger would be surprised as well. He had authorised the pilots to fly in New Zealand and accepted their intentions when he leased the aircraft. I wondered whether he had specifically briefed the pair for strip flying. It's one thing to land at a promulgated airport, quite another to fly into the often unpredictable conditions experienced on little country strips. There could be insurance repercussions if the pilots had strayed beyond the limits of their hire.

I parked into the wind and shut the engine down. I clambered out and took a minute or two to stretch my legs before climbing up to dip the wing tanks and check the fuel levels.

Jorge wasn't there waiting for me, which was unusual, nor was there any sign of FOG's two pilots. I looked at my watch. 3.50 pm. I hoped Jorge wasn't going to be late. Sod's Law if he was, of course.

It had been a year since David and I separated, a year of quiet living while I readjusted to singledom. I hadn't seen anyone significant, and hadn't wanted to. Tonight's dinner with Sam would be my first venture into the social world of dating. I wasn't certain it was a good idea. Sam was a nice guy but …

It was the 'but' that worried me. I wasn't sure whether the issue was Sam, or my response to him. I appreciated his sense of humour, and found him a pleasant colleague. We'd met at work where he had a habit of popping in for a visit in his spare time from running the flight information service in the airport tower. I liked him, but he didn't set my world ablaze. Still, at twenty-six, did I really expect a guy to sweep me off my feet? I'd already invested four years of my life in one unsatisfactory relationship.

David had once set me on fire, and there had been a time when we seemed very good together. We'd even talked about getting married. I eventually realised the months I'd waited for him to propose to me were, unfortunately, being replaced by an increasing number of months when such a proposal would be deeply unwelcome.

I'd been shocked two years ago when my mother's death forced me to understand I'd unconsciously fallen into a pattern of behaviour with David modelled on her own unsatisfactory relationship with my father. Luckily I'd recognised it in time.

I took stock of my situation. I wanted more from life than David would ever understand, and our expectations and ambitions were increasingly divergent. Finally, I gathered my courage, confronted him and severed the relationship. David, predictably, had no idea what I was talking about and blamed the whole debacle on mysterious 'women's issues', which rather proved my point.

I looked along the airstrip to the north. Still no sign of Jorge. I decided to follow the other track that led through the sand dunes down to the beach. Greville Harbour's particular geography means the beautiful crescent of the bay is separated from the airstrip by a wide stretch of dunes. The only chance I had of getting cell phone reception was to climb to the top of one and hope I picked up a signal. I plodded down the track, found a likely hill and climbed to its summit.

I phoned Jorge's mobile; it went straight to answerphone. Either he had it switched off, or more likely, he was out of range and already walking towards the plane. I shrugged and called Paraparaumu Aviation.

My boss answered, and I filled him in on FOG's presence on the strip. He sounded surprised at first, then amused.

"Crafty buggers," he commented. "No, I'm not worried about their competence, but they certainly didn't tell me they were planning to end up on D'Urville. I'm surprised they even found the strip. It's not that easy to spot from the air unless you know where it is. Ah well, no harm done, but I'll have a word when they get back."

He confirmed there had been no message from Jorge warning me he would be late. I sighed, hung up and looked round. Off the headland at the southern end of the bay I could see a small boat in the water. Matt and his family out fishing, I guessed.

I began the walk north along the sand towards Jorge's bach.

I was in a catch-22 situation. I couldn't see the airstrip from the beach, nor could anyone on the strip see me, but if Jorge arrived he would at least see the plane ready, and realise I had gone searching for him.

If I hadn't felt pressured by the need to be back in Paraparaumu in time for my date with Sam, I would have enjoyed the exercise. Greville is a lovely curve of sand, and I walked its length in solitude, the silence only broken by the calls of the seagulls.

I had reached the northern end of the beach, at the foot of the steps that led to the terrace and Jorge's bach, when I heard the roar of FOG's engine as she took off from the strip. I stood, gazing up, shielding my eyes from the setting sun, as the little Cub climbed out of the harbour and up over the sea. I could see her making the eastward turn which would bring her up over the range towards Cook Strait, and then a direct path back to her home airport.

I grinned. I'd missed seeing the pilots. They must have come back via the landward track.

I climbed the steps. Jorge's bach lay to the left. Ahead was the 'mystery house'. I had been flying into D'Urville for two years or more, and this house was always deserted. I had no idea who owned it.

With a shock, I saw the house was occupied. Windows and the front door were flung wide open, and a young couple were sitting on the deck, legs dangling over the edge into the tussock grass, while the man fed driftwood into their brazier. I reached up to wave.

The man gave a perceptible start when he saw me but replied with a tentative gesture of his own. His companion, whom I saw was very young, registered my presence with a sort of horror, sprang to her feet and bolted inside. She was a little too far away for me to be certain, but I got the impression she had been crying.

I shrugged, nodded again to the man and made my way to Jorge's.

He wasn't at home, which was fine if he was already at the strip waiting for me, but it was soon obvious to me that he hadn't locked the house up. I tried the back door, found it open and went in. The backpack Jorge normally carried was propped against the wall. With insufficient baggage to fill out its interior it had collapsed in its mid-section with a sad, sagging look of a failed fighter about it. The straps were undone and trailed loosely across the floor. I picked it up to check. Jorge had made no attempt to even begin packing.

I looked around. Jorge was a writer, and if what he said was true, he spent his days on D'Urville either wandering the hills or writing his novels. Early on he had discovered I was a reader – in that broad sense of the word that describes a person who reads everything from Victorian novels to the writing on cereal packets.

We had discussed books and explored our mutual interest in words during our flights to and from the island. It had become a game – a challenge between us, for each to bring a new and unusual word to the conversation every time I ferried him to the island. Today I had chosen 'solipsistic'. I was reasonably certain he wouldn't know the word, but sometimes he surprised me. Like many people for whom English is a second language, his vocabulary was considerable and eclectic.

A year or so back he'd shown me the cover design he'd chosen for his latest novel, featuring a man heavily clad in some space-age type of armour with a scantily dressed blonde, bound in chains, at his feet. I gathered the story was set in some dystopian future, was ultraviolent and possibly pornographic.

He had laughed at the expression on my face. "Trust me, Claire, there's a market for my books. They're very popular and sell particularly well in Japan and Germany."

It wasn't the kind of book that appealed to me, but I could see his life at the bach would be congenial for whatever muse inspired his work. With no Wi-Fi, television or phones to distract him, he could, as he said, churn out a couple of thousand words a day, and frequently more.

The sink was full of dishes, and his laptop sat open on his desk, a book beside it. With the automatic habit of a recidivist bibliophile I checked the title. *Horowhenua: its Maori place-names & their topographic & historical background.* I flicked through the pages. It looked interesting but didn't get me any nearer to finding Jorge. He wasn't the tidiest of men, but I had never known him leave the house without cleaning up and packing out the rubbish.

I wondered whether, by some bizarre series of errors, I had come on the wrong day. I pulled out my phone to call Roger, but there was no signal. I cursed, shoved the phone back into my pocket and left the bach.

The man at the mystery house was still tending his fire, which had now caught and was burning merrily in the grate. I waved again as I passed.

Feeling grumpy, I took the inland track back to the airstrip. The path led deeper into the dunes before emerging on the landward side of them, on the shores of the lagoon. This brackish store of swampy water was home to a wide variety of fowl, the most numerous and dramatic being the black swans. Flax, bulrushes and sedge lined the edges. It was an attractive spot, protected by the seaward dunes from any coastal breezes, so the temperature remained warmer than average all year long. This late in the season the Department of Conservation campsite here was empty. It was getting too cold at night to tempt punters in a tent. Even in high summer there were rarely more than two tents pitched on the site.

I strode along, in equal part perturbed and annoyed. Either I had got the wrong date, or something had happened to Jorge. I tried not to worry, but D'Urville is a bush-covered island of steep, mountainous terrain. A lot could go wrong for a middle-aged man, inexperienced in bush craft, who ventured unwisely into territory he couldn't handle.

I had swung past a series of sand dunes before I stopped, realising something in the recurring pattern of marram grass, tussock and sand looked odd. I traced my unease to a huddle of material half-visible in a bowl amongst the dunes and walked over to see the anomaly more clearly.

Jorge was lying sprawled in the hollow at the foot of a dune, just off the track. He was motionless, his head half turned away from me.

DEAR READER,

Thank you for reading *Helen Had a Sister* (previously published as *Princess of Sparta*). I hope you enjoyed it.

Nestra's story was one I always knew I would write. I have been fascinated by Ancient Greek myths and stories since I was a child. My father, who loved Classical Greek culture and literature, told me many of the myths as bedtime stories. When I was seven, my parents took me to Greece on holiday, and I vividly remember going to Delphi where the oracles were delivered; Crete, where the Minotaur was slain; and Delos where Apollo was born. The physical historical evidence of these sites made the stories even more compelling to my childish imagination.

At some point in my teens I was rereading *The Odyssey* and realised how interconnected the tales were. The Trojan War provided a focus around which other myths were massaged to make a coherent narrative. Generations of storytellers adapted the tales to fit this pivotal event. Thus Theseus, famous for slaughtering the Minotaur, is brought into the story as the first abductor of Helen of Sparta. The house of Atreides with its terrible history becomes Agamemnon's heritage. My own namesake, Penelope, the long-suffering wife of Odysseus, is cousin to Helen of Troy and her sister Clytemnestra.

These three women, with their vastly different reputations and fortunes, intrigued me, and I knew then it was a story I wanted to tell.

As an author and teller of stories I love feedback from my readers. You are the reason I write, so tell me what you liked, what you loved and what you hated. I'd love to hear from you.

You can write to me at penelope@penelopehaines.com.

Finally, I need to ask a favour of you. If you're so inclined, I'd appreciate a review of *Helen Had a Sister*. As you may know, reviews can be tough to come by. If you have the time, leave a review at Amazon.com or Goodreads.com. You, the reader, now have the power to make or break the book.

Thank you so much for reading *Helen Had a Sister*.

In gratitude,

Penelope

ACKNOWLEDGEMENTS

To each of you who helped me write *Helen Had a Sister*, some in small ways, others hugely, my heartfelt thanks.

First in line are those tolerant souls who read the earliest drafts and guided me into forming the whole into a coherent narrative. Renee van de Weert once again provided support, encouragement and suggestions. The wonderful team in the office, Kelly Pettitt and Ruth Holman, were pressed into service as beta readers, and I owe an inestimable debt to Kelly in particular for her frank but constructive criticism during the various revisions of the original draft. Kelly is also responsible for the cover artwork, the photograph of me inside the back cover and was a godsend as my personal IT division every time I ran into problems with the computer or with formatting.

Sue Reidy and Tina Shaw provided invaluable criticism and guidance during the draft process. They were patient and helpful in the advice they offered. I also owe thanks to Debbie Watson for early proofreading. Finally, my deepest thanks to Adrienne Morris who proofread and edited the final manuscript.

My gratitude to my husband Cavan who sustained me, helped in a thousand ways and never failed to encourage me.

My thanks to Reilly for spending the long hours with me, and wagging encouragement, Pascal who lay on my lap as I typed away at the keyboard, and Cash, on whose broad back I cantered away from the frustrations inherent in the creative process.

ABOUT THE AUTHOR

Penelope came to New Zealand as an eleven-year-old after a childhood spent in India and Pakistan. As an only child, reading was her hobby – she read everything that came her way, a habit which has continued throughout her life.

On leaving school she trained as a nurse, without fully considering that a brisk default attitude of 'pull yourself together and stop whining' might not be an ideal prerequisite for the industry. Conceding, at last, that nurturing was not her dominant characteristic, she changed career path and after graduating with a BA (Hons) in English Literature, moved into management consultancy, which better suited her personality type.

After some years of family life she worked as a commercial pilot and flight instructor, spending her days ferrying clients into strips in the Marlborough Sounds and discouraging students from killing her as she taught them to fly.

Penelope lives with her husband, dog, cat and horse in Otaki, New Zealand.

Death on D'Urville is the first novel in her *Claire Hardcastle* series.

Straight and Level takes place some three months after *Death on D'Urville*.

Stall Turns, the third in the series, continues to follow Claire's adventures.

The Lost One is her first novel.

All novels are available in various formats from Amazon.com.

Paperback editions can be purchased within New Zealand from Paper Plus, Unity Books and other reputable book stores and suppliers. Alternatively, they can be ordered from Penelope's website - www.penelopehaines.com, and you can visit Penelope on Facebook @penelopehainesbooks.

9 780473 551353